Topic relevant selected content from the highest rated entries, typeset, printed and shipped.

Combine the advantages of up-to-date and in-depth knowledge with the convenience of printed books.

A portion of the proceeds of each book will be donated to the Wikimedia Foundation to support their mission: to empower and engage people around the world to collect and develop educational content under a free license or in the public domain, and to disseminate it effectively and globally.

The content within this book was generated collaboratively by volunteers. Please be advised that nothing found here has necessarily been reviewed by people with the expertise required to provide you with complete, accurate or reliable information. Some information in this book maybe misleading or simply wrong. The publisher does not guarantee the validity of the information found here. If you need specific advice (for example, medical, legal, financial, or risk management) please seek a professional who is licensed or knowledgeable in that area.

Sources, licenses and contributors of the articles and images are listed in the section entitled "References". Parts of the books may be licensed under the GNU Free Documentation License. A copy of this license is included in the section entitled "GNU Free Documentation License"

All used third-party trademarks belong to their respective owners.

Contents

Articles

References

Article Licenses

Ariana Grande

Ariana Grande	
 Grande at the premiere of *The Twilight Saga: Breaking Dawn – Part 2* in November 2012	
Background information	
Birth name	Ariana Grande-Butera
Born	June 26, 1993 Boca Raton, Florida, U.S.
Genres	Pop, pop rock[1]
Occupations	Actress, singer, dancer, voice artist
Years active	2008–present
Labels	Universal Republic
Website	arianagrande.info [2][3]

Ariana Grande-Butera[4][5] (born June 26, 1993),[6][7] known professionally as **Ariana Grande**, is an American actress, singer, and dancer. She made her performance debut on Broadway at age 15, originating the role of Charlotte in *13* in 2008. Recently, she has gained attention for her role as Cat Valentine on the Nickelodeon sitcom *Victorious*, which she will reprise in *Sam & Cat*, a spinoff of *iCarly* and *Victorious*.

Early life

Grande was born and raised in Boca Raton, Florida.[8] She is of Italian descent, half Sicilian, half Abruzzese.[9] Her name was inspired by Princess Oriana from Felix the Cat. Grande's parents are Joan Grande and Edward Butera, a graphic designer.[10] She has an older brother, Frankie Grande, who is a performer and producer. He also was one of Grande's backup dancers on her first tour. Grande sang as a soloist in various symphonies, such as South Florida's Philharmonic, Pops and Symphonia Orchestras. She has sung various times in NYC's *Birdland* and sang the National Anthem on the first live broadcast of the Florida Panther's hockey league.[6]

Career

2003–10: Beginnings and Broadway

In her early years, she has been a soloist with various symphonies including South Florida's Philharmonic, Pops and Symphonia Orchestras, and has had repeated appearances singing at NYC's own Birdland.[11] Ariana performed the National Anthem for the first live Fox Sports broadcast of the Anthem for the Florida Panther's hockey league at age eight, her first National TV performance.[11]

In 2008, Grande played the role of Charlotte in the musical *13* on Broadway, for which she won a National Youth Theatre Association Award. When she joined the musical, Grande left her high school, North Broward Preparatory School, but continued to be enrolled. The school sent materials to her so she could study with tutors.[12][11]

In 2010, she created the original role of Miriam in the reading of the new musical, Cuba Libre, written and produced by Desmond Child.[11]

Grande at the film premiere of *Harry Potter and the Deathly Hallows – Part 2* in July 2011

2010–present: Victorious, debut album and other projects

Grande played the character Cat Valentine on the Nickelodeon television show Victorious, which premiered in March 2010. Grande was also featured in *Dream Magazine* as the cover girl for the August 2011 issue.[13] In 2011, Ariana voiced an animated fairy, Princess Diaspro, on the Nickelodeon series, *Winx Club*. Grande also made appearances as a panelist on *Figure It Out*. Grande starred as Snow White along with Charlene Tilton and Neil Patrick Harris in the Pasadena Playhouse's production of *A Snow White Christmas* from December 13–23, 2012.[14] In 2012, Grande sang a duet with MIKA on the single version of his track *Popular Song*.[15]

Sam & Cat

It was announced during the network's presentation at the Television Critics Association Summer Press Tour on August 3, 2012 that *Sam & Cat*, which would pair Grande from *Victorious* and Jennette McCurdy from *iCarly* together in a traditional "buddy sitcom" setting, where they would reprise their roles as Cat Valentine and Sam Puckett.[16] *Sam & Cat* was picked up by Nickelodeon on November 29, 2012.[17] The pilot suggests they will be roommates who launch a babysitting business for income. In the following month it was also announced that Victorious's current season (Season 3, which was split to a fourth season) will be the last.[18] Grande tweeted stating that she wasn't hoping for it to end and was looking forward to being on both shows. It was announced the third soundtrack was released on November 6, 2012 titled as "Victorious 3.0. *The first single is called "LA Boyz" (which was performed by Grande and Justice) and the music video was released October 18.*

Debut studio album

Grande is working on her first studio album, *Daydreamin'*,[19] which is due for release in early 2013. Grande commented on the album saying: "They can expect a lot of honesty. It's like a direct... you know, it's like it used to be pages from my diary, instead of keeping diary, I would write songs about what was happening in my life. So it's really personal. It's a Motown throwback and pop at the same time, so it's '50s and '60s inspiration mixed with today." The album was inspired by artists like Amy Winehouse, Mariah Carey, Whitney Houston, Alicia Keys, Fergie, Katy Perry, Madonna and other like these. Grande worked with artists like Sky Blue from LMFAO, 3OH!3, Kool Kojak, and Pebe Sebert on the album.[20] She was also working in the studio with Jonas Brothers singer Nick Jonas.[21][22][23] It was stated by Grande in an interview that the second single from her debut album would be released around Valentine's Day of 2013.

Philanthropy

At the age of 10, Grande co-founded the youth singing group, Kids Who Care, in South Florida, which performed for charitable fund-raising events, raising over $500,000 for charities in 2007 alone.[11]

In the summer of 2009, as a member of the charitable organization, Broadway in South Africa, Grande performed and taught music and dance to children in Gugulethu, South Africa along with her brother Frankie.[7][8][24]

Grande is also partnering with Kleenex on its "Shield Sneeze Swish" campaign.[20]

Personal life

In 2012, Grande began dating Jai Brooks, a member of the Australian YouTube group The Janoskians. They had a long distance relationship until December 2012, when they met for the first time in New York City.[25][26][27]

Stage and screen credits

Television

Year	Show	Role	Notes
2009	The Battery's Down	Bat Mitzvah Riffer	Minor role; 1 episode
2010–2013	Victorious	Cat Valentine	Main role
2011	iCarly ("iParty with Victorious")	Cat Valentine	Special guest star
2011	Winx Club	Princess Diaspro	Recurring role, voice only
2012	Figure It Out	Herself	Panelist
2013	Sam & Cat	Cat Valentine	Lead role

Films

Year	Film	Role	Notes
2013	Swindle [28]	Amanda	Main character

Broadway

Year	Show	Role	Notes
2008	13	Charlotte (u/s Patrice)	Original Broadway cast

Music video

Year	Main artist	Song	Notes
2010	Victoria Justice	"Freak the Freak Out"	Cameo
2011	Victoria Justice	"Beggin' on Your Knees"	Cameo
2011	Greyson Chance	"Unfriend You"	Cameo; main antagonist
2011	Victoria Justice	"All I Want Is Everything"	Cameo
2012	Ariana Grande	"Put Your Hearts Up"	Lead role
2012	Big Time Rush	"Time of Our Life"	Cameo
2012	Victoria Justice	"Make It In America"	Cameo
2012	Ariana Grande and Victoria Justice	"L.A. Boyz"	Lead role

Discography

Singles

Year	Song	Album
2011	"Put Your Hearts Up"	*Daydreamin*[19]
2013	"Do You Love Me (featuring Sky Blue of LMFAO)"[29]	*Daydreamin*[19]

Featured Singles

List of other charted songs, with selected chart positions

Title	Year	Peak chart positions	Album
		US [30]	
"Popular Song" (Mika featuring Ariana Grande)	2012	79	*The Origin of Love*

Other songs

Year	Song	Album
2009	"Suitcase"	non-album song[31]
	"Higher"	
	"Let It Rain"	
	"Stick Around (with Graham Phillips)"	
2012	"Baby It's Cold Outside" (with Larry Lovestein)	non-album song[31]

Album appearances

Year	Song	Artist(s)	Album	Appearance
2011	"Give It Up"	*Victorious* cast and Elizabeth Gillies	*Victorious* (soundtrack)	Lead vocalist
	"I Want You Back" (Jackson 5 cover)	*Victorious* cast		Backing vocals, additional vocals
	"Leave It All to Shine"	*Victorious* cast, *iCarly* cast, Victoria Justice and Miranda Cosgrove		Backing vocals, additional vocals
	"You're My Only Shorty" (demo)	Demi Lovato and Iyaz	*Unbroken*	Demo artist only, not featured in album
2012	"5 Fingaz to the Face"	*Victorious* cast	*Victorious 2.0*	Lead vocalist
	"Don't You (Forget About Me)"	*Victorious* cast		Backing vocals
	"Take Care"[32]	Leon Thomas III	*Metro Hearts*	Featured artist
	"L.A. Boyz"	*Victorious* cast	*Victorious 3.0*	Lead vocalist
	"Popular Song (Single Version)"	MIKA	*The Origin of Love*	Duet

Covers

Song	Artist
There's Hope[33]	India.Arie
ABC[34]	Jackson 5
California Gurls/Tik Tok[33]	Katy Perry/Kesha
Nothing Is Too Wonderful To Be True[33]	Dirty Rotten Scoundrels
Teenage Dream[33]	Katy Perry
Love The Way You Lie (Part 2)[33]	Rihanna
Grenade[33]	Bruno Mars
Born This Way/Express Yourself[33]	Lady Gaga/Madonna
Vienna[33]	Billy Joel
Hide And Seek[33]	Imogen Heap
Rolling In the Deep[33]	Adele
Last Dance[35]	Donna Summer
Chestnuts (with Elizabeth Gillies)[33]	Mel Tormé
Take Care (duet with Leon Thomas III)[33]	Drake & Rihanna
Gimmie Some Lovin'[36]	The Spencer Davis Group
Emotions[37]	Mariah Carey
Thinking About You[38]	Frank Ocean

Die In Your Arms[39]	Justin Beiber

Awards and Nominations

Year	Award	Category	Work	Result
2008	National Youth Theatre Association Awards	Best Actress	*13 (musical)*	Won[40]
2010	Hollywood Teen TV Awards	Teen Pick Actress: Comedy	*Victorious*	Nominated[41]
2012		Favorite Television Actress		Won[42]

References

[1] "Ariana Grande - Overview" (http://www.allmusic.com/artist/ariana-grande-mn0002264745). Allmusic. . Retrieved January 2, 2013.

[2] http://www.arianagrande.info/ariana/

[3] "Twitter: Ariana Grande (verified account)" (http://twitter.com/ArianaGrande/status/37679970436386816). February 16, 2011. . Retrieved 2011-02-16. "I hope you enjoy it nevertheless, thank you for everything. www.arianagrande.com. xx"

[4] "Twitter: Ariana Grande (verified account)" (https://twitter.com/#!/ArianaGrande/status/199002345944788993). May 5, 2012. . Retrieved 2012-05-08. "@pridelittlered Ariana Grande-Butera, everyone thinks Joan is my middle name but I don't actually have one! What's your middle name luv?"

[5] "Twitter: Ariana Grande (verified account)" (https://twitter.com/#!/ArianaGrande/media/slideshow?url=http://twitpic.com/8fcs90). February 3, 2012. . Retrieved 2012-04-03. "Oh my goodness. Look what I just found!.. This is my school ID from 8th grade. LOL. Had 2 share this with you guys."

[6] "Ariana Grande – about" (http://web.archive.org/web/20110721184425/http://arianagrande.info/site/?page_id=2). arianagrande.com. Archived from the original (http://arianagrande.info/site/?page_id=2) on 2011-07-21. . Retrieved 2012-03-06.

[7] "Twitter: Ariana Grande (verified account)" (http://twitter.com/ArianaGrande/status/17108571761). June 26, 2010. . Retrieved 2010-06-26. "I was born 17 years ago today. Woooop. :)"

[8] Laracy, Noah. "Ariana Grande: A *Back Stage* Exclusive". (http://www.backstage.com/bso/news-and-features-features/ariana-grande-a-back-stage-exclusive-1004089350.story) *Back Stage*, May 6, 2010. Retrieved 2010-06-23.

[9] "Twitter: Ariana Grande (verified account)" (http://twitter.com/ArianaGrande/status/40266680152240128). February 22, 2011. . Retrieved 2011-04-28. "I am Italian American, half Sicilian and half Abruzzese..."

[10] "BOCA KID GETS A PUCK AND ICE; 5-YEAR-OLD FINE AFTER BEING STRUCK 2ND TIME" (http://pqasb.pqarchiver.com/sun_sentinel/access/34975365.html?dids=34975365:34975365&FMT=ABS&FMTS=ABS:FT&type=current&date=Oct+10,+1998&author=JOSE+LAMBIET+South+Florida+Insider&pub=South+Florida+Sun+-+Sentinel&desc=BOCA+KID+GETS+A+PUCK+AND+ICE;+5-YEAR-OLD+FINE+AFTER+BEING+STRUCK+2ND+TIME&pqatl=google). Pqasb.pqarchiver.com. 1998-10-10. . Retrieved 2012-12-03.

[11] "Ariana Grande - About Ariana" (http://www.arianagrande.info/about.php). OfficalArianaGrande. . Retrieved 2012.

[12] "Ariana Grande: From Boca To Broadway". (http://www.girl2watch.com/ariana-grande-from-boca-to-broadway/) Girl2watch.com, May 4, 2010. Retrieved 2010-06-23.

[13] August Cover: Ariana Grande (http://thedreamagazine.com/august-cover-ariana-grande/).

[14] "Ariana Grande, Charlene Tilton and Neil Patrick Harris Headline A SNOW WHITE CHRISTMAS at Pasadena Playhouse, 12/13-23 – BroadwayWorld.com « Pasadena Playhouse" (http://pasadenaplayhouse.org/blog/2012/09/07/ariana-grande-charlene-tilton-and-neil-patrick-harris-headline-a-snow-white-christmas-at-pasadena-playhouse-1213-23-broadwayworld-com/). Pasadenaplayhouse.org. 2012-09-07. . Retrieved 2012-12-03.

[15] Popular Song - Single Premiere (http://www.josepvinaixa.com/blog/mika-popular-song-featuring-ariana-grande-single-premiere/), Retrieved 19/12/12.

[16] "Nickelodeon greenlights an 'iCarly' spinoff and other new shows" (http://www.latimes.com/entertainment/tv/showtracker/la-et-st-nickelodeon-greenlights-icarly-spinoff-20120803,0,3715048.story). . Retrieved 2012-08-12.

[17] Nordyke, Kimberly (2012-11-29). "Nickelodeon Greenlights Spinoff of 'iCarly,' 'Victorious'" (http://www.hollywoodreporter.com/live-feed/icarly-victorious-spinoff-sam-cat-395824). Hollywood Reporter. . Retrieved 2012-11-29.

[18] Big Time Rush (August 10, 2012). "M Exclusive: Victorious will NOT be returning for season four! – M Magazine" (http://www.mmm-mag.com/2012/08/m-exclusive-victorious-will-not-be-returning-for-season-four.html). Mmm-mag.com. . Retrieved August 10, 2012.

[19] "Do u have a name for the album yet??" (http://ask.fm/arianagrandefromfriday2nextfriday/answer/17941995192). Ask.fm. . Retrieved 2012-12-29.

[20] Lauren Joskowitz (2012-08-08). "Ariana Grande on debut album: 'It used to be pages from my diary'" (http://www.sheknows.com/ entertainment/articles/968169/ariana-grande-talks-about-debut-album-it-used-to-be-pages-from-my-diary). Sheknows.com. . Retrieved 2012-12-29.

[21] "Ariana Grande Writing W/ NICK JONAS!" (http://oceanup.com/2011/03/29/ariana-grande-writing-w-nick-jonas). oceanUP.com. . Retrieved 2013-01-05.

[22] Log nu in om een reactie te plaatsen. (2011-04-01). "Ariana Grande Talks Working With Nick Jonas" (http://www.youtube.com/ watch?v=5j1qCHshoO0). YouTube. . Retrieved 2013-01-05.

[23] "Nick Jonas" (http://nickjonline.com/2011/05/nick-jonas-again-was-in-the-beatlab-with-ariana-grande/). Nick J Online. 2011-05-06. . Retrieved 2013-01-05.

[24] Grande interview with WPIX TV (http://www.wpix.com/videobeta/2fcae32f-dba4-47c0-b9a1-0b8e160753e5/Entertainment/ Ariana-Grande-Talks-About-Victorious-), April 30, 2009. Retrieved 2010-06-23.

[25] "Ariana Grande Dating Jai Brooks" (http://www.bsckids.com/2013/01/ariana-grande-is-dating-austrialian-youtube-star-jai-brooks/). BSC Kids. .

[26] "Ariana Grande Twitlonger" (http://www.twitlonger.com/show/ki07pr). Ariana Grande Verified Twitter. .

[27] "Jai Brooks interview" (http://www.youtube.com/watch?feature=player_embedded&v=CFZc50411KA). Zach Sang Youtube. .

[28] New 'Nickelodeon' movie, *Swindle* with Ariana Grande (http://www.bsckids.com/2012/10/ ariana-grande-noah-munck-join-nickelodeons-swindle/)

[29] Michaels, Wendy (2012-05-15). "Ariana Grande Talks LMFAO Duet at Wango Tango on Cambio" (http://www.cambio.com/2012/05/ 15/ariana-grande-talks-lmfao-duet-at-wango-tango/). Cambio.com. . Retrieved 2012-12-03.

[30] http://www.billboard.com/news#/column/chartbeat/chart-highlights-whistle-to-blow-flo-rida-1007944972.story

[31] "Ariana Grande Profile and Biography" (http://celebritydays.com/ariana-grande-profile-and-biography.html). Celebrity Days. . Retrieved 2012-12-29.

[32] "Twitter / Leonthomas3: Ok ask and you shall receive" (http://twitter.com/Leonthomas3/status/208015426125438976). Twitter.com. . Retrieved 2012-12-03.

[33] "Covers" (http://www.youtube.com/playlist?list=PL420366E066F7F1F3). YouTube. . Retrieved 2012-12-29.

[34] "ABC (Jackson 5 cover)" (http://www.twitmusic.com/arianagrande/songs/abc-jackson-5-cover). Twitmusic.com. . Retrieved 2012-12-29.

[35] "Last Dance (Donna Summer cover)" (http://www.twitmusic.com/arianagrande/songs/last-dance-donna-summer-cover). Twitmusic.com. . Retrieved 2012-12-29.

[36] 0.00. "Ariana Grande Official's sounds on SoundCloud - Hear the world's sounds" (http://soundcloud.com/ariana-grande-official). Soundcloud.com. . Retrieved 2012-12-29.

[37] "Ariana Grande Covers "Emotions" By Mariah Carey I Nickelodeon News" (http://www.nickutopia.com/2012/08/18/ ariana-grande-covers-emotions-by-mariah-carey/). Nickutopia.com. . Retrieved 2012-12-29.

[38] "Thinking About You (Frank Ocean cover)" (http://www.twitmusic.com/arianagrande/songs/thinking-about-you-frank-ocean-cover--2). Twitmusic.com. . Retrieved 2012-12-29.

[39] Posted: 07/30/2012 4:57 pm Updated: 07/30/2012 5:42 pm (2012-07-30). "Ariana Grande Covers Justin Bieber's 'Die In Your Arms' (VIDEO)" (http://www.huffingtonpost.com/2012/07/30/ariana-grande-cover-justi_n_1720921.html). Huffingtonpost.com. . Retrieved 2012-12-29.

[40] "BIOGRAFÍA DE ARIANA GRANDE" (http://www.musica.com/letras.asp?biografia=41216). *Musica.com*. .

[41] "Hollywood Teen TV Awards" (http://hollywoodteenonline.com/2010/07/04/hollywood-teen-tv-awards/). .

[42] "Hollywood Teen TV Awards - Favorite Television Actress" (http://teentvawards.com/favorite-television-actress/). .

External links

- Official website (http://www.arianagrande.info/ariana/)
- Ariana Grande (http://www.imdb.com/name/nm3812858/) at the Internet Movie Database
- Ariana Grande (http://www.ibdb.com/person.asp?ID=480685) at the Internet Broadway Database

13 (musical)

13	
2008 Original Broadway Cast Recording	
Music	Jason Robert Brown
Lyrics	Jason Robert Brown
Book	Dan Elish Robert Horn
Productions	2007 Los Angeles 2008 Goodspeed Musicals 2008 Broadway 2012 London

13 is a non-musical with the book by Dan Elish, with Robert Horn as co-librettist. It is about a 12½ year old boy named Evan Goldman and his move from the big town of New York, New York, his struggle to be with the "in-crowd", turning 13 and becoming a man.

Productions

Pre-Broadway

The musical premiered on January 7, 2007 at The Mark Taper Forum in Los Angeles, California and ran through February 18, 2007. The production was directed by Todd Graff, with choreography by Michele Lynch, and the cast and band were all teenagers.[1] The original cast included Tinashe Kachingwe.[1][2] This production received a nomination for the 2007 LA Stage Alliance Ovation Awards, World Premiere Musical.[3] "The cast and band — all teenagers — includes Elizabeth Gillies, Ariana Grande, Ricky Ashley, Caitlin Baunoch, Molly Bernstein, Jenáe Burrows, Emma Degerstedt, Jamie Eblen, Julia Harriman, Jordan Johnson, Tinashe Kachingwe, Tyler Mann, Simone Haight, Sara Niemietz, Ryan Ogburn, J.D. Phillips, Ellington Ratliff, Chris Raymond, Charlie Rosen, Alex Scolari, Chloé Smith, Allie Trimm, Christian Vandal, Nehemiah Williams, Graham Phillips, and Seth Zibalese."[1]

The musical was next presented at the Norma Terris Theater in Chester, Connecticut, by Goodspeed Musicals from May 9, 2008 through June 8, 2008, with direction by Jeremy Sams and choreography by Christopher Gattelli. It stars most of the Original Broadway Cast, except Ashton Smalling as Kendra, Taylor Bright as Cassie and Kyle Crews as Malcom.[4]

2012 Adelaide Fringe

In March 2012, *13* made its South Australian debut when it was performed by Adelaide Youth Theatre for the Adelaide Fringe Festival at the Adelaide College of the Arts. It was directed by Rodney Hutton and musically directed by Michelle Nightingale. [5][6][7]

Broadway

The musical opened on Broadway at the Bernard B. Jacobs Theatre on September 16, 2008 in previews, with an official opening on October 5, 2008 and closed on January 4, 2009 after 105 performances and 22 previews.[8] The director and choreographer were as at Goodspeed, and most of the Broadway cast was also in the Goodspeed production (except Moro, Hammond and Williams). There is a teen band, as in prior productions.[9] This production received one Drama Desk Award nomination, for Outstanding Lyrics by Jason Robert Brown.

Off-Broadway

The musical opened Off-Broadway at the McGinn/Cazale Theatre on April 23, 2011, in a production by the Children's Acting Company. This is a six performance engagement featuring revisions made by Brown, Dan Elish and Robert Horn which were performed at French Woods Performing Arts Camp in summer 2009 and Theatre Under the Stars, Houston, in the fall 2009 as well as Indian Head camp in summer of 2010.[10]

Israel

In 2009-2010, the first production of *13* in Israel occurred in Jerusalem and had three re-mounts in larger venues in Jerusalem as well as national newspaper and television coverage.[11][12]

First UK Productions

The first UK performance of *13* was performed by Riverside Theatre Company, a youth theatre company from St Neots, performed at Comberton Village College on 17 July 2010.[13] Directed by Richard Mann, choreographed by Sara Johnson, and Ian Tipping and Jo Ryan were the musical directors.

References

[1] Hernandez, Ernio. "Middle School Musical: Jason Robert Brown's '13' Opens in Los Angeles" (http://www.playbill.com/news/article/104686.html) playbill.com, January 7, 2007

[2] TinasheNow.com Official Biography (http://www.tinashenow.com/?page_id=21) tinashenow.com

[3] Hernandez, Ernio. "Kaye, Fishburne, Felder Among Nominees for 2007 L.A. Stage Alliance Ovation Awards" (http://www.playbill.com/news/article/111309-Kaye-Fishburne-Felder-Among-Nominees-for-2007-LA-Stage-Alliance-Ovation-Awards) playbill.com, September 24, 2007

[4] Jones, Kenneth. "Teen Time! Cast Announced for Goodspeed Run of '13' Musical" (http://www.playbill.com/news/article/117016.html), playbill.com, April 22, 2008

[5] Nikki Gaertner. "New Adelaide Theatre Guide: South Australia's Only Comprehensive Internet Guide to Local Arts" (http://www.theatreguide.com.au/current_site/reviews/reviews_detail.php?ShowID=13musical&ShowYear=2012). Archived (http://www.webcitation.org/66306a4HW) from the original on 2012-03-09. . Retrieved 2012-03-06.

[6] (http://www.thebarefootreview.com.au/index.php?option=com_content&view=article&id=401:13-a-new-musical&catid=75:2012-fringe-festival&Itemid=53)

[7] "13 – A New Musical I BankSA Talk Fringe" (http://talkfringe.com/?fringe_events=13-a-new-musical#comment-774). Archived (http://www.webcitation.org/662zktWJL) from the original on 2012-03-09. . Retrieved 2012-03-06.

[8] Gans, Andrew and Jones, Kenneth. "New Musical 13 to Close on Broadway in January 2009" (http://www.playbill.com/news/article/123569.html), playbill.com, November 21, 2008

[9] Jones, Kenneth. "13, A New Musical Comes of Age on Broadway Sept. 16" (http://www.playbill.com/news/article/121334.html) Playbill.com, September 16, 2008

[10] Hetrick, Adam. After Broadway Growing Pains, 13 The Musical Returns to NYC in Revised Version April 23" (http://www.playbill.com/news/article/150151-After-Broadway-Growing-Pains-13-The-Musical-Returns-to-NYC-in-Revised-Version-April-23) playbill.com, April 23, 2011

[11] Dekel, Ayelet. (http://www.midnighteast.com/mag/?p=3573) "13 Mania Grips Jerusalem, March 1, 2010

[12] World News (http://wn.com/AVI_CHAI)

[13] Riverside Theatre Company (http://www.riversidetheatrecompany.co.uk/productions.php#previousproductions) Past productions details for first UK performance.

External links

• Official website (http://www.13themusical.com)
• *13* (http://www.ibdb.com/production.php?id=480453) at the Internet Broadway Database

Boca Raton, Florida

City of Boca Raton
— City —

Downtown Boca Raton skyline, seen northwest from the observation tower of the Gumbo Limbo Environmental Complex

Seal

Nickname(s): A City for All Seasons

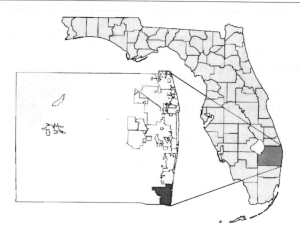

Location in Palm Beach County, Florida

Coordinates: 26°22′7″N 80°6′0″W

Country	United States
State	Florida
County	Palm Beach
Settled	1895
Incorporated (town)	May 1925
Government	

• **Type**	Commission-manager
• **Mayor**	Susan Whelchel (N)
Area	
• **Total**	29.1 sq mi (75.4 km^2)
• **Land**	27.2 sq mi (70.4 km^2)
• **Water**	1.9 sq mi (5.0 km^2)
Elevation	13 ft (4 m)
Population	
• **Total**	84,392 (2010 census)
• **Density**	2682.8/sq mi (1061.7/km^2)
Time zone	EST (UTC-5)
• **Summer (DST)**	EDT (UTC-4)
ZIP code(s)	
Area code(s)	561
FIPS code	12-07300[1]
GNIS feature ID	0279123[2]
Website	www.ci.boca-raton.fl.us [3]

Boca Raton (pron.: /ˈboʊkərəˈtoʊn/) is a city in Palm Beach County, Florida, USA, incorporated in May 1925. In the 2000 census, the city had a total population of 74,764; the 2006 population estimated by the U.S. Census Bureau was 86,396.[4] The Census 2010 count was down slightly, to 84,392.[5] However, the majority of the people under the postal address of *Boca Raton*, about 200,000[6] in total, do not actually reside within Boca Raton's municipal boundaries. As a business center, the city's daytime population increases significantly.

In terms of both population and land area, Boca Raton is the largest city between West Palm Beach and Pompano Beach, Broward County.

History

"Boca Raton" can be loosely defined as "Mouth of the Rat" or "Rat's Mouth" (In Spanish "boca" is mouth and "raton" is "mouse" and sometimes referred as "rat"). However, in nautical terms the word "boca" refers to an inlet. The original name "Boca de Ratones" appeared on eighteenth century maps associated with an inlet in the Biscayne Bay area of Miami. By the beginning of the nineteenth century, the term was mistakenly moved north to its current location on most maps and applied to the inland waterway from the closed inlet north for 8.5 miles (13.7 km), which was called the "Boca Ratones Lagoon". The word "ratones" appears in old Spanish maritime dictionaries referring to "rugged rocks or stony ground on the bottom of some ports and coastal outlets, where the cables rub against".[7] Therefore the abridged translation defining "Boca de Ratones" is "a shallow inlet of sharp-pointed rocks which scrapes a ship's cables".[8] The first settler was T. M. Rickards in 1895 who resided in a house made of driftwood on the east side of the East Coast Canal south of what is now the Palmetto Park Road bridge. He surveyed and sold land from the canal to beyond the railroad north of what is now Palmetto Park Road.[9]

Land boom

During the city's early history during the Florida land boom of the 1920s, Addison Mizner's Ritz-Carlton Cloister Inn was built in 1926,[10] later renamed the Boca Raton Resort & Club. It is today often referred to as the "pink hotel" and a 1969 addition is visible from miles away as a towering building on the Intracoastal Waterway.

War

Japanese farmers of the Yamato Colony converted the land west of the city into pineapple plantations beginning in 1904. During World War II, much of their land was confiscated and used as the site of the Boca Raton Army Air Force Base, a major training facility for B-29 bomber crews and radar operators. Much of the airbase was later donated to Palm Beach County and later become the grounds of Florida Atlantic University, many of whose parking lots are former runways of the airbase; when viewed from above, the site's layout for its previous use as an airfield is plainly evident. Boca Raton Airport's runway 5/23 was once part of the original airbase, and is still active to this day.

The Japanese heritage of the Yamato Colony survives in the name of Yamato Road (NW 51st Street) just north of the airport and at the Morikami Museum and Japanese Gardens northwest of the city. The headquarters building of the Army Air Forces Base has survived as the office building for the Cynthia Gardens apartment complex on Northwest 4th Avenue.

Post-war

In the late 1960s, the International Business Machines Corporation (IBM) announced their intentions to open a manufacturing plant in the area. In 1965, well before the extension of I-95 into Southern Florida, IBM, working in secret with the Arvida corporation, quietly purchased several-hundred acres of real estate just west of the CSX rail line and northwest of Florida Atlantic University in University Park. Originally situated in unincorporated Palm Beach County, the site was controversially annexed into Boca Raton almost a year following its dedication in 1970.[11]

The Boca Corporate Center and Campus was originally one of IBM's research labs where the PC was created. It is located on Yamato Rd (NW 51st St), and stands next to the Boca Raton Tri-Rail Station.

Construction of IBM's main complex began in earnest in 1967, and the mammoth manufacturing and office complex was dedicated in March 1970. The campus was designed with self-sufficiency in mind, and to that end sported its own electrical substation, water pumping station, and rail-spur. Among other very noteworthy IT accomplishments, such as the mass manufacture of the System/360 and development of the Series/1 mainframe computers, IBM's main complex was the birthplace of the IBM PC, which later evolved into the IBM Personal System/2, developed in nearby Delray Beach. Starting in 1987, IBM relocated their manufacturing for what became the IBM PC division to Research Triangle Park in Raleigh, North Carolina, and converted the cavernous manufacturing facilities into offices and laboratories, later producing products such as the OS/2 operating system and VoiceType Dictation, later known as ViaVoice voice-recognition software.

IBM maintained its facilities in the South Florida area until 1996, when the facility was closed and sold to Blue Lake Real Estate, who in turn sold it to T-REX Management Consortium. Today,

T-REX has revitalized the facility and its surrounding real estate into a highly successful and landscaped business/research park. What used to be IBM's Building 051, an annex separated from the former main IBM campus by Spanish River Boulevard was donated to the Palm Beach County School District and converted into Don Estridge High Tech Middle School. It is named for Don Estridge, whose team was responsible for developing the IBM PC. IBM later returned in July 2001 opening the current software development laboratory at Beacon Square off Congress Avenue.

Bluegreen Corporation, a real-estate and timeshare resort developer, has had its main office in Boca Raton since 1966.

In the 1980s, because of an explosion of development to the west of the historical center of the city, some eastern areas began to decay, including the downtown corridor. For instance, the old Boca Raton Mall, a shopping mall in the downtown area was beginning to experience higher vacancy, and occupancy by marginal tenants, due to the opening of Town Center at Boca Raton west of the city in 1980.

In 1991, the new downtown outdoor shopping and dining center, Mizner Park, was completed over the site of the old Boca Raton Mall. It has since become a cultural center for the southern Palm Beach County. Featuring a landscaped central park between the two main roads (collectively called Plaza Real) with stores only on the outside of the roads, Mizner Park resembles a Mediterranean suburban "town center" with a more contemporary look. It features many restaurants and is home to the Boca Raton Museum of Art which moved to the new facility in 2001."Boca Raton Museum of Art" [12] In 2002, a new amphitheater was built replacing a smaller one, providing a large-capacity outdoor venue where concerts and other performances are held.[13]

Mizner Park is a downtown attraction in Boca Raton's financial district. It is the furthest north part of Boca's *downtown* area, and home to 'Mizner Park Amphitheater'.

Mizner Park has significantly aided downtown revitalization. Many new eight to ten story mixed-use buildings have been constructed, are currently under construction or are proposed for the downtown area. The surrounding areas to the downtown have benefited from the downtown redevelopment.

The National Cartoon Museum (formally the International Museum of Cartoon Art) built a 25,000-square-foot (2,300 m^2) facility on the southwest edge of Mizner Park in 1996. Open for six years, the museum relocated to its original home in New York City in 2002. Building renovations for public uses, including the local public TV station, and private uses, such as a locally owned and operated bookstore were completed in 2008. In addition to the Mizner Park Cultural Arts Association's theater and space, the building is home to the Schmidt Family Foundation.

As development continued to focus to the west of the city in the 1980s and 1990s, the mall area, Town Center at Boca Raton, became the geographic center of what is referred to as Boca Raton, though this mall was not actually annexed into the city until 2004. The area referred to as Boca Raton, including the unincorporated area west of the city (and discussed below), is now almost entirely built out.

In 1999, the Simon Property Group bought Town Center at Boca Raton and redeveloped it. Nordstrom was added as the anchor department store for the new wing. Neiman Marcus is the newest department store tenant as of 2006. In-late 2006, Simon began the construction stage of an outdoor lifestyle center near the new wing. Town Center Mall has become a tourist attraction and the largest indoor mall in Palm Beach County.

Boca Raton has a strict development code, including the size and types of commercial buildings, building signs and advertisements which may be erected within the city limits. No outdoor car dealerships are allowed in the municipality, according to the city zoning code. Additionally, no billboards are permitted in the city. The only billboard was grandfathered in during a recent annexation. Corporations such as McDonald's have subdued their Golden Arches due to the code. The unincorporated areas still contain restaurants with the classic arches, but the heights of the signs have also been reduced. Many buildings in the area have Mediterranean and Spanish architectural themes, initially inspired in the area by Addison Mizner. The strict development code has resulted in several major thoroughfares without large signs or advertisements in the traveler's view; significant landscaping is in its place.

Geography

According to the United States Census Bureau, the city has a total area of 29.1 square miles (75.4 km²). 27.2 square miles (70.4 km²) of this is land and 1.9 square miles (5.0 km²) of it (6.63%) is water. Boca Raton is a 'principal city' (as defined by the Census Bureau) of the Miami metropolitan area. Like most South Florida cities, Boca Raton has a water table that does not permit building basements, but there are several high points in the city, such as 4th Avenue which is aptly named "High Street". The highest point in this area is the guard shack at Camino Gardens, which is 24 ft (7.3 m) above sea level. The Boca Raton Hotel's Beach Club rests at 23 ft (7 m) above sea level.[14]

Several small tunnels run under roads in Boca, but the roads are built up several feet at these locations, or are located on dunes. Several of these tunnels are under State Road A1A at Spanish River Park, from the west side of the road where parking is available to beachgoers, to the east side of the road, which is where the beach is located. A1A is already higher than the surrounding land here due to sand dunes formed by erosion and other natural features.[14]

Climate

Boca Raton's climate barely qualifies as a Tropical rainforest climate (Köppen climate classification Af), as its driest month (December) averages 62.5mm of precipitation, narrowly meeting the minimum standard of 60mm in the driest month needed to qualify for that designation.

Climate data for Boca Raton													
Month	**Jan**	**Feb**	**Mar**	**Apr**	**May**	**Jun**	**Jul**	**Aug**	**Sep**	**Oct**	**Nov**	**Dec**	**Year**
Average high °F (°C)	76 (24)	77 (25)	80 (27)	83 (28)	87 (31)	90 (32)	92 (33)	92 (33)	91 (33)	87 (31)	82 (28)	78 (26)	85 (29)
Average low °F (°C)	58 (14)	58 (14)	62 (17)	66 (19)	71 (22)	74 (23)	75 (24)	75 (24)	74 (23)	71 (22)	66 (19)	61 (16)	68 (20)
Precipitation inches (mm)	2.78 (70.6)	2.76 (70.1)	3.00 (76.2)	3.40 (86.4)	5.73 (145.5)	7.31 (185.7)	5.94 (150.9)	6.91 (175.5)	7.01 (178.1)	5.73 (145.5)	4.24 (107.7)	2.46 (62.5)	57.27 (1,454.7)
Source: [15]													

Demographics

Population		
Census	**Pop.**	**%±**
1940	723	—
1950	992	372%
1960	6,961	6017%
1970	29,538	3243%
1980	49,477	675%
1990	61,492	243%
2000	74,764	216%
2010	84,392	129%

Boca Raton Demographics

2010 Census	Boca Raton	Palm Beach County	Florida
Total population	84,392	1,320,134	18,801,310
Population, percent change, 2000 to 2010	+12.9%	+16.7%	+17.6%
Population density	2,877.2/sq mi	670.2/sq mi	350.6/sq mi
White or Caucasian (including White Hispanic)	88.5%	73.5%	75.0%
(Non-Hispanic White or Caucasian)	79.1%	60.1%	57.9%
Black or African-American	5.2%	17.3%	16.0%
Hispanic or Latino (of any race)	11.9%	19.0%	22.5%
Asian	2.4%	2.4%	2.4%
Native American or Native Alaskan	0.2%	0.5%	0.4%
Pacific Islander or Native Hawaiian	0.1%	0.1%	0.1%
Two or more races (Multiracial)	1.6%	2.3%	2.5%
Some Other Race	2.0%	3.9%	3.6%

As of 2010, there were 44,539 households, out of which 17.4% were vacant. As of 2000, 24.1% had children under the age of 18 living with them, 53.1% were married couples living together, 7.1% had a female householder with no husband present, and 37.2% were non-families. 29.5% of all households were made up of individuals and 11.6% had someone living alone who was 65 years of age or older. The average household size was 2.26 and the average family size was 2.81.

In 2000, the city population was spread out with 18.9% under the age of 18, 8.1% from 18 to 24, 26.4% from 25 to 44, 26.7% from 45 to 64, and 19.8% who were 65 years of age or older. The median age was 43 years. For every 100 females there were 95.1 males. For every 100 females age 18 and over, there were 92.8 males.

According to a 2007 estimate, the median income for a household in the city was $67,531, and the median income for a family was $92,057.[16] Males had a median income of $52,287 versus $33,347 for females. The per capita income for the city was $45,628. About 4.1% of families and 6.7% of the population were below the poverty line, including 6.0% of those under age 18 and 4.9% of those age 65 or over.

According to Forbes, Boca Raton has three of the ten most expensive gated communities in the U.S. The Royal Palm Yacht and Country Club holds the #1 spot, The Sanctuary takes #6, and Le Lac takes the #8 spot.[17]

As of 2000, English was spoken as a first language by 79.89% of the population, Spanish by 9.28%, French by 1.46%, Portuguese by 1.45%, French Creole by 1.29%, and Italian by 1.05% of the population. There is a substantial Jewish population in Boca Raton, and a small percentage of them add to the linguistic variety, with 0.36% of Boca Raton residents speaking Hebrew and 0.27% of the population speaking Yiddish at home.[18]

Culture and attractions

Boca Raton is known for its affluent social community and high income demographic. Boca Raton was the site of two now vanished amusement parks, Africa U.S.A. (1953–1961) and Ancient America (1953–1959). Africa U.S.A. was a wild animal park in which tourists rode a "Jeep Safari Train" through the park. There were no fences separating the animals from the tourists on the "Jeep Safari Train".[19] It is now the Camino Gardens subdivision one mile (1.6 km) west of the Boca Raton Hotel. A red wooden bridge from Africa USA can still be seen at the entrance to Camino Gardens. In the 1970s, peacocks could still be found in the subdivision, having escaped from the attraction. Ancient America was built surrounding a real Indian burial mound. Today, the mound is still visible within the Boca Marina & Yacht Club neighborhood on U.S. 1 near Yamato Road.[20]

Boca Raton is home to the Caldwell Theatre Company, the longest-running professional theater in South Florida, celebrating its 34th season in the recently inaugurated Count de Hoernle Theatre on South Federal Highway.[21]

Boca Raton has beaches along its eastern shore, notably Red Reef Park,[22] where snorkeling from the shore can bring a visitor to a living reef without the expense of renting a boat. Also in the 20-acre (81,000 m^2) park is Gumbo Limbo, an Environmental Education Center. A small fee is charged to enter the park.

Crime

Crime statistics

According to the Department of Justice, the following offenses occurred in Boca Raton in 2006.[23] The Federal Bureau of Investigation assembles this data each year through the Uniform Crime Reporting Program.[24]

Murders and nonnegligent manslaughters 3

Forcible rapes 13

Robberies 72

Aggravated assaults 150

Total violent crimes 238

Burglaries 799

Larceny-thefts 2,232

Motor vehicle thefts 170

Arson 2

Total property crimes 2,956

Estimated population 88,093

Technological issues

According to MessageLabs (an email security vendor), Boca Raton is the "spam capital of the world", being the source of a significant proportion of all spam generated worldwide, not surprising given the area's appeal, the personal fortunes of typical spammers, and the area's notorious past as a favorite of organized crime. According to the Miami Herald, the city has a long history of involvement in confidence tricks. Richard C. Breeden, former U.S. Securities and Exchange Commission chairman, once called the city "the only coastal city in Florida where there are more sharks on land than in the water". In the keynote address to a computer security conference on June 8, 2004, Bruce Sterling described the city as the "Capone-Chicago of cyber fraud".

On July 22, 2004, Boca Raton resident Scott Levine was charged with the largest computer crime indictment in United States history. Federal prosecutors allege that Levine unlawfully accessed Acxiom, a database of consumer data, to steal detailed personal information of millions of people.

Organized crime

In 2007 it was reported that there were nine known gangs operating in Boca Raton.[25]

Boca Raton has a connection to the Mafia. Although not known for violent crime, it is a popular hangout for many suspected Mafia members. According to a number of US Federal indictments, as of June 2004, the Gambino family continues to operate in Boca Raton. The television show, *The Sopranos*, featured the city in its plot ("Boca" and "...To Save Us All From Satan's Power"), and *Mafia Wife* author Lynda Milito resides in Boca Raton.[26][27][28]

Politics

The City of Boca Raton has a Council-Manager form of government. Information about the City government is available at the city website.[29]

The city council, including Mayor Susan Whelchel, is nonpartisan. As of July 2011, Allen West, a Republican, and Ted Deutch, a Democrat, both represent parts of the city in the United States Congress.

Economy

Office Depot, a supplier of office products and services, has its global headquarters on a 28-acre campus in the city.[30] The GEO Group, a company that operates prisons, also has its headquarters in Boca Raton based out of One Park Place.[31] Media companies American Media and FriendFinder Networks, hotel company Luxury Resorts and e-retailers Vitacost plus BMI Gaming are also based in Boca Raton.

Previously W. R. Grace and Company had its headquarters in unincorporated Palm Beach County, near Boca Raton.[32][33]

Top employers

According to the City's 2011 Comprehensive Annual Financial Report,[34] the top employers in the city are:

#	Employer	# of Employees
1	Florida Atlantic University	2,706
2	Office Depot (corporate headquarters)	2,250
3	Boca Raton Regional Hospital	2,250
4	Boca Raton Resort	1,800
5	City of Boca Raton	1,267
6	National Council on Compensation Insurance	800
7	The Continental Group	750
8	Tyco International	700
9	IBM	600
10	Applied Card Systems	550

Education

Public schools

Public education is provided and managed by The School District of Palm Beach County. Boca Raton is also home to several notable private and religious schools.

As of 2007, Boca Raton is served by four public high schools. Within the city's limits, Boca Raton Community High School serves the eastern part of the city. Spanish River Community High School serves the west-central part of the city limits and parts of unincorporated Boca Raton. Olympic Heights Community High School serves the western unincorporated areas. Finally, West Boca Raton Community High School serves the far-west unincorporated areas. Spanish River, Olympic Heights, and West Boca Raton also serve students from Delray Beach and Boynton Beach.[35]

The area is served by five public middle schools:

- Boca Raton Community Middle School,
- Don Estridge High Tech Middle School, a technology magnet school named for Don Estridge, the leader of a small group of engineers who developed the IBM Personal Computer in Boca Raton.
- Eagles Landing Middle School
- Loggers' Run Community Middle School
- Omni Middle School

The area is served by twelve public elementary schools:

- Addison Mizner Elementary (Founded in 1968. It is named after Addison Mizner.)
- Boca Raton Elementary
- Calusa Elementary
- Coral Sunset Elementary
- Del Prado Elementary
- Hammock Pointe Elementary
- J.C. Mitchell Elementary
- Sandpiper Shores Elementary
- Sunrise Park Elementary
- Verde Elementary
- Waters Edge Elementary
- Whispering Pines Elementary

An alternative to the Palm Beach County Public Schools in Boca Raton is the Alexander D. Henderson University School is located on the Florida Atlantic University campus. A. D. Henderson University School (ADHUS) is organized as a unique and separate school district; it is not part of the Palm Beach County School System. Henderson School is recognized as Florida Atlantic University School District #72, under the College of Education's administrative oversight.

University schools in Florida are authorized to provide instruction for grades K-12 and university students, support university research efforts, and test educational reforms for Florida schools. ADHUS is a public school and thus does not charge tuition. It is open to children who reside in Palm Beach County or Broward County and admission is by lottery. Student characteristics of gender, race, family income and student ability are used to match the student population profile to that of the state.[36]

Private schools

- Hillel Day School of Boca Raton
- Boca Raton Christian School
- Pine Crest School, based in Fort Lauderdale, has a campus in Boca Raton.
- Saint Jude Catholic School and Parish is an Elementary and Middle School founded in 1985. The Parish also has a Preschool founded in 1995.
- Saint Andrew's School
- Pope John Paul II High School
- Grandview Preparatory School is an independent college preparatory, nonsectarian, coeducational day school founded in 1997. Student enrollment is offered for Pre-Kindergarten through Grade 12.[37]
- Donna Klein Jewish Academy
- Boca Prep International School[38]
- Saint Joan of Arc Catholic School and Church
- Weinbaum Yeshiva High School
- Summit Private School, a Montessori school[39]
- Spanish River Christian
- Saint Paul Lutheran School
- Advent Lutheran School
- Torah Academy of Boca Raton
- Claremont Montessori School
- American Heritage School

Pope John Paul II High School is a Catholic school located in Boca Raton near Florida Atlantic University and Lynn University.

Higher education

- Florida Atlantic University, founded in 1961, held its first classes in Boca Raton in 1964. FAU is a member of the State University System of Florida and is the largest university in Boca Raton. It has over 29,000 students, 3,555 of which are residential students, and a Division I athletics program.
- Lynn University (originally founded as Marymount College, then renamed the College of Boca Raton in 1974, and finally Lynn University in 1991) is a four-year co-educational institution renamed to honor the Lynn (Eugene & Christine) family who continue to be benefactors of the university.
- Palm Beach State College has had a Boca Raton campus, adjacent to Florida Atlantic University, since 1971.

- Digital Media Arts College, founded in 2001, offers bachelor's and master's degrees in computer animation and graphic design.
- Everglades University

In recognition of the rapid growth of Boca Raton's universities, in particular Florida Atlantic University, the city of Boca Raton has recently been referred to as a "burgeoning college town." [40]

Libraries

The Boca Raton Public Library serves city of Boca Raton residents. A second municipal library building on Spanish River Boulevard west of I-95 was opened in January 2008.

The Glades Road Branch Library and the West Boca Branch Library serve Boca Raton residents who live outside the city limits. The West Boca Branch opened on February 20, 2009. It is located on State Road 7 just north of Yamato Road. The Glades Road Branch Library, formerly known as the Southwest County Regional Library, is located on 95th Street and Glades Road, between Lyons Road and State Road 7. It closed for renovations in early 2009 and reopened as the Glades Road Branch Library on May 29, 2010. County library card holders may use any of the sixteen branches in the Palm Beach County Library System and have access to many databases and downloadable e-books and audio books.

Transportation

Air

- The Boca Raton Airport (BCT) is a general aviation airport located immediately adjacent to Florida Atlantic University and Interstate 95. It has a control tower which is manned from 0700 to 2300. The Boca Raton Airport is publicly owned and governed by a seven member Authority appointed by the City of Boca Raton and the Palm Beach County Commission.
- Palm Beach International Airport (PBI) is located to the north near West Palm Beach.
- Fort Lauderdale-Hollywood International Airport (FLL) is located to the south in Dania Beach.

Highways

- Florida State Road A1A is a north-south road lying between the Intracoastal Waterway and the Atlantic Ocean.
- U.S. Highway 1 is a north-south highway passing through the city's downtown, commercial, and industrial districts in the eastern part of the city.
- U.S. Highway 441, also popularly known as State Road 7, is a north-south highway passing through commercial and residential districts west of the city limits.
- Interstate 95 bisects the city from north to south with four interchanges serving Boca Raton.
- Florida's Turnpike is a north-south highway passing through unincorporated Boca Raton, forming part of the city limits in the north, with one interchange at Glades Road.
- Florida State Road 808 (Glades Road) is an east-west road between US 441 and US 1.
- Other major east-west roads include Palmetto Park Road and Yamato Road.
- Other major north-south roads include Military Trail and Powerline Road.

Rail

- The Tri-Rail commuter rail system serves the city with its Boca Raton station located on the south side of Yamato Road just west of I-95.
- CSX Transportation and the Florida East Coast Railway also serve the city.

Water

Long before any settlers arrived, the original 1870 government survey of the area[41] showed that just west of and parallel to the Atlantic Ocean's coastal dune was the "Boca Ratones Lagoon", which extended south for nine miles (14.5 km) from just north of the present location of Atlantic Avenue in Delray Beach. Along the southern half of the lagoon were three wide areas each called a "Lake", which are now named (north to south) Lake Rogers, Lake Wyman, and Lake Boca Raton. At the southeast end of the lagoon was a short protrusion toward the south which would become the Boca Raton Inlet after a sandbar at its mouth was removed. The lagoon and lakes were part of a half-mile (0.8 km) wide swamp, west of which was scrub land a mile (1.6 km) wide (part of the Atlantic coastal ridge) where the Florida East Coast Railway (1896) and Dixie Highway (1923) were built. To the west of the scrub was a half mile or wider swamp within which flowed north to south the "Prong of Hillsborough River", which is now the El Rio Canal. It now forms the eastern border of Florida Atlantic University and the Old Floresta neighborhood. The prong entered the "Hillsborough River" at the present eastern end of the straight portion of the Hillsboro Canal (dredged 1911–14), which is the southern city limits. The river flowed southeast in several channels along the western edge of the present Deerfield Island, formerly called Capone Island (named for Al Capone who owned it during the 1930s), which did not become an island until the Royal Palm Canal was dredged along its northern edge in 1961.[42][43] Flowing south from the lagoon to the river along the eastern edge of the 'island' was a "Small boat Pass into Hillsboro' River", also called the Little Hillsboro. The river continued due south about four and a half miles (7.2 km) just inland of the coastal dune until it emptied into the Atlantic Ocean at the "Hillsborough Bar", now the Hillsboro Inlet.

The lagoon was dredged in 1894–95 to form part of the Florida East Coast Canal from Jacksonville to Biscayne Bay with a minimum depth of 5 feet (1.5 m) and a minimum width of 50 feet (15.2 m).[44] After 1895, the lagoon and canal were sometimes called the Spanish River. Between 1930 and 1935 the canal was improved to 8×100 feet (2.4×30.5 m) by the federal government and renamed the Intracoastal Waterway. It was improved again between 1960 and 1965 to 10×125 feet (3×38.1 m).[45] All three versions were subject to shoaling which reduced their depths below the specified minimum. Forming part of the northern city limits is the C-15 canal, connecting the El Rio Canal to the Intracoastal Waterway.

Notable residents, past and present

Reed Alexander, actor	Marilyn Manson, shock rocker
Jozy Altidore, soccer player	Leonard Marshall, football player
Carling Bassett-Seguso with husband Robert Seguso, both tennis players	Tucker Max, writer
Derek Bell, motor racing driver	Nicko McBrain, Iron Maiden drummer
Marc Bell, entrepreneur	Vince McMahon, professional wrestler & promoter
Yuniesky Betancourt, baseball player	Scott Mersereau, professional football player for the New York Jets
Jeanne Bice, founder of Quaker Factory[46]	Andy Mill, Olympic ski racer and ex-husband of Chris Evert
Ian Bishop, former English soccer player	Corina Morariu, tennis player
Ryland Blackinton, musician/guitarist for Cobra Starship	Jaclyn Nesheiwat, beauty queen, fashion model
Jon Bon Jovi, singer & musician	Paul Newman, entrepreneur
Jason Bonham, rock and roll drummer & son of Led Zeppelin drummer John Bonham	Greg Norman, golfer

- Ernest Borgnine, actor
- Don Brewer, drummer for Grand Funk Railroad
- Rebecca Brooke, actress
- Keith Byars, former football player
- Jennifer Capriati, tennis player
- Chris Carrabba, lead singer & guitarist of Dashboard Confessional
- Cris Carter, All-Pro football player
- Elena Dementieva, Russian tennis player
- Dion DiMucci, Rock & Roll Hall of Fame member
- Rashad Evans, former UFC Lightheavyweight Champion, current UFC fighter
- Chris Evert, tennis player
- Dr. Frank Field, TV personality, and NYC meteorologist for 5 decades
- Jeff Gordon, NASCAR racer
- Ariana Grande, actress, model and singer
- Taurean Green, basketball player
- John Grogan, author of *Marley & Me*
- Sébastien Grosjean, French tennis player
- Megan Hauserman, model & reality television actress
- John W. Henry, one of the owners of the Boston Red Sox
- Scott Hirsch, boxing manager & former e-mail spammer[48]
- Lisa Hunt, author & artist
- Ryan Hunter-Reay, IndyCar Series driver
- Žydrūnas Ilgauskas, basketball player
- Khori Ivy, former football player
- Dennis Kozlowski, former CEO of Tyco International
- Bernhard Langer, golfer
- Jesse Levine, tennis player
- Scott Levine, computer criminal
- Hector Lombard, former Bellator Middleweight Champion, current UFC fighter

- Petter Northug, Norwegian cross country skier
- Terrence Pegula, billionaire natural gas tycoon and owner of the Buffalo Sabres
- Sabby Piscitelli, football player for the Tampa Bay Buccaneers
- Maury Povich and wife, Connie Chung, tabloid and news media personalities
- Morgan Pressel, golfer
- Guillaume Raoux, tennis player[47]
- Mark Richt, head football coach of the University of Georgia
- Andy Roddick, tennis player
- Pete Rose, baseball player
- Frank Rosenthal, ex-Las Vegas casino owner & handicapper
- Marion Ryan, 1950s British singer
- Sheryl Sandberg, COO of Facebook
- Stephanie Moulton Sarkis, psychotherapist and author
- Ryan Shore, contemporary film composer
- Vince Spadea, tennis player
- Scott Stapp, lead singer for the rock band Creed
- Howard Stelzer, avant-garde composer & founder of Intransitive Recordings
- Anna Tatishvili, tennis player
- Horia Tecău, tennis player
- Sahaj Ticotin, lead singer for the rock band Ra
- Donald Trump, billionaire real estate mogul, has a second residence in Boca Raton
- Danny Valencia, baseball player
- Brian Voss, bowler
- Blair Walsh, All-Pro football kicker for the Minnesota Vikings
- Ernie Wise, UK comedian & half of the double act Morecambe and Wise had a holiday home here, where he spent much of his time after Morecambe's death in 1984.

Greater Boca Raton

A majority of postal Boca Raton lies outside of the actual city limits. This large unincorporated area to the west of the city limits is included in the Boca Raton mailing address and local telephone calling area. There are many large planned developments in the area, including gated communities, and a number of golf courses. This is a result in the later start of development in these areas, and the availability of large tracts of land. Many of these affluent communities are large enough to be designated as census-designated places, including Boca Del Mar and Boca Pointe, geographically in *Central Boca Raton*, and Avalon at Boca Raton, Boca Falls, Boca Winds, Cimarron, Hamptons at Boca Raton, Mission Bay, Loggers' Run, The Polo Club Boca Raton, Sandalfoot Cove, and Whisper Walk as *West Boca Raton*.

On November 2, 2004, the voters of the Via Verde Association, Waterside, Deerhurst Association (Boca South), Marina Del Mar Association, Rio Del Mar Association (both originally Boca Del Mar communities), and

Heatherwood of Boca Raton Condominium Association approved annexation into the Boca Raton city limits, increasing the city land area to 29.6 square miles (77 km^2).

Boca Raton in popular culture

Boca figures in many forms of popular culture.

Boca has been mentioned in many movies, including *All the President's Men*, *Back to the Future*, *Bewitched*, *Cats & Dogs*, *Marley and Me*, *The Mexican*, *Mr. 3000*, *Music and Lyrics*, *A Perfect Murder*, *Wag the Dog*, and *Wonderland*, and in many TV shows, such as *American Dad!*, *American Dragon: Jake Long*, *Code Name: The Cleaner*, *Dexter*, *Entourage*, *Lizzie McGuire*, *Nip/Tuck*, *The Golden Girls*, *Histeria!*, *Mad Men*, *MADtv*, *My Name Is Earl*, *The Nanny*, *Phil of the Future*, *Robot Chicken*, *The Sopranos*, *SpongeBob SquarePants*, *Two and a Half Men*, *The Venture Bros.*, *Weeds*, and *Wipeout*. These references usually have something to do with the large number of luxury resorts and condominiums in Florida, or the considerable number of retired persons residing in Florida (especially in the case of *Seinfeld*),.[49]

Boca Raton is almost idiomatically used for indicating retirement. For example, Fran Drescher's character in *The Nanny* is always pushing her parents to move to Boca, and Chelsea Handler frequently uses the city in reference to the elderly on her talk show, *Chelsea Lately*.

Development of Boca Raton features prominently in the 2008 Stephen Sondheim/John Weidman musical, *Road Show*, which centers on the lives of Addison Mizner and his brother Wilson Mizner.

Boca Raton has also been the stage and background for many movies filmed on location in Boca Raton, including *Paper Lion* (1968), *Paper Moon* (1973), *Caddyshack* (1980), *Caddyshack II* (1988), *Where the Boys Are '84* (1984), *Stella* (1990), *2 Fast 2 Furious* (2003) and *Sex Drive* (2008).

Photo Gallery

References

[1] "American FactFinder" (http://factfinder.census.gov). United States Census Bureau. . Retrieved 2008-01-31.

[2] "US Board on Geographic Names" (http://geonames.usgs. gov). United States Geological Survey. 2007-10-25. . Retrieved 2008-01-31.

[3] http://www.ci.boca-raton.fl.us/

[4] Census (http://www.census.gov/popest/cities/tables/ SUB-EST2006-04-12.xls)

[5] "Multimedia" (http://www.usatoday.com/news/nation/ census/profile/FL). *USA Today*. .

[6] Boca Raton Historical Society: Boca Raton's History (http:// www.bocahistory.org/boca_history/br_history.asp)

[7] The Spanish Maritime Dictionary of 1831

[8] Boca De Ratones: An Etymological Reassessment(Ruiz and Cobia, Feb. 14, 2012)

[9] Boca Raton Historical Society, *Spanish River Papers* (http:// www.bocahistory.org/pdf/span_river/SRP Jan 1973.pdf), 1.1 (January 1973).

[10] Curl, Donald W. and John P. Johnson. *Boca Raton; A Pictorial History*. Virginia Beach, VA: The Donning Company, 1990. p. 52

[11] Janie Gold, "Archer calls on Boca Raton to de-annex University Park" (http://news.google.com/newspapers?id=DYAyAAAAIBAJ& sjid=PLcFAAAAIBAJ&pg=5266,4338414&dq=university+park+boca+raton&hl=en), *The Palm Beach Post*, July 12, 1972, C1-C2.

[12] http://www.bocamuseum.org/index.php?submenu=about_us&src=gendocs&link=AboutUs&category=About%20Us

[13] http://www.miznerparkamp.com/

[14] Google Earth (http://earth.google.com/)

Old Dixie Seafoodis a popular local seafood market and deli famous for their Marlin dip and stone crab claws

[15] "Average weather for Boca Raton" (http://www.weather.com/outlook/travel/businesstraveler/wxclimatology/monthly/graph/
       USFL0040?from=36hr_bottomnav_business). Weather.com. May 2011. . Retrieved 14 August 2009.

[16] U.S. Census Bureau Fact Finder for Boca Raton (http://factfinder.census.gov/servlet/ACSSAFFFacts?_event=Search&
       geo_id=06000US0900173070&_geoContext=01000US|04000US09|05000US09001|06000US0900173070&_street=&_county=boca+
       raton&_cityTown=boca+raton&_state=04000US12&_zip=&_lang=en&_sse=on&ActiveGeoDiv=geoSelect&_useEV=&pctxt=fph&
       pgsl=060&_submenuId=factsheet_1&ds_name=ACS_2006_SAFF&_ci_nbr=null&qr_name=null&reg=null:null&_keyword=&
       _industry=)

[17] "Most Expensive Gated Communities In America 2004" (http://www.forbes.com/realestate/2004/11/19/cx_sc_1119home.html).
       Forbes. .

[18] Data Center Results (http://www.mla.org/map_data_results&state_id=12&county_id=&mode=&zip=&place_id=7300&cty_id=&
       ll=&a=&ea=&order=r)

[19] Virtual Tour of Arica U.S.A. (http://www.africa-usa.com/tour.htm). Retrieved August 27, 2006.

[20] Ancient America: one of Florida's lost tourist attractions (http://www.lostparks.com/ancientamerica.html). *lostparks.com.* Retrieved
       August 27, 2006.

[21] Caldwell Theatre Company (http://www.caldwelltheatre.com/)

[22] Red Reef Park (http://www.ci.boca-raton.fl.us/rec/parks/redreef.shtm)

[23] "2006 Crime in the United States, Table 8 (Florida)" (http://web.archive.org/web/20071010122134/http://www.fbi.gov/ucr/
       cius2006/data/table_08_fl.html). United States Department of Justice. September 2007. Archived from the original (http://www.fbi.gov/
       ucr/cius2006/data/table_08_fl.html) on 2007-10-10. . Retrieved 2007-11-01.

[24] "2006 Crime in the United States, Table 8, Data Declaration" (http://web.archive.org/web/20071010121818/http://www.fbi.gov/ucr/
       cius2006/data/table_08_dd.html). United States Department of Justice. September 2007. Archived from the original (http://www.fbi.gov/
       ucr/cius2006/data/table_08_dd.html) on 2007-10-10. . Retrieved 2007-11-01.

[25] "Where South Florida gangs are working" (http://web.archive.org/web/20070515090946/http://www.palmbeachpost.com/localnews/
       content/local_news/special_reports/gangs/gang_data.html), *The Palm Beach Post.*

[26] Boca Raton, Florida - Mafia Wife Interview with Lynda Milita | Boca Raton (http://bocaraton.com/index.aspx?pid=458)

[27] cbs4.com - Married To The Mob: Mafia Wife To Sue HBO (http://cbs4.com/entertainment/local_story_044082354.html)

[28] Lynda Milito from HarperCollins Publishers (http://www.harpercollins.com/authors/20964/Lynda_Milito/index.aspx)

[29] City of Boca raton website (http://www.myboca.us)

[30] Office Depot Press Release. (http://mediarelations.officedepot.com/phoenix.zhtml?c=140162&p=irol-newsarticle&id=933195&
       highlight=)

[31] " Contact Us (http://www.thegeogroupinc.com/contact.asp)." GEO Group. Retrieved on May 10, 2010.

[32] " Grace Announces Relocation To Columbia, Maryland (http://www.grace.com/media/NewsItem.aspx?id=138361)." W. R. Grace and
       Company. Retrieved on June 29, 2011. "The restructuring will entail a relocation of approximately 40 people, including senior management,
       from Grace's Boca Raton, Florida office to its Columbia, Maryland site. A few positions will be relocated to another Grace office in
       Cambridge, Massachusetts." and "Following the relocation, Grace will close its headquarters office at 1750 Clint Moore Road in Boca Raton,
       which currently employs approximately 130 people."

[33] " Boca Raton city, Florida (http://factfinder.census.gov/servlet/MapItDrawServlet?geo_id=16000US1207300&_bucket_id=50&
       tree_id=420&context=saff&_lang=en&_sse=on)." U.S. Census Bureau. Retrieved on June 29, 2011.

[34] City of Boca Raton CAFR (http://www.ci.boca-raton.fl.us/fin/pdf/CAFR2011.pdf)

[35] School District of Palm Beach County - High School Boundary Maps (http://cms.palmbeach.k12.fl.us/cms/document_display.
       cfm?document_id=1073) - Accessed December 17, 2007

[36] FAU - A.D. Henderson University School (http://www.adhus.fau.edu)

[37] "Grandview Preparatory School" (http://www.grandviewprep.net/aboutus.htm).

[38] "Boca Prep International School" (http://www.bocaprep.net/).

[39] "Summit Private School" (http://www.bocanews.com/local-news/boca-raton/
       4512-boca-raton-summit-school-kids-take-lead-on-world-environment.html).

[40] http://articles.sun-sentinel.com/2011-11-14/news/fl-boca-college-town-20111104_1_president-mary-jane-saunders-fau-college-town

[41] Bureau of Land Management, General Land Office Records (http://www.glorecords.blm.gov/SurveySearch/) Florida, Townships
       46–48, Range 43

[42] The Mysterious "Capone Island": Deerfield Island Park (http://www.royalpalm.com/art/pdfs/10_03_04.pdf) PDF (597KB)

[43] Deerfield Island - Spanish River Papers (http://www.bocahistory.org/pdf/span_river/SRP Winter 1986.pdf) PDF (2.47MB)

[44] A history of Florida's East Coast Canal: The Atlantic Intracoastal Waterway from Jacksonville to Miami (http://www.aicw.org/
       browardlegacy.pdf) PDF (3.8 MB)

[45] Aubrey Parkman, *History of the waterways of the Atlantic coast of the United States* (http://www.usace.army.mil/publications/misc/
       nws83-10/toc.htm), National Waterways Study, 1983, p.87.

[46] Tuckwood, Jan (2011-06-13). "Queen of the 'Quackers' turned world on with her sparkle" (http://www.palmbeachpost.com/news/
       queen-of-the-quackers-turned-world-on-with-1537222.html?viewAsSinglePage=true). *Palm Beach Post.* . Retrieved 2011-06-27.

[47] "ATP World Tour profile: Guillaume Raoux" (http://www.atpworldtour.com/Tennis/Players/Ra/G/Guillaume-Raoux.aspx). .
       Retrieved 2012-03-14.

[48] "Are Hurricanes Swamping Spammers?" (http://www.businessweek.com/bwdaily/dnflash/sep2004/nf20040915_0180_db035.htm). 2004-09-15. .

[49] Seinfeld, *The Wizard* (http://www.seinfeldscripts.com/TheWizard.htm), Air date: February 26, 1998 (Jerry: "Kramer, you can't live down here. This is where people come to die.")

External links

- City of Boca Raton (http://www.ci.boca-raton.fl.us/)
- Greater Boca Raton Chamber of Commerce (http://www.bocaratonchamber.com/)

Elizabeth Gillies

Elizabeth Gillies	
 Gillies at the 64th Primetime Emmy Awards in September 2012	
Born	Elizabeth Egan Gillies[1] July 26, 1993 Haworth, New Jersey, U.S.[2]
Other names	Liz Gillies
Occupation	Actress, singer, dancer, voice artist
Years active	2007–present

Elizabeth Egan "Liz" Gillies[1] (born July 26, 1993)[3] is an American actress, singer and dancer. She made her Broadway debut at age 15 in the musical *13* as the character Lucy.[4] She played the role of Jade West on *Victorious* and also voices the character Daphne on the animated series *Winx Club*.[5]

Career

Acting

Elizabeth Gillies started her acting career at age twelve when she went to a local open casting call and began appearing in commercials for companies such as Virgin Mobile.[6] She also received roles in *The Black Donnellys*. She starred in *The Clique* as Shelby Wexler. She was cast in *Harold*, as a supporting character.In summer 2008, she was cast as Lucy in a Goodspeed production of Jason Robert Brown's new musical about growing up, *13*. Later that year, *13* moved to Broadway, which made it the first Broadway production to have an all teen cast. She received the two big numbers "Opportunity" and "It Can't Be True" along with smaller parts in other songs, such as the title song, "Hey Kendra" and "Getting Ready". *13* ran through January 4, 2009.[7]

Gillies stars in the Nickelodeon sitcom *Victorious* as Jade West, the antagonist and frenemy to Tori Vega. Gillies also currently voices Daphne on the animated series *Winx Club* and recorded Winx Club's official song, "We Are Believix." She has guest starred in *White Collar* and *Big Time Rush* and was a contestant on the Nickelodeon game shows *BrainSurge* and *Figure It Out*.

Music

Gillies has appeared in several songs on the soundtracks *Victorious (soundtrack)* and *Victorious 2.0*, including *Give It Up (Victorious song)* (A duet with Ariana Grande), and *Take a Hint* (A duet with Victoria Justice that became the most popular song on the Victorious 2.0 Soundtrack.) She wrote the song *You Don't Know Me* which later appeared on *Victorious* and was featured in *Victorious 3.0*.[8][9]

She also has a YouTube account called LizGilliesOfficial, where she uploads covers of popular songs including: Wild Horses by The Rolling Stones, You and I by Lady Gaga, For No One by The Beatles, Jealous Guy by John Lennon, Father and Son by Cat Stevens and One and Only by Adele.[10] She has covered songs with Max Schneider (Somewhere Only We Know) and Ariana Grande (The Christmas Song).

In July of 2012, it was reported that Gillies was working on an album with alternative rock music.[11][12]

Filmography

Film

Year	Title	Role	Notes
2008	*Harold*	Evelyn Taylor	Supporting role
2008	*The Clique*	Shelby Wexler	Minor role
2011	*The Death and Return of Superman*	Eradicator Folks	YouTube short film

Television

Year	Title	Role	Notes
2007	*The Black Donnellys*	Young Jenny	Recurring role, 3 episodes
2007	*Locker 514*	Trinnie	
2010–2013	*Victorious*	Jade West	Main role
2011	*iCarly*	Jade West	Episode: "iParty with Victorious"
2011	*Winx Club*	Daphne[13]	9 episodes, Voice only
2011	*Big Time Rush*	Heather Fox	Episode: "Big Time Secret"
2011	*BrainSurge*	Herself	1 episode, contestant
2012	*White Collar*	Chloe Woods	Episode: "Upper West Side Story"
2012	*Figure It Out*	Herself	7 episodes, panelist

Year	Show	Role	Notes
2008-2009	*13*	Lucy Dunn	Original Broadway cast

I+ Broadway

Year	Main artist	Song	Notes
2010	Victoria Justice	"Freak the Freak Out"	Cameo
2011	Victoria Justice	"Beggin' on Your Knees"	Cameo
2011	Victoria Justice	"All I Want Is Everything"	Cameo
2011	Mickey Deleasa	"Time in the Day"	Cameo
2012	Big Time Rush	"Time of Our Life"	Cameo
2012	Victoria Justice	"Make It in America"	Cameo
2012	Herself	"We Are Believix"	Lead singer
2012	Herself	"You Don't know Me"	Lead singer

I+ Music videos

Discography

Year	Song	Album	Notes
2011	"Give It Up" (with Ariana Grande)	*Victorious* (soundtrack)	Lead vocalist
	"I Want You Back" (with the *Victorious* cast)		Backing vocals/additional vocals
	"All I Want Is Everything" (with the *Victorious* cast)		Backing vocals
	"Leave It All To Shine" (with the *Victorious* cast and *iCarly* cast)		Backing vocals/additional vocals
2012	"Don't You (Forget About Me)" (with the *Victorious* cast)	*Victorious 2.0*	Backing vocals
	"Take a Hint" (with Victoria Justice)		Lead vocalist
	"Shut Up 'N Dance" (with the *Victorious* cast)		Backing vocals/additional vocals
	"Five Fingaz to the Face" (with the *Victorious* cast)		Additional vocals
	"We Are Believix"[14]	Winx Club Deluxe Version (single)	Lead vocalist
	"You Don't Know Me"[8]	*Victorious 3.0*	Lead vocalist

References

[1] Brantley, Ben (October 6, 2008). "Stranger in Strange Land: The Acne Years" (http://theater.nytimes.com/2008/10/06/theater/reviews/ 06bran.html). *The New York Times*. . Retrieved September 15, 2011.

[2] "Elizabeth Gillies's Biography" (http://hairstyles.hairboutique.com/details.php?ID=41992). HairBoutique.com. . Retrieved September 15, 2011.

[3] Gillies, Elizabeth (July 25, 2011). "Twitter: Elizabeth Gillies (verified account)" (http://twitter.com/#!/LizGillies/status/ 95638167398526976). . Retrieved August 29, 2011. "Enjoying the last few hours of my childhood! Tomorrow I am a legal adult!"

[4] "13 Cast" (http://broadwayworld.com/article/13_A_New_Musical_Announces_Its_Teenage_Cast_and_Band_20080814). .

[5] Rohan, Virginia (June 7, 2011). "TV Mean Girl: Haworth's Elizabeth Gillies talks *iParty with Victorious*" (http://www.bergen.com/ TV_Mean_Girl_Haworths_Elizabeth_Gillies_talks_iParty_with_Victorious.html). *(201) magazine*. . Retrieved July 28, 2011.. "Elizabeth Gillies is not a diva. She just plays one on TV. The Haworth teen is nothing but charming as she chats on the phone about Jade, the gifted character with attitude she plays on Nickelodeon's *Victorious*.... Although *Victorious* shoots in Hollywood, whenever possible, she is back home in Haworth. 'We refuse to move. I'm an East Coast person,' says Gillies, who does her studies online. 'Right now, I'm taking some time, I'm finishing up school, chilling with my family.'"

[6] Rohan, Virginia. "TV Mean Girl: Haworth's Elizabeth Gillies talks "iParty with Victorious"" (http://www.bergen.com/ TV_Mean_Girl_Haworths_Elizabeth_Gillies_talks_iParty_with_Victorious.html). Bergen.com. . Retrieved 6 September 2012.

[7] "13 The Musical" (http://13themusical.com/). . Retrieved 10/13/12.

[8] "Victorious 3.0 Track List" (http://www.clevvertv.com/victoria-justice/36996/ victorious-3-0-even-more-music-from-the-hit-tv-show-out-nov-6.html). .

[9] Gillies, Liz. "Liz Gillies Tweet" (https://twitter.com/LizGillies/status/258337433572241408). Twitter (Verified Account). . Retrieved 10/16/12.

[10] "LizGillies Official YouTube" (http://www.youtube.com/user/LizGilliesOfficial). .

[11] "Twitter / LizGillies: @LizGOnline" (https://twitter.com/LizGillies/status/177227387476520961). . Retrieved July 27, 2012.

[12] "Liz Gillies Interview" (http://www.huffingtonpost.com/hannah-orenstein/elizabeth-gillies-victori_b_1711949.html). .

[13] Global Hit Animated Series 'Winx Club' Comes To Nickelodeon, Starting June 27 (http://tvbythenumbers.zap2it.com/2011/06/09/global-hit-animated-series-winx-club-comes-to-nickelodeon-starting-june-27/95196/)

[14] "Winx Club - Kids Music - Online Songs" (http://www.nick.com/music/album/winx-club-we-are-believix-album.html). . Retrieved July 27, 2012.

External links

- Elizabeth Gillies (http://www.imdb.com/name/nm2566697/) at the Internet Movie Database
- Elizabeth Gillies (http://www.ibdb.com/person.asp?ID=480687) at the Internet Broadway Database
- Elizabeth Gillies (https://twitter.com/LizGillies) on Twitter
- Elizabeth Gillies (https://www.facebook.com/people/Elizabeth-Gillies/160059308492) on Facebook

Figure It Out

Figure It Out	
Format	Children's game show
Created by	Kevin Kay Magda Liolis
Presented by	Summer Sanders (1997-99) Jeff Sutphen (2012-present)
Narrated by	Jeffrey "J" Dumas (1997-99) Elle Young (2012-present)
Country of origin	United States
No. of seasons	6
No. of episodes	218
Production	
Location(s)	Universal Studios Orlando, Florida (1997-1999) Paramount Studios Los Angeles, California (2012-present)
Running time	24 minutes
Broadcast	
Original channel	Nickelodeon
Picture format	480i (SDTV) (Seasons 1-4); 1080i (HDTV) (Season 5-present)
Original run	**Original Series** July 7, 1997 – December 12, 1999 **Revived Series** June 11, 2012 – present

Figure It Out is an American children's game show that airs on Nickelodeon. The original series, hosted by Summer Sanders, ran for four seasons from July 7, 1997 to December 12, 1999; the current revival of the show began running on June 11, 2012 and is hosted by Jeff Sutphen.

Kids with special skills or unique achievements compete as contestants on the show while a panel of four Nick celebrities try to guess the predetermined phrase that describes the contestant's talent. The series is a loose adaptation of *What's My Line?* and *I've Got a Secret*, both established panel shows created by Mark Goodson and Bill Todman.

A contestant on *Figure It Out*.

Shortly after the series aired its last first-run episode, *Figure It Out* began airing repeats on Nick GAS until the network ceased at the end of 2007 (2009 on Dish Network). The series was originally recorded at Nickelodeon Studios at Universal Studios in Orlando, Florida. The revival episodes are filmed on stage 19 at Paramount Studios in Los Angeles.[1]

Reruns of the Sanders-hosted series were among the shows carried on the now-defunct cable channel Nickelodeon Games and Sports for Kids; and also several episodes of the Sanders-hosted series have also aired as part of *The '90s*

Are All That, a 1990s-oriented rerun block that airs on TeenNick, as the series aired on the block from August 3, 2012, to August 5, 2012.

Gameplay

Each episode has two sets of three timed rounds (originally all 60 seconds in length; currently, rounds 2 and 3 are 45 seconds long), in which the panel takes turns asking yes-or-no questions to try to guess the contestant's talent. Each time a panelist mentions a word that is part of the phrase that describes the secret talent, the word is turned over on a game board displaying the puzzle. This game board was referred to as Billy the Answer Head during the original series run and is known simply as the "It" Board in the show's current adaptation.

This game board shows which words of the phrase are guessed, along with blanks denoting unguessed words. Prepositions and articles, such as "of" and "an," are provided automatically. The contestant wins a prize after each round that his or her talent remains unguessed; the prize for winning the third round is a trip. In Season 1 prizes consisted mainly of leftover props from then-defunct Nickelodeon shows such as All That, Legends of the Hidden Temple, and Global Guts. Merchandise prizes (such as a Nintendo 64) and gift cards for stores including Kids Foot Locker, Toys 'R' Us, and Loew's began to appear as prizes during later seasons. If Round 3 ends with at least one word left unrevealed, each panelist takes one final guess as to what the contestant's talent is (any correct words given during the final guess are revealed, as during the game). The game ends when a panelist guesses the secret talent or if no panelist guesses the secret talent correctly after the "last guess" stage.

During each Round, the panelists receive one clue as a hint to one of the words of the secret phrase. The clue usually takes the form of physical objects – such as dates to indicate a clue about calendars – sounds (rarely used), or pantomime (the "Charade Brigade" (Season 1-4), "Clue Force 3" (Season 5)), usually two or three cast members that act out a word from the phrase during Round 3) with "Clue Force 3" pictionary was sometimes use instead of pantomime.

At the end of the game, after the secret talent is revealed, the contestant demonstrates or displays his or her skill and discusses it with the host and panel.

Secret Slime Action

In each game, from the start of round 2, a randomly selected member of the studio audience plays for a prize (a merchandise prize, such as a Nintendo 64 or a mountain bike in season 1. A *Figure It Out*-branded article of clothing in seasons 2-6) if at least one or more panelists perform the action, those panelists will be slimed by the end of round 3.

The action designated as the Secret Slime Action is typically simple and almost guaranteed: touching a clue, looking to the left (which was reflexive, as clues were commonly wheeled out on a small track from a tunnel to the panel's left), using the phrase "Are you..." or "Is it...," looking to the audience behind the panel (who was sometimes used for clues), saying "I don't know," having a certain name, and even *being* a panelist were all used as actions. On one notable occasion, Steve Burns (from *Blue's Clues*) was slimed because the Secret Slime Action was "having a blue dog," and Jade Ramsey (from *House of Anubis*) was slimed because the Secret Slime Action was "having an identical twin sister." Despite this, and contrary to popular belief, the Secret Slime Action was not always performed in the original series. In the new version, Secret Slime Actions are almost impossible to miss and so far, there has not been a single show in which it was not performed during both halves of gameplay. In episode 14 of season six, there was finally an instance where it was not performed. The Secret Slime Action was **Saying "Wait"** for the first segment, and it was not performed.

Some Actions are logically unenforceable, such as "thinking about coconuts" or "thinking about mushroom soup." Especially in the latter seasons, a successful Action has mostly been a foregone conclusion – the variables have only been when it will be triggered, and by whom (not necessarily a panelist).

When the Secret Slime Action is triggered, all play stops (including the clock) while the panelist is slimed and the action revealed, after which gameplay resumes. The host knows of the action and sometimes tricks the panelists into performing it by making them say or touch something (in one episode, the action was "touching your head." Sanders touched her head and said, "Have you done something with your hair?," which caused the panel to touch their heads in reaction). In an episode, Sanders tried to trick Danny Tamberelli (from *The Adventures of Pete and Pete*) into saying the word "something", but Danny did not perform it.

Word of Honor

In the 2012 revival, prior to each game, one word of the contestant's secrets may be designated as the "Word of Honor." Should the panel guess this word, the contestant is slimed.[2] The clock is paused when the contestant is slimed.

Panelists

Either three or all four panelists are taken from Nickelodeon shows airing at the time. Regulars during the original run included *All That* cast members Amanda Bynes, Lori Beth Denberg (who left after Season 3), and Danny Tamberelli (who also starred in the Nick show *The Adventures of Pete and Pete*).

The first seat on the panel was usually reserved for an older-aged panelist, either an older actor from Nick (usually Kevin Kopelow of *All That*) or a non-Nickelodeon celebrity (such as Taran Noah Smith of *Home Improvement*). In several episodes, CatDog, rendered in CGI, and Cousin Skeeter, a puppet character, were panelists, but never at the same time. In Seasons 5 & 6, the first seat can be for anyone, but it's normally reserved for Matt Bennett or Ciara Bravo.

Other guest panelists included Coolio (semi-regular on the 1998 *Match Game*); Mike O'Malley (host of Nick's *Get the Picture* and *GUTS* from 1991–1995); Colin Mochrie (regular on *Whose Line Is It Anyway?*), who, along with Kevin Kopelow, was notably slimed for "having a shiny head"; Paul Wight (WWE's "The Big Show", then known as "The Giant"); Chris Jericho also from WWE; "Hacksaw" Jim Duggan (WWE Hall of Famer); and Rondell Sheridan (regular on the 1998 *Match Game*).

There was also an episode where Lori Beth and Summer switched roles for half of an episode. Summer took Lori Beth's seat as a panelist, and Lori Beth took Summer's role as the host for Game 1.

Now in the revival seasons (5 & 6), there are new regular panelists.

- Matt Bennett - Victorious
- Ciara Bravo - Big Time Rush
- Whole cast of How to Rock

List of panelists

Original run (Seasons 1–4)

- Alisa Reyes (1)
- Amanda Bynes (1-4)
- Danny Tamberelli (1-4)
- Josh Server (1-2)
- Kel Mitchell (2-3)
- Kenan Thompson (2-3)
- Lori Beth Denberg (1-3)
- Kenan Thompson (2-3)
- Vanessa Baden (1)
- Phil Moore (actor) (1-3)

- Aaron Carter (3)
- Adam Busch (1)
- Arjay Smith (2, 4)
- "Giant" Paul Wight (2)
- Bob Sanders (Summer's father) (3)
- Boris Cabrera (4)
- Brian Knobs (4)
- Carla Overbeck (4)
- Carrot Top (3)
- CatDog (4)
- Cedric Ceballos (3)
- Chris Jericho (3)
- Christy Knowings (2-4)
- Colin Mochrie (4)
- Coolio (3)
- Cousin Skeeter (3)
- Curtis Williams, Jr. (3)
- Dave Aizer (4)
- Dennis Haskins (3)
- Doug E. Doug (4)
- Eleanor Noble (3)
- Ellen David (3)
- Erin J. Dean (2-4)
- Evander Holyfield (4)
- "Hacksaw" Jim Duggan (4)
- Hardy Rawls (3)
- Irene Ng (1-4)
- Jack Hanna (4)
- Jenna Leigh Green (1)
- Jesse Camp (4)
- Joe Namath (2)
- Judy Grafe (3)
- Julius Erving (4)
- Kareem Blackwell (4)
- Kevin Kopelow (1-4)
- Kordell Stewart (2)
- Leon Frierson (2)
- Lindsay Felton (4)
- Marc Weiner (1)
- Mark Saul (4)
- Meagan Good (3)
- Michelle Trachtenberg (2-3)
- Mike Maronna (3)
- Mike O'Malley (1-2)
- Moira Quirk (1-2)
- Mýa (4)
- Neil Smith (2)

- Penny Hardaway (2)
- Preslaysa Edwards (1)
- Richard Simmons (4)
- Robert Ri'chard (3)
- Rondell Sheridan (4)
- Schuyler Fisk (4)
- Shane Sweet (2, 4)
- Sherman Hemsley (4)
- Steve Burns (4)
- Steve Purnick (2)
- Summer Sanders (2)
- Tara Lipinski (4)
- Taran Noah Smith (1-2)
- Tiffany Roberts (4)
- Travis White (3)
- Shannon Miller

Revival (Season 5–present)

- Alex Heartman (3 episodes)
- Ana Mulvoy Ten (6 episodes)
- Ariana Grande (2 episodes)
- Ashley Argota (6 episodes)
- Avan Jogia (2 episodes)
- Camille Spirlin (TBA)
- Candace Parker (Special Guest) (1 episode only)
- Carlos Knight (5 episodes)
- Carlos Pena, Jr. (2 episodes)
- Challen Cates (3 episodes)
- Christopher O'Neal (6 episodes)
- Ciara Bravo (Regular Panelist) (11 episodes)
- Cristian Puento (Watch & Win Winner) (1 episode only)
- Cymphonique Miller (5 episodes)
- Daniella Monet (2 episodes)
- Drake Bell (4 episodes)
- Elizabeth Gillies (4 episodes)
- Eric Lange (2 episodes)
- Gracie Dzienny (5 episodes)
- Halston Sage (4 episodes)
- Jacob Bertrand (TBA)
- Jade Ramsey (6 episodes)
- Jake Weary (2 episodes)
- James Maslow (2 episodes)
- Jennette McCurdy (4 episodes)
- Kendall Schmidt (1 episode)
- Kirk Fox (3 episodes)
- Leon Thomas III (4 episodes)
- Logan Henderson (1 episode)

- Lucas Cruikshank (2 episodes)
- Lulu Antariksa (7 episodes)
- Marcus Canty (Special Guest) (1 episode only)
- Matt Bennett (Regular Panelist) (9 episodes)
- Max Schneider (7 episodes)
- Metta World Peace (Special Guest) (1 episode only)
- Michael Eric Reid (3 episodes)
- Nathan Kress (2 episodes)
- Noah Crawford (5 episodes)
- Noah Munck (6 episodes)
- Rachel Crow (4 episodes)
- Ramy Youssef (1 episode)
- Ryan Potter (9 episodes)
- Samantha Boscarino (5 episodes)
- Stephen Kramer Glickman (3 episodes)
- Tanya Chisholm (1 episode)
- Victoria Justice (2 episodes)
- Victory Van Tuyl (TBA)

Format changes

For Season 3 (Fall 1998), the series became *Figure It Out: Family Style*, featuring two or three contestants who were related, typically parent-child or siblings. Sometimes on the 2nd half, the panel can have a family member of the contestant. Sometimes, the Charade Brigade can have family members of the panelists and the host. *Figure It Out: Family Style* also features Little Billy. If the panelists figured out the contestants' secret, then Little Billy (a miniature version of Billy the Answer Head with hair and on wheels) would come out. Summer reads a question about the family's talent and then each panelist try to guess one (almost impossible) answer. If they can't figure it out (no panel ever did since they simply treated it as a free-for-all most times by guessing answers intended for comedic response), then the answer in Little Billy would reveal and which gives the family another chance to win a prize (usually the Figure It Out apparel used for the Secret Slime Action Rounds).

- Season 4 - Fall 1999: The show was retitled *Figure It Out: Wild Style* and focused solely on talents involving animals; in addition, Billy the Answer Head was reshaped into various animals. During these episodes, the panelists went wild with hair, wigs, and make-up, sporting a different, distinctive look. Lori Beth Denberg never appeared in any of those episodes, because she left Nickelodeon and went on to The Steve Harvey Show, so during these episodes, panelists such as Steve Burns, Shane Sweet, Erin J. Dean, Christy Knowings, Irene Ng and Kareem Blackwell replaced Lori Beth in the chair on the right end.

- Season 5 - Summer 2012: The show was retitled once more to "Figure It Out," and Jeff Sutphen took over as host. The set, host, panelists, theme music, and logo were all modified to serve Nickelodeon's contemporary audience. Gameplay was also slightly modified to include the Word of Honor component and to shorten the lengths of rounds two and three (originally, all rounds were 60 seconds; in the newer version, rounds two and three are 45 seconds). Also, Billy the Answer Head was changed to the "It Board", the Clue Express was renamed the "Clue Coaster," and the Charade Brigade was changed to "Clue Force III" featuring Lorenz Arnell, Gevorg Manoukian, and Julia Srednicki.

- Season 6 - Fall 2012: The show was brought back after the long gap in the summer. The style of the show stays the same, but with some changes, such as a fifth seat and slime spewer added to the panel desk for the kid panelist who won a summer contest to appear for one whole episode (the fifth panel desk is gone before and after the winning kid's episode), the previous "Clue Express" was bought back, and more swirly colored arrows were added. Plus, the slime is more greener then ever.

Some of the panelists from Season 5 never appeared in this season (such as the three main characters from Supah Ninjas, Stephen Glickman from Big Time Rush, Jade Ramsey from Anubis, & Victorious's Victoria Justice & Eric Lange) Later in this season, one or two episodes will have celebrities from the recently new show Marvin Marvin. The panelists are Lucas Cruikshank from his other show Fred, along with special guests Victory Van Tuyl from her other show Supah Ninjas, Camille Spirlin, & Jacob Bertrand.

Cardinal Games released a board game based on the series in 1998. Cardinal games included "Name That Thingy", "Name That Critter", "The Drench Bench", "The Last Laugh" "Lightning Letters", "Little Billy" and "The Secret Panel Match Up."

Famous contestants

On April 7, 1998, future country music singer/songwriter Hunter Hayes was a contestant on *Figure It Out* when he was six years old. His talent was playing the accordion.[3]

References

[1] "Nickelodeon Figure It Out: Figure This Out" (http://www.cattlecallauditions.com/nickelodeon-figure-it-out-figure-this-out/). cattlecallauditions.com. . Retrieved 2012-06-06.

[2] "Ready, Set, Slime! Nickelodeon Premieres Figure It Out on Monday, June 11, at 7 P.M. (ET/PT)" (http://markets.on.nytimes.com/research/stocks/news/press_release.asp?docTag=201205181629PR_NEWS_USPRX____NY10239&feedID=600&press_symbol=280669). The New York Times. . Retrieved 2012-06-06.

[3] http://www.youtube.com/watch?v=mPpjNgdT2dk

External links

- Official website (http://www.nick.com/shows/figure-it-out/)
- *Figure It Out* (http://www.imdb.com/title/tt0127994/) at the Internet Movie Database
- *Figure It Out* (http://www.tv.com/shows/figure-it-out/) at TV.com

Freak the Freak Out

"Freak the Freak Out"	
Single by Victorious cast featuring Victoria Justice	
from the album *Victorious: Music from the Hit TV Show*	
Released	November 19, 2010
Format	Digital download
Recorded	2010; The Backhouse (Los Angeles, California); Rocket Carousel (Los Angeles, California)
Genre	Electro-rock, electropop
Length	3:54
Label	Columbia, Nick
Writer(s)	Michael Corcoran, C.J. Abraham, Nick Hexum, Zack Hexum, Dan Schneider
Producer	Backhouse Mike, The Super Chris
Victoria Justice chronology	

"Make It Shine" (2010)	"Freak the Freak Out" (2010)	"Beggin' on Your Knees" (2011)

"**Freak the Freak Out**" is a song performed by American pop recording artist Victoria Justice. It was produced by The Super Chris and Michael Corcoran, who also co-wrote the song with C.J. Abraham, Nick Hexum, Zack Hexum, Dan Schneider, for *Victorious* (2011), the soundtrack to the Nickeloden television series, *Victorious*. It was released as the album's second single on November 19, 2010 through Columbia Records. Musically, the song is a fast-paced electro-rock with influences of electropop and teen pop lyrics, and the lyrics speak of getting the attention of a distant boyfriend.

The song was met with generally positive reviews from critics, with the majority of them praising its message and aggressive sound. "Freak the Freak Out" has currently charted on the *Billboard* Hot 100 at number 50, remaining as the highest peaking song from the soundtrack. The accompanying music video portrays Justice with the *Victorious* cast at a night club dancing, singing and enjoying the moment.

Background

"Freak the Freak Out" is the second single released from the soundtrack *Victorious* (2011), for the television series of the same name on Nickelodeon. It was first heard on the series's one hour special, "Freak the Freak Out", which premiered on November 26, 2010 in North America, a few days after the single's release. The scene where the song was performed features Justice, disguised as a very ugly girl Louise Nordoff, who comes up on stage to sing and later reveals her true self as a part of a plan to win a bet with the two main antagonists in the episode, Hayley (Jillian Clare) and Tara (Jamie Snow). They won a previous contest only because Hayley's father owns the karaoke place. Justice continues singing as Elizabeth Gillies and Ariana Grande, playing Jade West and Cat Valentine, come up on stage and dance beside her.

The song was written by Michael Corcoran, C.J. Abraham, Nick Hexum, Zack Hexum, Dan Schneider.[1] It also featured addition production by Greg Wells on additional production.[1] The mixing for the song was provided by Greg Wellstook place at Rocket Carousel in Los Angeles, California.[1] Backhouse Mike and The Super Chris produced the track along with providing all the instruments on the song.[1] Michael Corcoran also provided the guitars.[1] Corcoran was also included on the programming for the song with CJ Abraham, both of which engineered the track in The Backhouse in Los Angeles.[1] Corcoran and Abraham provided additional vocals along with Niki Watkins, Nick and Zack Hexum.[1]

Composition

"Freak the Freak Out" is an electro-rock song that contains influences of teen pop and electropop. The song runs through a dance-rock oriented beat and features a more aggressive sound than the rest of the album's songs, at one point received comparisons to American recording artist Katy Perry's musical stylings.[2] Much of the song features relentless beats, synthesized instrumentations, nonstop simple, and repetitive choruses,[3] The theme of this song is center around managing relationships.[2] The lyrics are about getting the attention of a distant partner, who doesn't listen.

Critical reception

Bob Hoose and Steven Isaac of *Plugged In Online* condemned the song for its objectionable content, mainly noting the title's second "freak" was, stated by Hoose and Isaac, "a not-so-subtle substitute for an intended obscenity."[2] Joe DeAndrea of *AbsolutePunk* praised the song, along with "Beggin' on Your Knees", for its catchy nature, further commenting that "They will get stuck in your head and you'll probably feel a little ashamed, but no worries: it's the good type of ashamed! Like eating chocolate cake in a bathtub alone on a Friday night. But really, it's easier to accept it when you realize that the songs aren't all that worse than what is currently on the radio."[4]

Performances

Justice performed this song in the Macy's Thanksgiving Day Parade in 2010. Also, the song was performed in a *Victorious* episode of the same title as the song.

Music video

The music video premiered on Nickelodeon on November 19, 2010, after the iCarly episode "iStart a Fan War". The video opens with Justice talking on the phone with someone outside of the club. She is upset that her friend isn't coming to the club, but decides to go in anyway. As she walks around the club, she sees the *Victorious* cast socializing with other people. They are also shown dancing individually on the dance floor in another part of the club. There are also interspersed shots of Justice singing the song while sitting down, singing parts of the song into her phone, performing the song in a room with people dancing behind her and at the DJ booth.

In a shorter version of the music video, there are interspersed shots of Justice recording the song in a studio.

Credits and personnel

- Victoria Justice – vocals
- Michael Corcoran - songwriting, production, instrumentation, guitars, programming, engineering, background vocals
- The Super Chris - production, instrumentation
- C.J. Abraham - songwriting, programming, engineering, background vocals
- Nick Hexum - songwriting, background vocals
- Zack Hexum - songwriting, background vocals
- Dan Schneider - songwriting
- Niki Watkins - background vocals
- Greg Wells - additional production, mixing

Credits are taken from *Victorious* liner notes.[1]

Chart performance and certifications

"Freak the Freak Out" debuted at #78 on the *Billboard* Hot 100. It fell off the next week, but re-entered at #58 and peaked at #50.

Chart (2010–2011)	Peak position
U.S. *Billboard* Hot 100[5]	50
U.S. Top Heatseekers[6]	1

It is Gold in the U.S. according to the RIAA, However her label incorrectly certified it as an album.[7]

It was also confirmed that the song sold over 600,000 digital copies in the U.S.[8]

References

[1] *Victorious* (CD). Victorious and Victoria Justice. United States: Columbia. 2011.

[2] Hoose, Bob. "Victorious: Music From the Hit TV Show" (http://www.pluggedin.com/music/albums/2011/varioussoundtrack-victoriousmusicfromthehittvshow.aspx). *Plugged In Online*. Focus on the Family. . Retrieved 1 November 2011.

[3] Ruhlmann, William. "Victorious - Victorious Cast" (http://www.allmusic.com/album/victorious-r2142243/review). *All Music Guide*. Rovi Corporation. . Retrieved 1 November 2011.

[4] DeAndrea, Joe. "Victorious Cast featuring Victoria Justice - Victorious - Album Review" (http://www.absolutepunk.net/showthread.php?s=7921ea84222fe283672059a22f6b78c5&t=2383532). *AbsolutePunk*. AbsolutePunk, LLC. . Retrieved 1 November 2011.

[5] Billboard.com, Top 100 Music Charts (http://www.billboard.com/charts/hot-100?chartDate=2011-02-05&order=drop#/charts/hot-100?chartDate=2011-02-05&order=drop)". Accessed 25 March 2011.

[6] "Victorious Cast Album & Songs Chart History | Billboard.com" (http://www.billboard.com/charts/hot-100?chartDate=2011-02-05&order=drop#/artist/victorious-cast/chart-history/1632337?f=887&g=Singles). *Billboard*. . Retrieved 28 November 2012.

[7] Riaa.com

[8] Justin Bieber, Cee Lo Green, Jennifer Hudson, Victoria Justice And The Band Perry Join Lineup for TNT's Christmas in Washington, Hosted by Conan O'Brien (http://tvbythenumbers.zap2it.com/2011/11/15/justin-bieber-cee-lo-green-jennifer-hudson-victoria-justice-and-the-band-perry-join-lineup-for-tntâs-christmas-in-washington-hosted-by-conan-oâbrien/110819/)

Graham Phillips (actor)

Graham Phillips	
Born	Graham David Phillips April 14, 1993 Laguna Beach, California, USA
Occupation	Actor, Singer
Years active	2002 - present

Graham David Phillips (born April 14, 1993) is an American actor and singer. Beginning his acting career at the age of nine, Phillips is known for a variety of film, stage and television roles; as Jordan Baxter in the Universal Pictures feature film *Evan Almighty*, as Evan Goldman in the Broadway musical *13*, and as Zach Florrick on the CBS television series *The Good Wife*.

Personal life

Phillips was born in Laguna Beach, California. During his K-9 school years he attended St. Margaret's Episcopal School in San Juan Capistrano, California. He entered Princeton as a freshman in the fall of 2012.

Stage

Phillips starred as Evan Goldman in the musical comedy *13* on Broadway at the Bernard B. Jacobs Theatre which opened October 5, 2008 and closed January 4, 2009. It was directed by Jeremy Sams, choreographed by Christopher Gattelli, with music and lyrics by Jason Robert Brown and book by Dan Elish and Robert Horn.

Prior to his role in *13*, Phillips played the title role in *The Little Prince* with the New York City Opera at Lincoln Center. The *New York Times* critic called Phillips' performance in the title role "smashing."[1] From there Phillips went directly into the world premiere of "An American Tragedy" at the Metropolitan Opera where he played the part of Young Clyde, both opening and closing the opera with a solo.

Phillips' other professional stage credits include *A Christmas Carol: The Musical* on Broadway performed at Madison Square Garden where he sang the role of Tiny Tim to Jim Dale's Scrooge; *The Ten Commandments: The Musical* with Val Kilmer at the Kodak Theatre in Los Angeles. Phillips, at ten years old, was the second youngest person to sing the National Anthem to open a Los Angeles Dodgers baseball game (behind 9 year old Jessica Tivens in 1990). He has also debuted original songs composed by Martin Charnin and John Kander in New York.

Film and television

Phillips had a co-starring role as Jordan Baxter, the middle son, in the feature film *Evan Almighty* starring Steve Carell, Morgan Freeman and Lauren Graham which premiered June 22, 2007. In the fall of 2007 he completed working on the feature film *Stolen Lives* starring Josh Lucas. Phillips also played the lead role in *Ben 10: Race Against Time*. This live-action movie was the #1 telecast in Cartoon Network history.

Phillips' television credits include *The Good Wife*, *Crossing Jordan*, *Judging Amy*, *The King of Queens*, *White Collar*, and a Hallmark Movie, *Love's Long Journey*.

Phillips, along with the rest of the cast of *The Good Wife*, has received three Screen Actors Guild Award nominations for "Outstanding Performance by an Ensemble in a Drama Series".[2][3] He has also received three Young Artist Award nominations; "Best Performance By a Leading Young Actor in a TV Movie, Miniseries or Special" for his role in *Ben 10: Race Against Time*, "Best Performance by a Supporting Young Actor in a Feature Film" for his role in *Evan Almighty*, and "Best Supporting Young Actor in a TV Series" for his role in *The Good*

Wife.[4]

Musical

Phillips, portraying Evan, was the original cast member of the Broadway musical *13*, co-starring Elizabeth Gillies and Ariana Grande. He appeared twice on *The Today Show* as a soloist. Phillips recorded a solo composed by Alan Menken and Stephen Schwartz for the film *Noel* starring Robin Williams and Susan Sarandon. He also was a soloist on Meat Loaf's 2006 album *Bat Out of Hell III: The Monster Is Loose.*[5]

Filmography

Film			
Year	**Film**	**Role**	**Notes**
2004	*Noel*	Boy Soprano	
2005	*Love's Long Journey*	Jeff Huff	
2006	*The Ten Commandments: The Musical*	Moses' Son	
2007	*Evan Almighty*	Jordan Baxter	Nominated – Young Artist Award for Best Performance by a Supporting Young Actor in a Feature Film - Comedy or Musical
	Ben 10: Race Against Time	Ben Tennyson	Nominated – Young Artist Award for Best Performance by a Leading Young Actor in a TV Movie, Miniseries or Special
2009	*Stolen Lives*	Mark Wakefield	
2011	*Goats*	Ellis	completed; premiered at Sundance 2012

Television			
Year	**Television**	**Role**	**Notes**
2009–2012	*The Good Wife*	Zach Florrick	2010: Nominated – Screen Actors Guild Award for Outstanding Performance by an Ensemble in a Drama Series 2011: Nominated – Screen Actors Guild Award for Outstanding Performance by an Ensemble in a Drama Series 2011: Nominated — Young Artist Award for Best Supporting Young Actor in a TV Series – Comedy or Drama[4] 2012: Nominated – Screen Actors Guild Award for Outstanding Performance by an Ensemble in a Drama Series

Guest Appearances			
Year	**Title**	**Role**	**Episodes**
2002	*The King of Queens*	Winthrop	Mentalo Case
2004	*Judging Amy*	Toby Carroll	Legacy
2006	*Crossing Jordan*	Jonah Wheeler/Kyle	Mace vs. Scalpel
2012	*White Collar*	Evan	Upper West Side Story

References

[1] Midgette, Anne (November 14, 2005). "From Grown-Ups, a 'Little Prince' for Children" (http://www.nytimes.com/2005/11/14/arts/music/14prin.html). *The New York Times*. .

[2] "Nominations Announced for the 18th Annual Screen Actors Guild Awards" (http://www.sagawards.org/media-pr/11213). December 14, 2011. .

[3] "The 17th Annual Screen Actors Guild Awards" (http://www.sagawards.org/awards/nominees-and-recipients/17th-annual-screen-actors-guild-awards). December 16, 2010. .

[4] "32nd Annual Young Artist Awards - Nominations / Special Awards" (http://www.youngartistawards.org/noms32.html). The Young Artist Foundation. 2011. . Retrieved 2011-03-15.

[5] "It's Evening in America". *Vanity Fair*. May 2012. Page 158.

External links

- Graham Phillips (http://www.imdb.com/name/nm1775177/) at the Internet Movie Database

Greyson Chance

Greyson Chance

Chance in concert at the Hard Rock Cafe in Boston, Massachusetts on September 20, 2011

Background information	
Birth name	Greyson Michael Chance
Born	August 16, 1997[1] Wichita Falls, Texas, USA[2]
Origin	Edmond, Oklahoma, USA[2]
Genres	Pop rock, piano rock
Occupations	Singer-songwriter
Instruments	Piano, vocals
Years active	2010–present
Labels	eleveneleven, Maverick, Streamline, Geffen
Website	greyson-official.com [3]

Greyson Michael Chance (born August 16, 1997)[1] is an American pop rock singer, songwriter, pianist whose April 2010 performance of Lady Gaga's "Paparazzi" at a sixth-grade music festival became a hit on YouTube,[4] gaining over 48 million views as of September 12, 2012. Two of his original compositions, "Stars" and "Broken Hearts", gained over 5 and 7 million views respectively on his YouTube channel.[5] His début single, "Waiting Outside the Lines", was released in October 2010. Chance's début album, *Hold On 'Til the Night,* was released on August 2, 2011.

Personal life

Chance was born on August 16, 1997 in Wichita Falls, Texas, and currently resides in Edmond, Oklahoma. He is the youngest child of Scott and Lisa Chance. Chance has an eighteen-year-old sister, Alexa, and a twenty-year-old brother, Tanner, both of whom also do music. Chance began playing the piano at the age of 8 and has had three years of piano lessons. He, however, had no formal vocal training.

Of his inspiration, Chance said, "I love artists who are able to communicate their emotions through music and sing from the heart. That's what I'm hoping to do with my songs." He was emboldened by Lady Gaga after seeing her performance of "Paparazzi" at the 2009 MTV Video Music Awards. He stated, "I was awestruck by her performance. I love her sense of drama and theatricality. Plus, she's an amazing singer and piano player." Chance was also inspired by the artists Christina Aguilera, Augustana, John Legend, Elton John, and John Lennon.

Appearances

Chance's "Paparazzi" cover video was posted to YouTube, on April 28, 2010, and for almost two weeks the video generated low views. At least two social websites, GossipBoy.ca and reddit.com, posted video embeds on May 10, 2010. Ellen DeGeneres first saw the video after Chance's brother, Tanner Chance, wrote to her show suggesting she watch it.[6] The video had about 10,000 views when DeGeneres first saw it.[7] While explaining her reasons for naming her new record label *eleveneleven*, she listed as one reason the fact that she first saw Chance's "Paparazzi" cover on May 11, 2010. Also, she states that 11 is Greyson's soccer jersey number.[8] On the afternoon of May 11, *Yahoo! Music* reported: "As of this writing, the video has got more than 36,000 views so far, and he's even been invited to perform on *The Ellen DeGeneres Show*.[4]

On May 12, 2010 Greyson Chance taped an interview and performance of "Paparazzi" for *Ellen* in Los Angeles.[9] It was broadcast on May 13.[10][11] During the interview, Chance received a phone call from Lady Gaga,[12] who the boy says is his "true inspiration."[13] This first appearance on *Ellen* was followed by a second appearance on the show, airing May 26, 2010, on which Chance performed his original song "Broken Hearts", received a $10,000 award for winning *Ellen's Wonderful Web of Wonderment* contest, a brand new Yamaha piano, and was announced as DeGeneres's first signed artist to her new recording label eleveneleven.[14] Chance now has many fans on online social sites such as Facebook and Twitter.[15] He is the 28th most subscribed musician of all time on YouTube, with a 286,000 subscriber base, as of January 3, 2011.[16] Greyson Chance also appeared at We Day (also known as Me to We Day 2010) in downtown Toronto at the Air Canada Centre, where he performed "Fire" by Augustana.[17]

In the media

On the morning of May 11, 2010, Chance's cover video of "Paparazzi" was embedded at RyanSeacrest.com, which reported finding the video via BuzzFeed, a website that attempts to track and predict emerging viral internet memes.[18] Later in the day, *TVGuide*,[19] *The Huffington Post*,[20] and Yahoo! Music's video blog, Video Ga Ga,[4] also posted articles embedding the video; *TVGuide* mentioned in its article that a Facebook fan page had already been started for Chance. That afternoon, Ryan Seacrest and DeGeneres linked the video on their Twitter accounts,[21][22] as did celebrity Ashton Kutcher[23] later that evening.

On May 12, 2010, DeGeneres' announcement of Chance's booking, on *The Ellen DeGeneres Show*, was broadcast at different times across the U.S. and posted to her website.[24] *Wall Street Journal*[25] and *Los Angeles Times*,[26] among other mainstream media, posted articles embedding the video and announcing the forthcoming appearance. That evening, ABC World News broadcast a report on Chance which was introduced by Diane Sawyer, who said the story struck ABC News as "part *Billy Elliot* and part *Glee*."[27] Also that evening, Guy Oseary, an L.A.-based entertainment manager whose clients include Madonna, Demi Moore, and Ashton Kutcher, recommended Greyson's "Paparazzi" video on Twitter.[28]

Greyson at the film premiere of Harry Potter and the Deathly Hallows – Part 2 in July 2011.

On May 13, 2010, Chance's appearance on *The Ellen DeGeneres Show* was broadcast, and mainstream media, including CBS[29] and *People*,[30] reported on the appearance. That morning, Ryan Seacrest posted another link on Twitter, this time to the video of Chance appearing on *The Ellen DeGeneres Show*.[31] Not only has he received attention from DeGeneres and Seacrest but also, on May 14, singer, songwriter, and author David Archuleta linked the video on Twitter claiming that Greyson "is talented."[32]

On May 15, 2010, Greyson Chance created an official MySpace page[33] and an official Twitter[34] account. The same day, Crazed Hits, a music industry "tip-sheet" run by Alex Wilhelm, while citing no sources, reported that Interscope Records had signed 12-year-old Chance to a record deal.[35] The same day, NewsOK posted a video, "Three Things to Know about Greyson Michael Chance", and an article in which Chance's father, was quoted as saying the family would spend the weekend deciding how they wanted to proceed before signing any contracts.[36]

On May 18, 2010, the *New York Post* reported on the deal with Interscope Records, citing Chance's sister and father as confirming the deal; *The Post* also reported that calls made to Chance's school were being referred to Guy Oseary.[37] On May 25, Ellen DeGeneres announced that she had formed a record label called eleveneleven and Chance was her first artist.[38] Guy Oseary who manages Madonna's career and Troy Carter, who manages Lady Gaga's career, would be co-managers of Greyson Chance's career, but no partnership with a major recording label had been finalized.[39]

The chronology of events has resulted in media analysis of the marketing phenomenon separately from musical or biographical elements. On May 15, 2010, *The Christian Science Monitor* published an article by staff writer Gloria

Goodale; citing Chance's quick rise to media attention and the establishment of various official and fan websites for Chance, as well as concerns raised by music industry analyst Jeff Snyder about the quality of the video itself, Goodale asked "whether there's a Big Media hand behind sixth grader Greyson Michael Chance."[15] On May 18, 2010, Goodale followed this up with a second article focusing on the modern "age of media manipulation", which she introduced by saying, "Reports so far suggest that the Greyson Chance YouTube video is legit."[40] On May 18, 2010, ITN News posted a video report to its YouTube channel, in which many of the same questions were raised; highlighting aspects of Chance's "Paparazzi" video, media industry analyst Alan Stevens pointed out the growing inability within our modern media culture to distinguish between videos which are produced by amateurs and videos which are produced by professionals but made to appear amateur in origin.[41]

His debut single title "Waiting Outside the Lines" was released to iTunes on October 26, 2010. It was released digitally in the UK on December 9. The single also contained a studio version of his cover of Lady Gaga's "Paparazzi". In early December 2010 he visited both Paris and London, appearing on local radio stations and giving private concerts in both cities.[42][43]

On February 5,[44] Greyson Chance entered the National spotlight again with an appearance/performance of "Waiting Outside The Lines" on the CBS *Early Show*, while stopping through New York on his tour with Miranda Cosgrove.

On May 17, 2011 his new single "Unfriend You" was released to iTunes.[45]

On April 9, he started the Waiting 4U tour with Australian pop/R&B singer Cody Simpson in Ivins, Utah. The tour ended on May 18, 2011 in Portland, Oregon.

On May 23, Greyson visited *The Ellen DeGeneres Show* to premiere his new single, "Unfriend You". After the performance, Greyson revealed a solid release date for his upcoming debut album, *Hold On 'Til the Night*, which was released on August 2, 2011. The music video features a cameo from *Victorious* star, Ariana Grande.[46]

On September 15, he again appeared on *The Ellen DeGeneres Show* to talk about his album, and also revealed that he had taken his first steps into acting, portraying a younger version of Jimmy Chance, the protagonist of *Raising Hope*, in the series' second season premiere.[47]

In November 2011, Greyson undertook a tour of Southeast Asia to promote his album, which had just been released in the region. Starting in Kuala Lumpur, Malaysia, where in addition to a showcase performance he was invited to perform at the Anugerah Industri Muzik (Malaysian Music Industry Awards) show (the first foreign artist so invited since 1999), Greyson also gave performances in Singapore; Kota Kinabalu (Borneo, Malaysia); Manila, Philippines; and Jakarta, Indonesia.[48][49][50]

In March 2012, Greyson returned to Asia, this time with his full four-part band, and gave full concert performances in Kuala Lumpur, Singapore, Jakarta, and Manila, before going on without the band on a promotional tour to Taiwan, Hong Kong, and Bangkok, Thailand. In early July he was back in the region for promotional and TV appearances in Hong Kong and Changsha (Hunan Province, China). In August he performed at the MTV-CCTV Mandarin Music Awards show in Beijing, and won the award for Most Popular New International Artist of the Year.[51]

Discography

Studio albums

Year	Album	Peak position	Sales
		US [52]	
2011	*Hold On 'til the Night* • Released: August 2, 2011 • Label: eleveneleven, Maverick, Geffen, Streamline • Format: CD, digital download	29	• US: 16,000

Extended play

Year	Album	Peak position	Sales
		US	
2012	*Truth Be Told, Part 1* • Released: October 26, 2012 • Label: Geffen • Format: Digital download	—	

Singles

from *Hold On 'til the Night*

- "Waiting Outside the Lines" (peaked at #112 in Billboard 100)
- "Unfriend You"
- "Hold On 'til the Night"
- "Take a Look at Me Now"

from *Truth Be Told, Part 1*

- "Sunshine & City Lights"

Music videos

Year	Song	Director
2010	"Waiting Outside the Lines"	Sanaa Hamri
2011	"Unfriend You"	Marc Klasfeld[53]
2011	"Hold On 'til the Night"	Dano Cerny, Marielle Tepper
2012	"Sunshine & City Lights"	Clarence Fuller

Tours

- Waiting 4U Tour
- Dancing Crazy Tour
- Asia Tour 2011

Awards and recognition

Year	Category	Work	Award	Result
2010	Choice Web Star	Himself	Teen Choice Awards	Nominated
	Icon of Tomorrow		J-14 Teen Icon Awards	Nominated
	Teen Pick: YouTube Artist		Hollywood Teen TV Awards	Nominated
2011	Favorite Viral Video Star		People's Choice Awards	Nominated
	Rockin' New Artist of the Year		Youth Rock Awards	Nominated
2012	Most Popular New International Artist of the Year		MTV-CCTV Mandarin Music Awards	Won

References

[1] "21 Under 21: Greyson Chance" (http://www.billboard.com/features/21-under-21-greyson-chance-1004116423.story?sms_ss=blogger). *Billboard*. Prometheus Global Media. September 23, 2010. . Retrieved January 2, 2011.

[2] "Greyson Chance : Biography" (http://www.greyson-official.com/bio/). *Greyson-official.com*. . Retrieved January 2, 2011.

[3] http://www.greyson-official.com/

[4] "Little Lord Gaga: Greyson Michael Chance's "Paparazzi" Is A Web Sensation" (http://new.music.yahoo.com/blogs/videogaga/39067/little-lord-gaga-greyson-michael-chances-paparazzi-is-a-web-sensation/), Yahoo! Music. May 11, 2010.

[5] "Greyson Chance's YouTube channel" (http://www.youtube.com/user/greyson97). . Retrieved February 2, 2011.

[6] "See Greyson Chance at Home" (http://ellen.warnerbros.com/videos/?autoplay=true&mediaKey=eeff7182-dbbb-4a66-afdc-6c31b6521ee8&isShareURL=true), EllenTV.com, May 25, 2010.

[7] "Ellen DeGeneres Starts Record Label Just to Sign Greyson Chance" (http://www.people.com/people/article/0,,20388495,00.html) People.com, May 26, 2010.

[8] "Ellen Explains Her New eleveneleven Record Label" (http://ellen.warnerbros.com/2010/05/ellen_explains_her_new_eleveneleven_record_label_0528.php) EllenTV.com, May 28, 2010.

[9] "Clip from the Future: 12-year-old Web Sensation Greyson Chance performs on The Ellen DeGeneres Show (http://ellen.warnerbros.com/2010/05/12-year-old-web-sensation-greyson-chance-0512.php/), EllenTV.com, May 12, 2010.

[10] "Greyson Chance performs on The Ellen DeGeneres Show (http://ellen.warnerbros.com/music/greyson-chance.php), EllenTV.com. May 13, 2010.

[11] "Greyson Michael Chance Rocks Ellen" (http://www.cbsnews.com/stories/2010/05/13/entertainment/main6480145.shtml), CBSNews.com. May 13, 2010

[12] "Lady Gaga phones 12-year-old YouTube star" (http://news.bbc.co.uk/1/hi/entertainment_and_arts/10116841.stm), *BBC News*. May 14, 2010.

[13] "Prodigy Greyson Michael Chance on Ellen – Lady Gaga's Paparazzi" (http://www.nationalledger.com/artman/publish/article_272631756.shtml). *National Ledger* (Phoenix AZ). May 13, 2010. . Retrieved May 19, 2010.

[14] "Video of the Day: Greyson Chance Returns to 'Ellen'" (http://ellen.warnerbros.com/2010/05/greyson_chance_returns_to_ellen_vod_0526.php?adid=greyson_chance_returns_to_ellen_vod_0526_sphere_ellen) EllenTV.com, May 26, 2010.

[15] Goodale, Gloria (May 15, 2010). "Is Greyson Chance's Serendipitous YouTube Rise a Ruse?" (http://www.csmonitor.com/USA/2010/0515/Is-Greyson-Chance-s-serendipitous-Youtube-rise-a-ruse/), *The Christian Science Monitor* (Boston MA).

[16] "greyson97's Channel" (http://www.youtube.com/user/greyson97). Youtube.com. Retrieved on 2012-08-22.

[17] "Home" (http://www.freethechildren.com). Free The Children. May 21, 2010. . Retrieved December 18, 2010.

[18] "Justin Bieber Look-alike Plays Lady Gaga's 'Paparazzi" (http://ryanseacrest.com/2010/05/11/justin-bieber-look-alike-plays-lady-gagas-paparazzi-video/), RyanSeacrest.com, May 11, 2010.

[19] "Sixth Grader Wows Crowd with Lady Gaga Cover" (http://www.tvguide.com/News/Greyson-Gaga-Paparazzi-1018320.aspx), *TV Guide*, May 11, 2010.

[20] "13-Year-Old's 'Paparazzi' Cover Woos The Ladies" (http://www.huffingtonpost.com/2010/05/11/13-year-olds-paparazzi-co_n_571836.html), *The Huffington Post*, May 11, 2010.

[21] "u cant really go wrong singing..." (http://twitter.com/RyanSeacrest/status/13806833060) Ryan Seacrest on Twitter, May 11, 2010.

[22] "Never been more excited..." (http://twitter.com/TheEllenShow/status/13806721331), Ellen DeGeneres on Twitter when she announced Chance's forthcoming appearance on her show, May 11, 2010.

[23] "Watch the 1 girl in the back row..." (http://twitter.com/aplusk/status/13827306741), Ashton Kutcher on Twitter, May 11, 2010.

[24] "Greyson Chance's Unbelievable Performance" (http://ellen.warnerbros.com/2010/05/greyson_chances_unbelievable_performance_0512.php), EllenTV.com, May 12, 2010.

[25] "Lady Gaga Fan Greyson Michael Chance to Perform on Ellen" (http://blogs.wsj.com/speakeasy/2010/05/12/lady-gaga-fan-greyson-michael-chance-to-perform-on-ellen/), *Wall Street Journal* blog, May 12, 2010.

[26] "Paparazzi prodigy Greyson Michael Chance booked by Ellen" (http://latimesblogs.latimes.com/gossip/2010/05/paparazzi-prodigy-greyson-michael-chance-booked-by-ellen.html/) *Los Angeles Times* blog, May 12, 2010.

[27] "6th Grader Takes Chance, Becomes Sensation" (http://abcnews.go.com/WNT/video/6th-grader-takes-dare-sensation-10631403), *ABC World News*, May 12, 2010.

[28] "Check this video out – 'Paparazzi'" (http://twitter.com/guyoseary/status/13896200472), Guy Oseary on Twitter, May 12, 2010.

[29] "Greyson Michael Chance Rocks Ellen" (http://www.cbsnews.com/stories/2010/05/13/entertainment/main6480145.shtml/), *CBS News*, May 13, 2010.

[30] "Is Greyson Chance the Next Justin Bieber (or Lady GaGa)?" (http://www.people.com/people/article/0,,20368867,00.html), *People*, May 13, 2010.

[31] "The kid just keeps getting better!" (http://twitter.com/RyanSeacrest/status/13926635468), Ryan Seacrest on Twitter, May 13, 2010.

[32] "David Archuleta acknowledges Greyson's talent." (http://twitter.com/DavidArchie/status/13995739121), David Archuleta on Twitter, May 14, 2010.

[33] "The OFFICIAL MySpace Page of Greyson Chance!" (http://www.myspace.com/greysonchance), Greyson Chance on MySpace, May 15, 2010.

[34] "My first tweet!" (http://twitter.com/greysonchance/status/14076708184), Greyson Chance on Twitter, May 15, 2010.

[35] "Interscope sign YouTube Star" (http://www.crazedhits.com/interscope-sign-12-year-old-youtube-star/), CrazedHits.com, May 15, 2010.

[36] Williams, John A. (May 15, 2010). "Gaga songsters parents put brakes on fame for now" (http://newsok.com/gaga-songsters-parents-put-brakes-on-fame-for-now/article/3461566?custom_click=rss/), *The Oklahoman* (Oklahoma City).

[37] Kemp, Adam; Li, David K. (May 18, 2010). "Gaga over kid singer: Label signs Lady Lovin Web Phenom, 12" (http://www.nypost.com/p/news/national/label_signs_lady_lovin_web_phenom_V8vMmBwSUyHEfHOvyzSfVP#ixzz0oJ8O1Ivj/), *New York Post*.

[38] "A Message from Ellen" (http://ellen.warnerbros.com/2010/05/a_message_from_ellen_0525.php), EllenTV.com. May 25, 2010.

[39] Herrera, Monica (June 4, 2010). "Search on for the next Justin Bieber" (http://www.thestar.com/entertainment/music/article/817698--search-on-for-the-next-justin-bieber), *Toronto Star*.

[40] Goodale, Gloria (May 18, 2010). "Greyson Chance: What is real in an age of media manipulation?" (http://www.csmonitor.com/USA/Society/2010/0518/Greyson-Chance-What-is-real-in-an-age-of-media-manipulation/), *The Christian Science Monitor* (Boston MA).

[41] "Is Greyson Chance Manufactured?" (http://www.youtube.com/watch?v=i1MBBRpYY3k&feature=player_embedded), ITN News on YouTube, May 18, 2010.

[42] "Greyson Chance – Live – Paparazzi de Lady Gaga – Le 6/9 NRJ" December 10, 2010 (http://le-6-9.nrj.fr/videos-3344/media/video/300850-greyson-chance-live-paparazzi-de-lady-gaga-le-6-9-nrj.html). Le-6-9.nrj.fr. Retrieved on 2012-08-22.

[43] "Greyson Chance on BBC Radio" December 12, 2010 (http://www.greysonchanceweb.com/2010/12/greyson-chance-on-bbc-radio/). Greysonchanceweb.com (2010-12-12). Retrieved on 2012-08-22.

[44] "Greyson Chance performs and interviews with CBS Early Show" (http://www.greysonchancezone.com/greyson-chance-videos/greyson-chance-interview-videos/greyson-chance-explains-waiting-outside-the-lines-to-cbs-backstage/) GCZ – February 5, 2011

[45] iTunes – Unfriend You (http://itunes.apple.com/us/album/unfriend-you-single/id436389528). Itunes.apple.com. Retrieved on 2012-08-22.

[46] Greyson Chance 2nd Day of UnFriend You Video Shoot with Ariana Grande July 13th 2011 – Greyson Chance What's New! – Greyson Chance Fans | Fan Site Blog (http://greysonchancefans.com/whats-new/2011/6/14/greyson-chance-2nd-day-of-unfriend-you-video-shoot-with-aria.html). Greyson Chance Fans (2011-06-14). Retrieved on 2012-08-22.

[47] The Ellen DeGeneres Show, Thursday September 15, 2011; Episode: Eva Longoria/Greyson Chance.

[48] Hanis Maketab (November 19, 2011). "SHOWBIZ: Chance encounter" (http://www.nst.com.my/life-times/live/showbiz-chance-encounter-1.7811). *New Straits Times* (Kuala Lumpur). . Retrieved December 13, 2011.

[49] "Greyson Chance to perform here on Nov 13" (http://news.asiaone.com/News/Latest+News/Showbiz/Story/A1Story20111102-308279.html). *My Paper* (Singapore). November 2, 2011. . Retrieved December 13, 2011.

[50] Belmonte, Maureen Marie (November 21, 2011). "Greyson on seizing that 'Chance' of a lifetime" (http://www.mb.com.ph/articles/342081/greyson-seizing-chance-a-lifetime). *Manila Bulletin*. . Retrieved December 13, 2011.

[51] Chen Nan (August 31, 2012). "Young heartthrob remains down to earth" (http://www.chinadaily.com.cn/cndy/2012-08/31/content_15722619.htm). *China Daily*. . Retrieved October 27, 2012.

[52] Hold on 'Til the Night – Greyson Chance (2011) (http://www.billboard.com/#/album/greyson-chance/hold-on-til-the-night/1522664). billboard.com

[53] Gottlieb, Steven (May 20, 2011). "Video Static: Music Video News: IN PRODUCTION: Greyson Chance – Marc Klasfeld, dir." (http://www.videostatic.com/vs/2011/05/in-production-greyson-chance-marc-klasfeld-dir.html). Video Static.. . Retrieved July 17, 2011.

External links

- Official website (http://www.greyson-official.com/)
- Greyson Chance (http://www.imdb.com/name/nm3976550/) at the Internet Movie Database

iCarly

iCarly	
Genre	Teen sitcom
Created by	Dan Schneider
Starring	Miranda Cosgrove Jennette McCurdy Nathan Kress Jerry Trainor Noah Munck
Theme music composer	Michael Corcoran
Opening theme	"Leave It All to Me", sung by Miranda Cosgrove and Drake Bell
Country of origin	United States
Language(s)	English
No. of seasons	7
No. of episodes	109 (List of episodes)
Production	
Executive producer(s)	Dan Schneider
Producer(s)	Robin Weiner (supervising producer; co-executive producer season 5–7) Joe Catania Bruce Rand Berman (season 2–7) Jake Farrow (season 5–7) Matt Fleckenstein (season 5–7) Arthur Gradstein (season 5–7)
Location(s)	Nickelodeon on Sunset Hollywood, California (2007–2012) KTLA Studios Hollywood, California (2012)
Camera setup	Videotape (filmized); Multi-camera
Running time	23 minutes (regular episode)
Production company(s)	Schneider's Bakery Nickelodeon Productions
Distributor	Nickelodeon

Broadcast	
Original channel	Nickelodeon
Picture format	480i (SDTV) 1080i (HDTV)
Audio format	Stereo
Original run	September 8, 2007 – November 23, 2012
Chronology	
Followed by	*Sam & Cat*, *Gibby*
Related shows	*Victorious*
External links	
Website [1]	

iCarly is an American teen sitcom that ran on Nickelodeon from September 8, 2007 until November 23, 2012. The series was created by Dan Schneider and follows teenager Carly Shay and her best friends Sam Puckett and Freddie Benson as they create and star in their own web show.

The show focuses on a girl named Carly Shay who creates her own web show called *iCarly* with her best friends Sam and Freddie. It stars Miranda Cosgrove as Carly, Jennette McCurdy as Sam, Nathan Kress as Freddie, Jerry Trainor as Spencer, and Noah Munck as Gibby. The show was taped at Nickelodeon on Sunset (season 1–5) and KTLA Studios (Season 6–7) in Hollywood, California. The show was originally rated TV-Y7, and later changed to TV-G.

On May 17, 2012, it was announced that the show's seventh season was the last for *iCarly* and that a series finale event would air in November 2012.[2] The series finale, "iGoodbye" aired on November 23, 2012.

Development

iCarly is the fourth series created by Dan Schneider for Nickelodeon. Schneider originally wanted to make a new TV series starring Miranda Cosgrove; the original idea was that she play a normal girl who, in a twist of fate, gets cast to star in her favorite TV show, *Starstruck*. The pilot was written (and turned in to Nickelodeon), which was about Carly, a regular girl who gets cast to star in her favorite TV show. However, things started to take a turn. During a casual meeting in his den with his wife and his friend Steve, Schneider decided that it would be much better if Carly had her own show – a show she could run herself, the way she wanted, and do whatever she wanted to do which would become a web show. In November 2006, Schneider threw out his *Starstruck* script and wrote a brand new pilot called *iCarly* during December. The pilot was shot in January 2007.[3]

During production of *Zoey 101*, Schneider came up with the idea of the show and its name with his friend and producer of *The Big Bang Theory*, Steve Molaro. He was trying to think of a good title for the new series about kids who start their own web show. However, *iCarly* was not going to be the original name for the show. In fact, the pilot script followed the lead girl's name was "Sam" but the URL for iSam was already taken. Schneider tried other girl's names and bought the URL for iJosie, but he decided he did not like the name. Schneider tried *iCarly* and loved the name for the lead character. The names of the two lead girls were then changed from Sam and Kira to Carly and Sam.[4]

Plot

When Carly and her sassy best friend Sam act funny at a school talent show audition, tech-savvy Freddie tapes it and posts it online without telling them. After seeing the girls' strong chemistry and banter, the online audience clamors for more and the iCarly webcast is born. While grappling with typical issues of adolescence, Carly, Sam, and Freddie find out that they have also become online celebrities as their show — which features talent contests, recipes, problem-solving, and random dancing — garners international accolades.

Carly lives in Seattle, Washington with her 26-year-old brother and guardian Spencer and produces the show in a makeshift third-floor studio loft in their apartment. Their mother has never been seen or mentioned, but their father, Steven Shay, is a U.S. Air Force officer temporarily stationed on a submarine, and is often mentioned but is only seen in person during the series finale episode, *iGoodbye*.

Exterior shots of the Shays' apartment building, Bushwell Plaza, are digitally altered images of the Eastern Columbia Building in Los Angeles.

Characters

Main characters

- **Carly Shay** (Miranda Cosgrove) is the host of her own popular web show, *iCarly*, which she produces with her two best friends, Sam and Freddie.
- **Sam Puckett** (Jennette McCurdy) is one of Carly's best friends and co-host of *iCarly*.
- **Freddie Benson** (Nathan Kress) is also one of Carly's good friends and neighbor. He is the technical producer of *iCarly*.
- **Spencer Shay** (Jerry Trainor) is Carly's eccentric older brother and legal guardian.
- **Gibby** (Noah Munck) (Recurring Season 1–3, Main Cast 4–7) is an odd friend of Carly, Sam and Freddie.

Recurring characters

- **Marissa Benson** (Mary Scheer) is Freddie's overbearing and overprotective mother (often referred to by Sam as Freddie's "freakish mother").
- **Lewbert** (Jeremy Rowley) is the doorman for the building in which Carly, Spencer, and Freddie live, characterized by his annoying, protective behavior and a large wart on his face. He is often being pranked by the kids on *iCarly*.
- **Nevel Papperman** (Reed Alexander) is a critic who runs the nevelocity.com website, a site that reviews other websites, including iCarly.com. He is Carly's nemesis and has constantly tried to sabotage *iCarly* in exchange for a kiss from Carly.
- **T-Bo** (BooG!e) is the manager at the Groovy Smoothie. He often annoys customers into buying random foods (i.e. bell peppers, bagels, tacos), which are always impaled on a stick. Starting in "iQ", he began renting a room from Freddie's mother.
- **Guppy** (Ethan Munck) is Gibby's younger brother and often tags along with Gibby.
- **Chuck Chambers** (Ryan Ochoa) is a child in the Shays' apartment building who constantly torments Spencer.
- **Principal Franklin** (Tim Russ) is the principal at Ridgeway Secondary School, the school where Carly, Sam, and Freddie attend. He is very fair and is a big fan of iCarly.
- **Ms. Francine Briggs** (Mindy Sterling) is a very strict English teacher at Ridgeway Secondary School who shows an obvious dislike for children.
- **Mr. Howard** (David St. James) is a strict and unenthusiastic teacher who hates almost everything including his wife.

Episodes

Season	Episodes	Originally aired		Prod. line	DVD releases
		Season premiere	**Season finale**		
1	25	September 8, 2007	July 25, 2008	1xx	September 23, 2008 (Volume 1)[5] April 21, 2009 (Volume 2)[6]
2	25	September 27, 2008	August 8, 2009	2xx	August 18, 2009 (Volume 1)[7] January 4, 2011 (Volume 2)[8] April 5, 2011 (Volume 3)[9]
3	20	September 12, 2009	June 26, 2010		
4	13	July 30, 2010	June 11, 2011	3xx	August 30, 2011 (Season 3)[10]
5	11	August 13, 2011	January 21, 2012	4xx	July 10, 2012 (Season 4)[11]
6	6	March 24, 2012	June 9, 2012	5xx	TBA
7	9	October 6, 2012	November 23, 2012		TBA

Multi-part installments

Title	Type	Air date	Synopsis	Viewers
"iGo to Japan"	Television movie	November 8, 2008	After the iCarly crew is nominated for "Best Comedy Category," Carly, Sam, Freddie, Spencer, and Mrs. Benson fly away to Japan to attend the iWeb Awards show. However, their trip soon turns into an adventure with many twists after meeting with their competing webshow hosts *Kyoko and Yuki.*	7.6[12]
"iDate a Bad Boy"	Two-part special	May 9, 2009	When Spencer's motorcycle is "stolen" by Griffin, their new neighbor who claims he was only "borrowing" it, Carly immediately hates him for his wrongdoing whereas Spencer gives him a chance and drops the charges. Eventually, much to Carly's dismay, Spencer begins mentoring Griffin. However, after getting to know him, Carly actually falls for Griffin and makes out with him passionately. Spencer walks in on them and becomes angry and grounds her until oollege. Eventually, Spencer realizes he was being over-protective and allows them to resume dating, as long as they don't take their relationship too far. While they are dating, however, Carly finds out a big secret about Griffin that she does not like at all; he collects "PeeWee Babies." This leaves Carly conflicted, and she has to decide if she should continue dating him or end their relationship. Meanwhile, Freddie attempts to build Sam a website after making a contract deal with her, and Sam experiences nightmares about a monster eating her soup, leading Spencer to help her get over her dream through confrontation.	7.1[13]
"iFight Shelby Marx"	Two-part special	August 8, 2009	When Carly jokingly challenges the champion martial arts fighter, Shelby Marx, during a web show, Shelby arrives at the Shay loft along with her manager, etc., to accept her challenge. It turns out to be the manager's idea and it is not a real fight, but an exhibition fight intended for fun. However, during a press conference, Carly accidentally knocks Shelby's grandmother down during a mock fight, which Shelby takes really seriously, prompting her to decide to fight for real. Later, Carly explains that it was all an accident and that she was pushed. Shelby accepts her apology, they make up, and the fight is an exhibition match once again. Meanwhile, Spencer has allergies and a doctor gives him pills to get rid of them forever. However, he must first be able to cope with troublesome side effects for a certain period of time.	7.9[13]

"iQuit iCarly"	Two-part special	December 5, 2009	After the iCarly crew agrees to help the web show hosts for the *Fleck and Dave Show*, they make a video for a website video contest. Fleck and Dave fight which leaves their friendship in jeopardy due to their conflicts with each other. The iCarly crew attempts to bring them back together as friends, which only leads to conflict for Carly and Sam when their comparison of conflicts with each other with Fleck and Dave's conflicts eventually breaks them up, even to the point where the web show is put in jeopardy. Meanwhile, Spencer becomes determined to win a boat through a televised contest in which a contestant must be able to answer the most boat-themed questions correctly and send them in, which Spencer eventually wins. Gibby tags along in his attempt to find parking for the boat, only to stumble upon a mishap with someone else's parkway space and lose the boat through force to the person's baseball team.	9.9[13]
"iPsycho"	Two-part special	June 4, 2010	The iCarly crew is getting ready for Webicon when they stumble upon an iCarly video mail from a girl named Nora Dirshlitt. She has a somewhat sad life and invites the iCarly crew to her upcoming birthday party. Feeling sympathetic, the crew divides their time to take a trip to Webicon to attend Nora's birthday party. The clown at the party suffers an aneurysm and is immediately hospitalized, with no guarantee of surviving, leaving Nora very sad. Feeling very sorry for Nora, the gang decides to do a web show in order to convince Nora's peers at School that the crew are really at her party. After the party, Nora decides to take advantage of the crew and locks them up in a basement studio hoping this will boost her popularity and help her gain more friends, leaving Carly, Sam, and Freddie in a sticky situation – from which they must escape. Meanwhile, Gibby decides to camp at the Shay loft, after not being able to attend his camp for another year due to age.	8.2[14]
"iStart a Fan War"	Two-part special	November 19, 2010	The iCarly crew once again head to Webicon for a panel, while Carly has a crush on a guy named Adam at Ridgeway High School. While Carly converses with Adam via video chat, Adam mentions that fans create forums and discuss whether Freddie should be with Carly or Sam. The fans call themselves "Creddies" and "Seddies". During the panel at Webicon, Sam starts a fan war between Creddies and Seddies which gets out of hand. This not only makes things bad at the panel, but makes things bad for Carly and Adam's connection. Meanwhile, Spencer tags along with them at Webicon dressed as Aruthor from "World of Warlords" to win a costume contest, only to meet a man dressed as Aruthor's mortal enemy, Aspartamay.	5.0[15]
"iParty with Victorious"	Television movie/Crossover special	June 11, 2011 (original) August 27, 2011 (extended)	Carly is happier than ever since she is now in a steady relationship with a boy named Steven, in which nothing goes wrong. He divides his time between his divorced parents in Seattle and Los Angeles. Unknown to the iCarly gang, Steven goes to Los Angeles where it is revealed that he is dating another girl named Tori Vega (from *Victorious*) at the same time. However, Robbie Shapiro (also from *Victorious*), posts a picture to TheSlap.com of Steven and Tori together. Sam immediately suspects he is dating another girl, leading the iCarly crew to head to Los Angeles on an adventure to set things straight after seeing an open invite online from Rex (from *Victorious*) to a party by André Harris (from *Victorious*) thanks to Kenan Thompson, where the gang meets with the *Victorious* gang.	7.3[16] (original) 3.7[17] (extended)
"iStill Psycho"	Two-part special	December 31, 2011	Nora is released from prison, and is having a welcome home party. The iCarly gang rushes to court to try to keep Nora behind bars at any cost but fail. The iCarly trio plus Spencer and Gibby go to the party, but this time Nora and the rest of her family are in on trapping them. Freddie finds a way to contact his mother but will she be able to save the day?	5.5[18]
"iShock America"	Two-part special	October 6, 2012	Jimmy Fallon invites the gang to New York after Carly dedicates a webshow to him parodying his famous skits. Gibby bought street pants and caused a few problems during the show. While the gang starts dancing, Gibby's street pants fall down and he isn't wearing underwear, causing the NCC to show up. People start to blame Jimmy for the incident by saying he deliberately wanted Gibby's pants to fall. Carly and her friends do an episode of iCarly saying it was their fault and not Jimmy's. They have to pay $500,000 or the NCC will shut down iCarly. So Jimmy blogs asking America for their spare change to help the iCarly gang get $500,000. Jimmy got the iCarly gang to the studios and the fans got them more than $500,000.	3.6[19]

"iGoodbye"	Two-part special	November 23, 2012	Carly is expecting her father Colonel Shay to arrive in Seattle to escort her to the Father-Daughter Air Force Dance, only to receive his email saying he will actually be unable to make it. To comfort her, Spencer asks to escort her to the dance, and she accepts. Meanwhile, prior to the dance, he attempts to repair a motorcycle for Socko's cousin Ryder. Sam instantly marvels at the vehicle and volunteers to assist Spencer in fixing it. Shortly after this, however, Spencer becomes sick from being sneezed at by Lewbert, the apartment building's doorman, and is unable to take his sister to the dance. Meanwhile, Freddie and Gibby are at the mall to create a replica of the latter's head, after losing his original copy at a pawn shop in Las Vegas. They are informed by Sam over the phone of Spencer's illness and offer to escort Carly to the dance, to which she cries as a sign of rejecting the offer. Colonel Shay arrives at Carly's home, much to her sudden and pleasant surprise, and escorts her to the dance. Upon returning, Colonel Shay informs everyone that he has to return to his base in Italy and invites her to travel with him. Despite her initial reluctance, Carly accepts the offer, and the gang streams their last iCarly webcast together with Colonel Shay present. Sam receives the motorcycle from Spencer after Socko changes his mind about giving it to his cousin. Carly and Freddie kiss each other for the last time in the iCarly studio alone before she departs. On an airplane, Carly is seen viewing a montage of archived iCarly webcasts as she and her dad are bound towards Italy. This is the final part of the iCarly series.	6.4[20]

iParty with Victorious

A crossover between *iCarly* and *Victorious* was completed in 2010; *iParty with Victorious* aired on June 11, 2011. The crossover is considered a 3-part episode of *iCarly*. A two-hour extended version debuted August 27, 2011.

Season 5 onward

In late January 2011, while doing press for her North American Dancing Crazy concert tour, Miranda Cosgrove began telling news sources that she was looking forward to returning to Hollywood to begin filming a 5th season of *iCarly*.[21][22][23] On January 27, 2011, Cosgrove told Cleveland Live News "We're getting ready to start the next season, right after the tour. I would be willing to do the show as long as people like it and as long as it works."[21] On January 28, 2011, Reuters news agency also reported that Cosgrove was preparing to begin filming a 5th season of *iCarly*,[22] and on February 3, 2011 Cosgrove told The Middletown Press, when speaking of the show and her co-stars Jennette McCurdy and Nathan Kress, "I've known them since I was little. I can't wait to get back. I'm really comfortable doing iCarly. It's like my home away from home."[23] Cosgrove concluded her Dancing Crazy concert tour on February 24, 2011, and Jennette McCurdy finished her Generation Love mall tour on April 14, 2011.[24] The entire cast did not even get together until the 2011 Kids' Choice Awards. Miranda Cosgrove recently confirmed that filming would resume shortly.[25] At the 2011 Kids' Choice Awards, Jerry Trainor stated that filming would resume in May.[26]

On April 14, 2011, Nickelodeon officially announced the 5th and final production season renewal of *iCarly* to begin in 2012 with the episodes airing later that year.[27] These episodes would air as the show's sixth season due to the second season production of 45 episodes being split into two broadcast seasons.[28][29] The third production season originally consisted of 26 episodes as ordered in early 2010, however half that amount was shot from May to September 2010 that aired as the show's fourth season. Dan Schneider then shot the next half in May 2011 to July which became a whole new season production that aired as the show's fifth season later that year. However, due to Miranda's leave for a tour on July 15, 2011, only eleven episodes were produced and the last two were held over and produced during filming of the show's final season.

The final season, Season 7, began on March 24, 2012 with a total of fifteen episodes to air.[30] However, after a four month hiatus after six episodes of the season aired from March to June, "iShock America" was promoted as the start of a new season for the last batch of episodes,[31][32] effectively splitting the season into two. The series ended on

November 23, 2012 with the episode "iGoodbye".

Broadcast history

- *Nickelodeon* (September 8, 2007 – present)
- *TeenNick* (October 18, 2009 – present)

International releases

Country/Region	Official TV Network(s)	Series Premiere	Series Finale
United States	Nickelodeon TeenNick	September 8, 2007 October 18, 2009	November 23, 2012[33][34][35] 2013
Canada	Nickelodeon YTV	October 8, 2007 (YTV) November 3, 2009 (Nickelodeon)	December 1, 2012 (YTV)
Australia	Nickelodeon	October 29, 2007	December 2012
Germany	Nickelodeon	February 23, 2008	2013
United Kingdom	Nickelodeon	March 8, 2008	2013
Turkey	Nickelodeon	March 29, 2008	2013
Brazil	Nickelodeon	April 10, 2008	2013
Mexico	Nickelodeon Canal 5	April 16, 2008 January 2, 2009	2013
Argentina	Nickelodeon	April 16, 2008	2013
Chile			
Colombia			
Ecuador			
Honduras			
Peru			
Panama			
Uruguay			
Venezuela			
Dominican Republic			
Spain	Nickelodeon	May 17, 2008	2013
Netherlands	Nickelodeon		
Italy	Nickelodeon	June 15, 2008	2013
Poland	Nickelodeon	April 26, 2009	2013
Russia	Nickelodeon	May 1, 2009	January 30, 2013
France	Nickelodeon	September 2, 2009	2013
Greece	Nickelodeon	September 3, 2010	May 5, 2013

Internationalization

Some minor alterations have been made for transmission in markets where the series is dubbed. In the German version (but not on all transmitted episodes) the intro music lyrics are in German. Episode titles are usually the same when the series is dubbed.

DVD releases

Note: The season DVDs are released by the production seasons.

DVD Title	Region 1	Discs	Episodes	Extras
iCarly: Season 1, Vol. 1	September 23, 2008	2	1–12, 16	"Leave It All to Me" by Miranda Cosgrove
iCarly: Season 1, Vol. 2	April 21, 2009	2	13–15, 17–25	Behind the Slime with the cast of iCarly; Behind-the-Scenes Extras; Pilot episode of *True Jackson, VP*
iCarly: Season 2, Vol. 1	August 18, 2009	2	26–38	Featurette for The Making of "iGo to Japan" & Behind The Scenes with the iCarly Cast on Season 2!
iCarly: iFight Shelby Marx[36]	March 30, 2010	1	"iFight Shelby Marx", "iDate a Bad Boy", "iLook Alike", "iCarly Awards"	Special bonus episode: Pilot episode of *Big Time Rush*
iCarly: iSaved Your Life[37]	June 8, 2010	1	"iSaved Your Life", "iQuit iCarly", "iThink They Kissed", "iTwins", "iMove Out"	Behind the scenes with the cast of iCarly; iQuit iCarly window stunt; Meet Chuck; Favourite Birthday moments; Welcome to my boat
iCarly: iSpace Out[38][39]	August 31, 2010	1	"iSpace Out", "iWas a Pageant Girl", "iEnrage Gibby", "iBelieve in Bigfoot", "iFix a Popstar", "iWon't Cancel The Show"	Special bonus episode: Pilot episode of *Victorious*
iCarly: Season 2, Vol. 2[40]	January 4, 2011	2	39–52	Behind the Scenes with the Cast
iCarly: Season 2, Vol. 3[41]	April 5, 2011	3	53–70	Special bonus episode: Pilot episode of *T.U.F.F. Puppy* iSaved Your Life – Extended Version
iCarly: The i <3 iCarly Collection[42]	July 19, 2011	3	Collection includes all of "iSpace Out", "iSaved Your Life", and "iFight Shelby Marx" DVDs released previously separately	Special bonus episode: Pilot episode of *Big Time Rush*. Behind the scenes with the cast of iCarly; iQuit iCarly window stunt; Meet Chuck; Favorite Birthday moments; Welcome to my boat. Special bonus episode: Pilot episode of *Victorious*
iCarly: The Complete 3rd Season[43]	August 30, 2011	2	71–83	Carly's Hot New Room Tour, Meet Sam's Mother, Archenemies profiles
iCarly: The Complete 4th Season[44]	July 10, 2012	2	84–94	5 Bonus Episodes of *How to Rock*

Other media

Music

Columbia Records and Nickelodeon Records have released a soundtrack for the show entitled *iCarly*. It includes the theme song and four original songs by Miranda Cosgrove. Several tracks by guest artists and cast dialogue are also included. A follow-up soundtrack, titled *iSoundtrack II*, came out on January 24, 2012.[45]

Website

In reality, the iCarly.com website contains many promotional videos by the cast (as their respective characters), as well as content created and sent in by viewers. Other features on the site include characters' blogs, pictures from the set, songs, games, and comments from viewers. Many fictional websites from this show redirect to this page. For example, Zaplook [46], SplashFace [47], ToonJuice, CraigsMix [48], Nevelocity [49], GirlyCow.com, WebFlicks.com, RadioDingo.com, PillowMyHead.com, AggressiveParenting.com, SamPuckett.com, TheValerieShow.com, SendMeaSack.com, Beavecoon.org, NeverWatchiCarly.com, iSnarly.com, SprayYourChildren.com, and any other website mentioned on the show redirect to this page.

Video games

An animated PC hidden object game, *iCarly: iDream in Toons*, was released by Nickelodeon on their *Nick Arcade*. Jerry Trainor is the only actor from the cast who lends his voice to the game, the rest of the characters' speech being dubbed with typing sounds on a keyboard.

On May 13, 2009, Nickelodeon announced they had reached an agreement with Activision to produce an *iCarly video game* for the Nintendo DS and Wii. The game was released October 28, 2009. The cast lend their voices in the videogame. A sequel, iCarly 2: iJoin the Click, was released on November 16, 2010 for the same platforms.

On January 11, 2010, the official iCarly Facebook page announced the release of an application called "Sam's Remote" exclusively for iPhone and iPod Touch. This app consists of Sam's remote, which she uses on live casts of iCarly in the show, where one pushes different buttons and they make silly sound effects. Available through the iTunes App Store for $1.99 download.

Books

iCarly Reader series

Book
1. iDon't Wanna Fight!
2. iHatch Chicks!

iCarly Novel series

Book	Episode(s)
1. iHave a Web Show!	iPilot iWant More Viewers
2. iWanna Stay!	iSpy a Mean Teacher iWanna Stay with Spencer
3. iWant a World Record!	iWant a World Record iGot Detention
4. iAm Famous!	iPromote Tech-Foots iCarly Saves TV
5. iAm Your Biggest Fan!	iAm Your Biggest Fan iNevel
6. iGo to Japan!	iGo to Japan
7. iKiss!	iKiss iThink They Kissed iOMG iLost My Mind
8. iMove Into Carly's Apartment!	iSam's Mom iMove Out iChristmas

Proposed spin-off series

Two spin-off series have been proposed as pilots for Nickelodeon, and were both announced during the network's presentation at the Television Critics Association Summer Press Tour on August 3, 2012.[50]

The first is *Sam & Cat*, which would pair Ariana Grande from *Victorious* and Jennette McCurdy together in a traditional "buddy sitcom" setting as their characters, Cat Valentine and Sam Puckett. The pilot suggests they will be roommates who launch a babysitting business for income. The show was picked up by Nickelodeon on November 29, 2012.[51]

The second would spin-off Noah Munck's character Gibby Gibson into a self-titled sitcom named *Gibby* where the character works at a recreation center as a mentor to four middle school students.[52][53]

Reception

Critical

iCarly received mixed reviews from critics. Carey Bryson of About.com, gave the show 2 1/2 stars, concluding "The show's comedic elements don't all rest on the irreverent, though, there are some clever storylines and even a few touching moments. Overall, the show has some great comedy, interesting stories, and fun actors."[54] The show was awarded 3 stars by Common Sense Media reviewer Emily Ashby. Emily praised that "[t]he show isn't designed to be educational, per se, but young viewers will learn a bit about interacting with media."[55]

On the more positive side, Hollywood.com's Michelle Lee considered the show to be the best sitcom since arrested development: "Like the Lost fan rejecting every Lost-like show that came after it, I resented all of the shaky single-camera docu-style comedies that came after Arrested's demise. Because, frankly, my favorite dead show did it better. I needed something completely different to break me out of my comedy funk and get me back on that horse. And it worked."[56]

On TV.com, the show has received mixed reviews from users. Despite some negative reviews of *iCarly*, the series has an 8 (Great) rating on the website.[57] The first airing of the episode, at 8:30 PM on Saturday, September 8th drew 5.65 million viewers. This is the second highest of any Nickelodeon live action show only trailing behind Victorious whose premiere drew 5.7 million viewers.

The second airing at 11:30am on Sunday, September 9th drew 7.35 million viewers for a total of 13 million.

Awards and nominations

Year	Award	Category	Recipient	Result	Ref.
2008	2008 Kids' Choice Awards	Favorite TV Show	*iCarly*	Nominated	[58][59]
	2008 UK Kids' Choice Awards	Favorite Kids' TV Show	*iCarly*	Nominated	[60][61]
		Favorite Female TV Star	Miranda Cosgrove	Nominated	[60][61]
	2008 Australian Kids' Choice Awards	Fave Comedy Show	*iCarly*	Nominated	[62]
		Fave International TV Star	Miranda Cosgrove	Nominated	[62]
	Young Artist Award	Best Performance in a TV Series – Leading Young Actress	Miranda Cosgrove	Nominated	[63]
		Best Performance in a TV Series – Supporting Young Actor	Nathan Kress	Nominated	[63]
		Best Performance in a TV Series – Supporting Young Actress	Jennette McCurdy	Nominated	[63]
	British Academy Children's Awards	International	*iCarly*	Nominated	[64]
	Casting Society of America	Outstanding Achievement in Casting - Children's Series Programming	Sharon Chazin Lieblein Leah Buono Krisha Bullock	Nominated	[65]

2009	2009 Kids' Choice Awards	Favorite TV Show	*iCarly*	Won	[66]
		Favorite TV Actress	Miranda Cosgrove	Nominated	[66][67]
	2009 Australian Kids' Choice Awards	Fave Comedy Show	*iCarly*	Won	[68]
		Fave International TV Star	Miranda Cosgrove	Nominated	[68]
	Primetime Emmy Award	Outstanding Children's Program	*iCarly*	Nominated	[69]
	Teen Choice Award	Choice TV Actor: Comedy	Jerry Trainor	Nominated	[70]
		Choice TV Actress: Comedy	Miranda Cosgrove	Nominated	[70]
		Choice TV Sidekick	Jennette McCurdy	Nominated	[70]
		Choice TV Show: Comedy	*iCarly*	Nominated	[70]
	Young Artist Award	Best Performance in a TV Series (Comedy or Drama) – Leading Young Actor	Nathan Kress	Nominated	[71]
		Best Performance in a TV Series (Comedy or Drama) – Leading Young Actress	Miranda Cosgrove	Won	[71]
		Best Performance in a TV Series (Comedy or Drama) – Supporting Young Actress	Jennette McCurdy	Nominated	[71]
		Outstanding Young Performers in a TV Series	Miranda Cosgrove Nathan Kress Jennette McCurdy Noah Munck	Nominated	[71]
	British Academy Children's Awards	BAFTA Kid's Vote: TV	*iCarly*	Nominated	[72]
	Casting Society of America	Outstanding Achievement in Casting - Children's Series Programming	Krisha Bullock	Nominated	[73]
2010	2010 Kids' Choice Awards	Favorite TV Show	*iCarly*	Won	[74]
		Favorite TV Actress	Miranda Cosgrove	Nominated	[75]
	2010 Australian Kids' Choice Awards	Fave TV Show	*iCarly*	Won	[76]
		LOL Award	Cast of *iCarly*	Won	[76]
		Fave TV Star	Miranda Cosgrove	Nominated	[76][77]
		Big Kid Award	Jerry Trainor	Nominated	[76][77]

	Primetime Emmy Award	Outstanding Children's Program	*iCarly*	Nominated	[78]
	Teen Choice Award	Choice TV Actress: Comedy	Miranda Cosgrove	Nominated	[79]
	Television Critics Association Award	Outstanding Achievement in Youth Programming	*iCarly*	Nominated	[80][81]
	Young Artist Award	Best Performance in a TV Series (Comedy or Drama) – Leading Young Actress	Miranda Cosgrove	Nominated	[82]
		Best Performance in a TV Series (Comedy or Drama) – Supporting Young Actor	Nathan Kress	Nominated	[82]
		Best Performance in a TV Series – Guest Starring Young Actor 13 and Under	Joey Luthman	Nominated	[82]
		Outstanding Young Performers in a TV Series	Miranda Cosgrove Nathan Kress Jennette McCurdy Noah Munck	Nominated	[82]
	Hollywood Teen TV Awards	Teen Pick Actor: Comedy	Nathan Kress	Nominated	[83]
		Teen Show Pick: Comedy	*iCarly*	Nominated	[83]
	Kids Choice Awards Mexico 2010	Favorite Show	*iCarly*	Won	[84]
		Favorite International Female Personality	Miranda Cosgrove	Won	[84]
	Meus Premios Nick Brazil 2010	Favorite TV Show	*iCarly*	Won	[85]
	British Academy Children's Awards	BAFTA Kid's Vote: TV	*iCarly*	Nominated	[86]
	Casting Society of America	Outstanding Achievement in Casting - Children's Series Programming	Krisha Bullock	Nominated	[87]
2011	2011 Kids' Choice Awards	Favorite TV Show	*iCarly*	Won	[88]
		Favorite TV Actress	Miranda Cosgrove	Nominated	[88][89]
		Favorite TV Sidekick	Jennette McCurdy	Won	[88]
			Noah Munck	Nominated	[88][89]
	2011 UK Kids' Choice Awards	Nick UK's Favourite Show	*iCarly*	Nominated	[90]
		Nick UK's Funniest Person	Jerry Trainor	Won	[90]
	2011 Australian Kids' Choice Awards	LOL Award	Jennette McCurdy	Won	[91]
		Fave TV Star	Miranda Cosgrove	Nominated	[91][92]
		Fave TV Show	*iCarly*	Nominated	[91][92]
	Primetime Emmy Award	Outstanding Children's Program	*iCarly*	Nominated	[93]
		Outstanding Hairstyling For A Multi-Camera Series Or Special	Episode: iStart A Fan War	Nominated	[94]
		Outstanding Makeup For A Multi-Camera Series Or Special (Non-Prosthetic)	Episode: iStart A Fan War	Nominated	[95]

	Teen Choice Awards	Choice TV Show: Comedy	*iCarly*	Nominated	[96][97]
		Choice TV Actress: Comedy	Miranda Cosgrove	Nominated	[96][97]
		Choice TV: Female Scene Stealer	Jennette McCurdy	Nominated	[96][97]
	Television Critics Association Award	Outstanding Achievement in Youth Programming	*iCarly*	Nominated	[98][99]
	Young Artist Award	Best Performance in a TV Series (Comedy or Drama) – Leading Young Actress	Miranda Cosgrove	Nominated	[100]
		Best Performance in a TV Series – Guest Starring Young Actress 10 and Under	Ashley Switzer	Nominated	[100]
	Gracie Allen Awards	Outstanding Female Rising Star In A Comedy	Miranda Cosgrove	Won	[101]
	People's Choice Awards	Favorite Family TV Movie	Episode: iPsycho	Nominated	[102][103]
	Youth Rocks Awards	Rockin' Ensemble Cast (TV/Comedy)	*iCarly*	Nominated	[104][105]
	Kids' Choice Awards Mexico 2011	Favorite International Show	*iCarly*	Nominated	[106][107]
	Kids' Choice Awards Argentina 2011	Favorite TV International Show	*iCarly*	Won	[108]
	Meus Premios Nick 2011	Favorite TV Show	*iCarly*	Nominated	[109][110]
		Character Funny	Spencer Shay	Nominated	[109][110]
			Sam Puckett	Won	[110]
	Casting Society of America	Outstanding Achievement in Casting - Children's Series Programming	Krisha Bullock	Nominated	[111]
2012	2012 Kids' Choice Awards	Favorite TV Show	*iCarly*	Nominated	[112]
		Favorite TV Actress	Miranda Cosgrove	Nominated	[112]
		Favorite TV Sidekick	Jennette McCurdy	Won	[112]
			Nathan Kress	Nominated	[112]
			Jerry Trainor	Nominated	[112]
	Primetime Emmy Award	Outstanding Children's Program	*iCarly*	Nominated	[113]
	Teen Choice Award	Choice TV Actress: Comedy	Miranda Cosgrove	Nominated	[114][115]
	Television Critics Association Award	Outstanding Achievement in Youth Programming	*iCarly*	Nominated	[116][117]
	Young Artist Award	Best Performance in a TV Series – Recurring Young Actress 17–21	Victoria Justice	Nominated	[118]
	Hollywood Teen TV Awards	Favorite Television Actress	Miranda Cosgrove	Nominated	[119]
		Favorite Television Show	*iCarly*	Nominated	[120]
	Writers Guild of America	Children's - Episodic & Specials	Episode: iLost My Mind	Nominated	[121]

	Producers Guild Awards	Children's Programs	*iCarly*	Nominated	[122]
	Kids Choice Awards Mexico 2012	Favorite International Show	*iCarly*	Won	[123]
	Kids' Choice Awards Argentina 2012	Favorite TV International Show	*iCarly*	Nominated	[124]
	Meus Prêmios Nick Brasil 2012	Favorite TV Show	*iCarly*	Nominated	[125][126]
	British Academy Children's Awards	International	*iCarly*	Nominated	[127]
	Casting Society of America	Outstanding Achievement in Casting - Children's Series Programming	Krisha Bullock Jennifer Treadwell	Nominated	[128]
2013	Producers Guild Awards	Outstanding Children's Program	*iCarly*	Nominated	[129][130]

References

[1] http://www.nick.com/shows/icarly

[2] "Exclusive: iCarly Is Coming to an End, Cast to Film Together for Final Time in June – Today's News: Our Take" (http://www.tvguide.com/News/iCarly-Series-Finale-1047581.aspx). TVGuide.com. October 1, 2008. . Retrieved 2012-05-20.

[3] "DanWarp: 30 Questions – 30 Answers from Dan" (http://danwarp.blogspot.com/2009/05/30-questions-30-answers-from-dan.html). Danwarp.blogspot.com. 2009-05-02. . Retrieved 2012-11-24.

[4] "Dan Answers Fan questions" (http://danwarp.blogspot.com/2012/02/ianswer-your-questions.html). Danwarp.blogspot.com. 2012-07-08. . Retrieved 2012-12-26.

[5] "iCarly DVD news: Announcement for iCarly – Season 1, Volume 1" (http://www.tvshowsondvd.com/news/iCarly-Season-1-Volume-1/9809). *TVShowsOnDVD.com*. . Retrieved June 8, 2009.

[6] "iCarly DVD news: Release Date Change for iCarly – Season 1, Volume 2" (http://www.tvshowsondvd.com/news/iCarly-Season-1-Volume-2/11253). *TVShowsOnDVD.com*. . Retrieved June 8, 2009.

[7] "iCarly DVD news: Announcement for iCarly – Season 2, Vol. 1" (http://www.tvshowsondvd.com/news/iCarly-Season-2-Volume-1/11923). *TVShowsOnDVD.com*. . Retrieved June 8, 2009.

[8] "iCarly DVD news: iCarly – 'Season 2, Vol. 2' Announced: Date, Cost, Extras and Package Art" (http://www.tvshowsondvd.com/news/iCarly-Season-2-Volume-2/14605). *TVShowsOnDVD.com accessdate=2010-10-27*. .

[9] "Announcement for DVDs of 'Season 2, Vol. 3' to Finish Off the Season" (http://www.tvshowsondvd.com/news/iCarly-Season-2-Volume-3/14949). *TVShowsOnDVD.com*. . Retrieved January 24, 2011.

[10] iCarly – The Complete Season 3 is Announced for DVD! (http://www.tvshowsondvd.com/news/iCarly-Season-3/15473) – TVShowsonDVD.com

[11] iCarly – 'Season 4' DVDs Include Visits from The First Lady, 'Sheldon,' and Bonus 'How To Rock' Eps (http://www.tvshowsondvd.com/news/iCarly-Season-4/16814)-TVShowsonDVD.com

[12] Starr, Michael. (November 12, 2008) 'Icarly' Breaks Records (http://www.nypost.com/p/entertainment/tv/item_gfbUXwTeEILG3RJKrkynwJ;jsessionid=34EA3A5D678AEF7EDC3CEDEBDFD1F53A). NYPOST.com. Retrieved November 25, 2011.

[13] "Top 100 Most-Watched Telecasts On Basic Cable For 2009 – Ratings" (http://tvbythenumbers.zap2it.com/2009/12/29/espn-domination-top-100-most-watched-telecasts-on-basic-cable-for-2009/37284/). Tvbythenumbers.zap2it.com. . Retrieved 2012-12-26.

[14] "Football, Yankees, 'iCarly,' 'Video Music Awards' Lead Cable's Top Telecasts Of 2010 – Ratings" (http://tvbythenumbers.zap2it.com/2011/01/02/football-yankees-icarly-video-music-awards-lead-cables-top-telecasts-of-2010/76966/). Tvbythenumbers.zap2it.com. . Retrieved 2012-12-26.

[15] "Friday Cable Ratings: iCarly > Celtics-Thunder; Sanctuary, Friday Night Smackdown! Drop Back +Big Time Rush & More – Ratings" (http://tvbythenumbers.zap2it.com/2010/11/22/friday-cable-ratings-icarly-celtics-thunder-sanctuary-friday-night-smackdown-drop-back-big-time-rush-more/73059/). Tvbythenumbers.zap2it.com. . Retrieved 2012-12-26.

[16] Nickelodeon's "iParty With Victorious" TV Event Draws 7.3 Million Viewers (http://tvbythenumbers.zap2it.com/2011/06/13/nickelodeonâs-âiparty-with-victoriousâ-tv-event-draws-7-3-million-viewers/95423), Tvbythenumbers.zap2it.com (June 13, 2011)

[17] "Cable Top 25: 'VMAs,' 'Jersey Shore,' 'The Closer,' 'Rizzoli & Isles' Top Weekly Cable Viewing – Ratings" (http://tvbythenumbers.zap2it.com/2011/08/30/cable-top-25-vmas-jersey-shore-the-closer-rizzoli-isles-top-weekly-cable-viewing/101779/). Tvbythenumbers.zap2it.com. . Retrieved 2012-12-26.

[18] "Cable Top 25: 'Monday Night Football' Saints/Falcons On Top One Last Time" (http://tvbythenumbers.zap2it.com/2012/01/04/cable-top-25-monday-night-football-saintsfalcons-on-top-one-last-time/115251/). Tvbythenumbers.zap2it.com. . Retrieved January 31, 2012.

[19] "Saturday's Cable Ratings: College Football Tops Demos for ESPN" (http://www.thefutoncritic.com/ratings/2012/10/09/saturdays-cable-ratings-college-football-tops-demos-for-espn-243110/cable_20121006/). http://www.thefutoncritic.com. . Retrieved October 6, 2012.

[20] "Friday Cable Ratings:'Gold Rush' Wins Night, 'iCarly:Goodbye', 'Jungle Gold', 'Duck Dynasty', 'WWE Smackfown' & More" (http://tvbythenumbers.zap2it.com/2012/11/27/friday-cable-ratingsgold-rush-wins-night-icarlygoodbye-jungle-gold-duck-dynasty-wwe-smackfown-more/158869/). Tvbythenumbers.zap2it.com. . Retrieved 2012-12-11.

[21] "Miranda Cosgrove of 'iCarly' is headed to Cleveland" (http://www.cleveland.com/popmusic/index.ssf/2011/01/miranda_cosgrove_of_icarly_is.html). *Cleveland Live News*. . Retrieved February 14, 2011.

[22] "Miranda Cosgrove Taps Rivers Cuomo for "High Maintenance" EP" (http://www.reuters.com/article/2011/01/28/us-mirandacosgrove-idUSTRE70R8ZT20110128). Reuters. January 28, 2011. . Retrieved February 14, 2011.

[23] "iCarly's Miranda Cosgrove to perform in Connecticut" (http://www.middletownpress.com/articles/2011/02/03/entertainment/doc4d4a17dc591f2129594318.txt?viewmode=fullstory). *The Middletown Press*. . Retrieved February 14, 2011.

[24] "Jennette McCurdy – *Generation Love* mall tour dates" (http://www.jennettemccurdy.com/appearances.html). *JennetteMcCurdy.com*. . Retrieved April 2, 2011.

[25] Gonna start filming... (http://twitter.com/MirandaBuzz/status/55494526642556928) – MirandaBuzz twitter

[26] iCarly Spoilers INTERVIEW (http://tv.sky.com/icarly-spoilers)

[27] iCarly Renewed For Another Season (http://www.tvguide.com/News/iCarly-Renewed-Season-1031856.aspx) – TVGuide.com

[28] "DanWarp: iCarly: Second Season? Third Season? Huh?!?" (http://danwarp.blogspot.com/2009/09/icarly-second-season-third-season-huh.html). Danwarp.blogspot.com. September 1, 2009. . Retrieved February 8, 2012.

[29] "Nathan Kress Exclusive Interview" (http://www.thestarscoop.com/interviews/nathan-kress-exclusive-interview/). The Star Scoop. August 4, 2009. . Retrieved 2012-02-28.

[30] (http://www.danwarp.blogspot.com/2012/02/ianswer-your-questions.htm)

[31] "iCarly.com" (http://www.icarly.com/iVideo/video_27173-ishock-america/chan_2/cat_89). iCarly.com. . Retrieved 2012-11-24.

[32] "Timeline Photos" (http://www.facebook.com/photo.php?fbid=10151041945846755&set=a.76376866754.92068.53523601754&type=1&theater). Facebook. . Retrieved 2012-11-24.

[33] "Exclusive: iCarly Is Coming to an End, Cast to Film Together for Final Time in June – Today's News: Our Take" (http://www.tvguide.com/News/iCarly-Series-Finale-1047581.aspx). TVGuide.com. 2012-05-17. . Retrieved 2012-12-11.

[34] "iCarly Episode – iGoodbye Part 1" (http://www.tvguide.com/tvshows/icarly-2012/episode-14-season-5/igoodbye/289614). TV Guide. . Retrieved 26 October 2012.

[35] "iCarly Episode – iGoodbye Part 2" (http://www.tvguide.com/tvshows/icarly-2012/episode-14-season-5/igoodbye/289614). TV Guide. . Retrieved 26 October 2012.

[36] "iCarly DVD news: Announcement for iCarly – iFight Shelby Marx" (http://www.tvshowsondvd.com/news/iCarly-iFight-Shelby-Marx/13205). TVShowsOnDVD.com. . Retrieved May 24, 2010.

[37] "DVD: iCarly: iSaved Your Life (DVD)" (http://www.tower.com/icarly-isaved-your-life-dvd/wapi/115099002). Tower.com. . Retrieved May 24, 2010.

[38] "iCarly DVD news: Announcement for iCarly – iSpace Out!" (http://www.tvshowsondvd.com/news/iCarly-iSpace-Out/13876). TVShowsOnDVD.com. . Retrieved September 6, 2010.

[39] "iCarly iSpace Out (a J!-ENT DVD Review)" (http://www.nt2099.com/J-ENT/news/blu-ray-dvd-reviews/dvd-reviews-film-tv/icarly-ispace-out-a-j-ent-dvd-review/). J! ENT Entertainment Worldwide. . Retrieved August 10, 2010.

[40] "iCarly DVD news: Season 2, Vol 2 Announced: Date, Cost, Extras & Package Art" (http://www.tvshowsondvd.com/news/iCarly-Season-2-Volume-2/14605). TVShowsOnDVD.com. . Retrieved October 30, 2010.

[41] "Announcement for DVDs of 'Season 2, Vol. 3' to Finish Off the Season" (http://www.tvshowsondvd.com/news/iCarly-Season-2-Volume-3/14949). TVShowsOnDVD.com. . Retrieved January 24, 2011.

[42] The I <3 iCarly Collection. "The I <3 iCarly Collection: Nathan Kress, Jerry Trainor, Miranda Cosgrove, Jennette McCurdy" (http://www.amazon.com/dp/b004Yvo62E). Amazon.com. . Retrieved 2012-12-26.

[43] "iCarly DVD news: Announcement for iCarly – Season 3" (http://www.tvshowsondvd.com/news/iCarly-Season-3/15473). Tvshowsondvd.com. . Retrieved 2012-12-26.

[44] "iCarly DVD news: 'Season 4' DVDs Include Visits from The First Lady, 'Sheldon,' and Bonus 'How To Rock' Eps" (http://www.tvshowsondvd.com/news/iCarly-Season-4/16814). Tvshowsondvd.com. . Retrieved 2012-12-26.

[45] "iCarly: iSoundtrack II – Music From And Inspired By The Hit TV Show: iCarly: Music" (http://www.amazon.com/iCarly-iSoundtrack-Music-Inspired-Show/dp/B005WOAEA0/ref=sr_1_2?s=music&ie=UTF8&qid=1325974855&sr=1-2). Amazon.com. . Retrieved February 8, 2012.

[46] http://zaplook.com/

[47] http://splashface.com/

[48] http://craigsmix.com/

[49] http://nevelocity.com/

[50] "Nickelodeon greenlights an 'iCarly' spinoff and other new shows" (http://www.latimes.com/entertainment/tv/showtracker/la-et-st-nickelodeon-greenlights-icarly-spinoff-20120803,0,3715048.story). . Retrieved August 12, 2012.

[51] Nordyke, Kimberly (2012-11-29). "Nickelodeon Greenlights Spinoff of 'iCarly,' 'Victorious'" (http://www.hollywoodreporter.com/live-feed/icarly-victorious-spinoff-sam-cat-395824). Hollywood Reporter. . Retrieved 2012-11-29.

[52] Snierson, Matt (July 2, 2012). "Nickelodeon greenlights spin-off pilots for 'iCarly,' 'Victorious' from creator Dan Schneider – EXCLUSIVE" (http://insidetv.ew.com/2012/08/02/nickelodeon-icarly-spinoff-victorious/). Ew.com. . Retrieved 2012-07-02.

[53] "Sam & Cat,' 'Gibby' Get Pilots From Nickelodeon Starring Arian Grande, Jennette McCurdy And Noah Munck" (http://www.ibtimes.com/articles/369896/20120802/sam-cat-gibby-grande-mccurdy-nickelodeon-munck.htm). Entertainment & Stars. 2012-07 02. . Retrieved 2012-07-02.

[54] Bryson, Carey. iCarly – TV Show Review (http://kidstvmovies.about.com/od/icarly/fr/icarly.htm), About.com

[55] Alshey, Emily Common Sense Media Review (http://www.commonsensemedia.org/tv-reviews/icarly)

[56] Lee, Michelle (November 19, 2012). 'iCarly': the Best Sitcom Since 'Arrested Development'? (http://www.hollywood.com/news/iCarly_Best_Sitcom_Arrested_Development/44576189). Hollywood.com. Accessed from December 8, 2012.

[57] Karantzalis, Athena. "iCarly" (http://www.tv.com/shows/icarly/). Tv.com. . Retrieved 2012-12-26.

[58] "2008 Nickelodeon Kids' Choice Awards - Nominees" (http://www.nickkcapress.com/2008KCA/nominees.php). Nickkcapress.com. . Retrieved 2012-12-26.

[59] "2008 Nickelodeon Kids' Choice Awards - Winners" (http://allieiswired.com/archives/2008/03/nickelodeon-kids-choice-awards-2008-winners-list-pictures-and-video/). Allieiswired.com. . Retrieved 2012-12-26.

[60] "2008 UK Nickelodeon Kids' Choice Awards - Nominees" (http://nickalive.blogspot.com.ar/2008/08/nickelodeon-kids-choice-awards-uk-2008.html). Nickalive.blogspot.com.ar. 2008-08-30. . Retrieved 2012-12-26.

[61] "2008 UK Nickelodeon Kids' Choice Awards - Winners" (http://www.popsugar.co.uk/Winners-Photos-From-Inside-2008-Nickelodeon-UK-Kids-Choice-Awards-Feat-Evanna-Lynch-Bonnie-Wright-Josh-Peck-McFly-2005867). Popsugar.co.uk. 2008-09-14. . Retrieved 2012-12-26.

[62] "2008 Nickelodeon Australian Kids' Choice Awards" (http://jonasbrothersla.superforo.net/t4410-nickelodeon-australia-kids-choice-awards). Jonasbrothersla.superforo.net. . Retrieved 2012-12-26.

[63] "29th Annual Young Artist Awards" (http://www.youngartistawards.org/noms29.html). *Young Artist Awards.* . Retrieved February 16, 2011.

[64] "2008 Bafta Children's Awards - Winners" (http://www.bafta.org/awards/childrens/nominations-childrens-awards-in-2008,593,BA.html). *Bafta Children's Awards.* .

[65] Casting Society of America 2008 - Winners (http://www.imdb.com/event/ev0000154/2008)

[66] "2009 Nickelodeon Kids' Choice Awards – Winners" (http://www.nickkcapress.com/2009KCA/winners.php). *Kids' Choice Awards.* . Retrieved February 16, 2011.

[67] "2009 Nickelodeon Kids' Choice Awards – Nominees" (http://www.nickkcapress.com/2009KCA/nominees.php). *Kids' Choice Awards.* . Retrieved February 16, 2011.

[68] "2009 Nickelodeon Kids' Choice Awards Australian - Winners" (http://www.take40.com/news/17653/2009-nickelodeon-kids'-choice-awards-winners!). Take40.com. 2009-11-13. . Retrieved 2012-12-26.

[69] "61st Primetime Emmy Awards" (http://www.emmys.com/nominations/2009/Outstanding Children's Program). *Primetime Emmy Awards.* . Retrieved February 16, 2011.

[70] "2009 Teen Choice Awards" (http://www.imdb.com/event/ev0000644/2009). *IMDb.com.* . Retrieved February 16, 2011.

[71] "30th Annual Young Artist Awards" (http://www.youngartistawards.org/noms30.html). *Young Artist Awards.* . Retrieved February 16, 2011.

[72] "Children's in 2009" (http://awards.bafta.org/award/2009/childrens). *Bafta Children's Awards.* .

[73] "Casting Society of America 2009 - Winners" (http://www.imdb.com/event/ev0000154/2009). .

[74] "2010 Nickelodeon Kids' Choice Awards – Winners" (http://www.nickkcapress.com/2010KCA/releases/winners/). *Kids' Choice Awards.* . Retrieved February 16, 2011.

[75] "2010 Nickelodeon Kids' Choice Awards – Nominees" (http://www.nickkcapress.com/2010KCA/releases/hostnoms/). *Kids' Choice Awards.* . Retrieved February 16, 2011.

[76] "Nickelodeon Kids' Choice Awards Australian 2010 - Winners" (http://www.take40.com/news/20473/Nickelodeon). .

[77] "Nickelodeon Kids' Choice Awards Australian 2010 - Nominees" (http://www.take40.com/news/19949/2010-nickelodeon-kid's-choice-awards-nominations-list!). .

[78] "62nd Primetime Emmy Awards" (http://www.emmys.com/nominations?tid=123). *Primetime Emmy Awards.* . Retrieved February 16, 2011.

[79] "2010 Teen Choice Awards" (http://theenvelope.latimes.com/news/env-teen-choice-scorecard-2010-htmlstory,0,3151807.htmlstory). *Los Angeles Times.* . Retrieved February 16, 2011.

[80] "2010 Television Critics Association Awards" (http://tvcritics.org/2010/06/04/the-television-critics-association-announces-2010-tca-awards-nominees/). *Television Critics Association.* . Retrieved February 16, 2011.

[81] "2010 Television Critics Association Awards Winners" (http://tvcritics.org/2010/07/31/the-television-critics-association-announces-2010-tca-awards-winners/). *Television Critics Association.* . Retrieved February 16, 2011.

[82] "31st Annual Young Artist Awards" (http://www.youngartistawards.org/noms31.html). *Young Artist Awards*. . Retrieved February 16, 2011.

[83] "Hollywood Teen TV Awards" (http://hollywoodteenonline.com/2010/07/04/hollywood-teen-tv-awards/). .

[84] "MASGUAU – Ganadores de los Kids' Choice Awards México 2010" (http://masguau.com/2010/09/04/ ganadores-de-los-kids-choice-awards-mexico-2010/). Masguau.com. . Retrieved 2012-12-11.

[85] "Meus Premios Nick 2010 – Variados 2" (http://www.youtube.com/watch?v=mJdtuSd_AWo). YouTube. 2010-09-29. . Retrieved 2012-12-11.

[86] "2010 Bafta Children's Awards - Winners" (http://www.bafta.org/awards/childrens/awards2010,1452,BA.html#jump19). *Bafta Children's Awards*. .

[87] "Casting Society of America 2010 - Winners" (http://www.imdb.com/event/ev0000154/2010). .

[88] "2011 Nickelodeon Kids' Choice Awards - Winners" (http://www.digitalspy.co.uk/ustv/news/a312484/ nickelodeon-kids-choice-awards-2011-the-winners.html). *Digital Spy*. .

[89] "2011 Nickelodeon Kids' Choice Awards - Nominees" (http://nickkcapress.com/2011KCA/release/2011_host). .

[90] "2011 UK Nickelodeon Kids' Choice Awards" (http://www.funkidslive.com/news/nickelodeon-kids-choice-awards-2011-winners/). .

[91] "2011 Nickelodeon Kids Choice Awards Australian - Winners" (http://www.clevvertv.com/awards-show-2/27891/ 2011-kids-choice-awards-australia.html). .

[92] "2011 Nickelodeon Kids Choice Awards Australian - Nominees" (http://www.revistateen.com/ Â¡se-anuncian-los-nominados-a-los-kids-choice-awards-de-australia/). .

[93] "63th Primetime Emmy Awards" (http://www.emmys.com/nominations/2011/Outstanding Children's Program). *Primetime Emmy Awards*. .

[94] "63th Primetime Emmy Awards" (http://www.emmys.com/nominations/2011/Outstanding Hairstyling For A Multi-Camera Series Or Special). *Primetime Emmy Awards*. .

[95] "63th Primetime Emmy Awards" (http://www.emmys.com/nominations/2011/Outstanding Makeup For A Multi-Camera Series Or Special (Non-Prosthetic)). *Primetime Emmy Awards*. .

[96] "2011 Teen Choice Awards - Nominees" (http://www.dtodoblog.com/2011/06/lista-de-nominados-teen-choice-2011.html). .

[97] "2011 Teen Choice Awards - Winners" (http://elbazardelespectaculo.blogspot.com.ar/2011/08/ teen-choice-awards-2011-ganadores-lista.html). .

[98] "Television Critics Association Awards 2011 - Nominees" (http://tvcritics.org/2011/06/13/ the-television-critics-association-announces-2011-tca-awards-nominees/). .

[99] "Television Critics Association Awards 2011 - Winners" (http://www.capituloanterior.com/714/ lista-de-ganadores-de-los-television-critics-association-awards-2011). .

[100] "32nd Annual Young Artist Awards" (http://www.youngartistawards.org/noms32.html). *Young Artist Awards*. .

[101] "2011 Gracie Awards Winners" (http://www.thegracies.org/2011-grace-awards.php). *Thegracies*. .

[102] "People's Choice Awards 2011 - Nominees" (http://www.buzzsugar.com/ Full-List-2011-Peoples-Choice-Award-Nominations-2010-11-09-114556-11904931). .

[103] "People's Choice Awards 2011 - Winners" (http://elbazardelespectaculo.blogspot.com.ar/2011/01/ premios-people-choice-awards-2011_06.html). .

[104] "Youth Rocks Awards - Rockin' Ensemble Cast (TV/Comedy)" (http://youthrocksawards.com/?cat=32). *Youth Rocks Awards*. .

[105] "Youth Rocks Awards - Winners" (http://oceanup.com/2011/december/08/youth-rocks-awards-2011-winners). .

[106] "Kids Choice Awards México 2011 - Nominees" (http://tvnotiblog.com/lista-de-nominados-kids-choice-awards-mexico-2011/). .

[107] "Kids Choice Awards México 2011 - Winners" (http://tvnotiblog.com/ganadores-de-los-kids-choice-awards-mexico-2011/). .

[108] "Kids Choice Awards Argentina 2011 - Winners" (http://exitoina.com/ 2011-10-12-76250-todos-los-ganadores-de-los-kids-choice-awards/). .

[109] "Meus Prêmios Nick 2011 - Nominees" (http://www.anmtv.xpg.com.br/ nickelodeon-anuncia-os-finalistas-do-meus-premios-nick-2011/). .

[110] "Meus Prêmios Nick 2011 - Winners" (http://www.anmtv.xpg.com.br/ nickelodeon-divulga-os-vencedores-do-meus-premios-nick-2011/). .

[111] "Casting Society of America 2011 - Winners" (http://www.imdb.com/event/ev0000154/2011). .

[112] "2012 Nickelodeon Kids' Choice Awards - Winners" (http://solofamososonline.com/2012/04/ lista-completa-de-ganadores-kids-choice-awards-2012/). .

[113] "64th Primetime Emmy Awards" (http://www.emmys.com/nominations/2012/Outstanding Children's Program). *Primetime Emmy Awards*. .

[114] "2012 Teen Choice Awards - Nominees" (http://www.revistateen.com/conoce-los-nominados-para-los-teen-choice-awards-2012/). .

[115] "2012 Teen Choice Awards - Winners" (http://entretenimiento.starmedia.com/alfombra-roja/lista-ganadores-teen-choice-awards-2012. html). .

[116] "Television Critics Association Awards 2012 - Nominees" (http://tvcritics.org/2012/06/07/ the-television-critics-association-announces-2012-tca-award-nominees/). .

[117] "Television Critics Association Awards 2012 - Winners" (http://www.forbes.com/sites/jennifereum/2012/07/30/ winners-revealed-2012-television-critics-association-awards/). .

[118] "33rd Annual Young Artist Awards – Nominations / Special Awards" (http://www.youngartistawards.org/noms33.html). Youngartistawards.org. 2012-05-06. . Retrieved 2012-12-11.

[119] "Hollywood Teen TV Awards - Favorite Television Actress" (http://teentvawards.com/favorite-television-actress/). .

[120] "Hollywood Teen TV Awards - Favorite Television Show" (http://teentvawards.com/favorite-television-show/). .

[121] "Writers Guild of America 2012 - Winners" (http://www.hollywoodreporter.com/news/wga-writers-guild-awards-winners-list-292639).

[122] "Producers Guild Awards 2012 - Winners" (http://www.tvtonight.com.au/2012/01/producers-guild-of-america-awards-2012-winners. html). .

[123] "Kids Choice Awards Mexico 2012 - Winners" (http://entretenimiento.starmedia.com/alfombra-roja/ lista-ganadores-kids-choice-awards-mexico-2012.html). .

[124] "Kids Choice Awards Argentina 2012 - Winners" (http://elbazardelespectaculo.blogspot.com.ar/2012/10/ premios-kids-choice-awards-argentina.html). .

[125] "Nominees at Meus Prêmios Nick 2012" (http://iritmo.blogspot.com.ar/2012/08/nominados-oficiales-los-meus-premios.html). *Nick News*. .

[126] "Winners at Meus Prêmios Nick 2012" (http://iritmo.blogspot.com.ar/2012/10/ganadores-de-los-meus-premios-nick-2012.html). *Nick News*. .

[127] "2012 Bafta Children's Awards - Winners" (http://www.bafta.org/awards/childrens/nominations-winners-2012,3492,BA. html#jump08). *Bafta Children's Awards*. .

[128] "Casting Society of America 2012 - Winners" (http://www.imdb.com/event/ev0000154/2012). .

[129] "Producers Guild Awards 2013 - Nominees" (http://www.wetpaint.com/network/articles/ list-of-2013-producers-guild-awards-tv-nominations). .

[130] "2013 Producers Guild Awards Winners: Argo, Homeland, Modern Family & More" (http://www.eonline.com/news/382141/ 2013-producers-guild-awards-winners-argo-homeland-modern-family-more). .

External links

- Official website (http://www.icarly.com/)
- Nickelodeon page (http://www.nick.com/shows/icarly)
- YTV (Canada) website (http://www.ytv.com/programming/shows/iCarly/)
- *iCarly* (http://www.imdb.com/title/tt0972534/) at the Internet Movie Database
- *iCarly* (http://www.tv.com/shows/icarly/) at TV.com
- *iCarly* Wiki (http://icarly.wikia.com/wiki/ICarly_Wiki)

iParty with Victorious

"iParty with Victorious"	
iCarly episode	
Episode no.	Season 4 Episode 11-13
Directed by	Steve Hoefer
Written by	Dan Schneider
Produced by	Dan Schneider Joe Catania
Featured music	Leave It All To Me Make it Shine Number One Give It Up Leave It All To Shine
Production code	311-313
Original air date	June 11, 2011 August 27, 2011 (uncut version)
Running time	90 min. (approximately) 69 min. (without commercials) 86 min. (Uncut version)

"**iParty with Victorious**" is a 2011 three-part crossover episode of *iCarly* and *Victorious*. Although it is a crossover, the episode only counts as an *iCarly* episode. The episode aired on June 11, 2011, at 8/7c. It premiered in Los Angeles on June 4, 2011, and was released on DVD on August 30, 2011.[1] iParty with Victorious song mash up called *Leave It All To Shine* premiered on May 22, 2011 on Nickelodeon and was online (YouTube) on June 7, 2011. The episode was watched by 7.3 million viewers. It also marked Kenan Thompson's brief return to Nickelodeon. iParty With Victorious was released on the 3rd season DVD of iCarly and on the second Volume of Victorious' first season DVD. The normal length version was released on both DVD sets.

Plot

Carly (Miranda Cosgrove) is dating a boy named Steven Carson (Cameron Deane Stewart), who divides his time between his divorced parents in Seattle and Los Angeles. Every other month, Steven goes off to Los Angeles, where he is dating another girl named Tori Vega (Victoria Justice), who attends Hollywood Arts, a high school for the performing arts. Robbie Shapiro (Matt Bennett), a socially awkward friend of Tori's, posts a picture of Steven and Tori online, which Carly stumbles upon. She initially denies the fact that Steven is cheating on her, but Sam (Jennette McCurdy) seeks to prove it is indeed true. She finds Rex, Robbie's ventriloquist dummy, has tweeted about a party held at Kenan Thompson's house, in Hollywood.

Spencer (Jerry Trainor) drives the group to Los Angeles, where Carly, Sam, Freddie (Nathan Kress), Gibby (Noah Munck), and Spencer visit Spencer's ex-girlfriend, who happens to be a skilled make-up artist, and receive disguise makeovers to avoid being noticed from iCarly by others. They then head off to the house of actor and comedian, Kenan Thompson, where Andre Harris (Leon Thomas III), another friend of Tori's, is hosting a party that they suspect Steven and Tori are attending. The iCarly members enter Kenan's party house during the party and split up in search of Steven. Spencer, meanwhile, relaxes in Kenan Thompson's jacuzzi and meets Sikowitz (Eric Lange), Beck (Avan Jogia) and Jade (Elizabeth Gillies). Much to her chagrin, Carly eventually catches Steven and watches him kiss Tori, before she admits Sam is correct about Steven cheating on her. Sinjinn Van Cleef (Michael Eric Reid) another student at Hollywood Arts falls into the jacuzzi when a surfing machine malfunctions.

The iCarly members remove their disguises, and Tori walks in and immediately recognizes them from iCarly. After explaining Steven's actions, Carly and Tori devise a plan to humiliate Steven for revenge. Steven is lured into a closet where he thinks he will make out with Tori. Instead, when he enters the closet, he finds himself on an iCarly webcast with Carly, Sam, Kenan, and Tori, who reveal to iCarly's one million audience members Steven had been dating both Carly and Tori at the same time. Steven becomes embarrassed and leaves. Then Sam beats Rex in a rap battle. Later, the iCarly cast joins Tori and her friends in karaoke, where they sing *Leave It All to Shine*.

Production

Dan Schneider has confirmed that because of the success of the film, he decided to give Nickelodeon an uncut, 2-hour version of it which contains material the production team edited out after filming. It aired August 27, 2011.

The episode "iParty With Victorious" was confirmed as an iCarly movie, not a TV crossover probably because of the lowercase "i" in the title which appeared in all iCarly episodes known (ex."iPilot","iQuit iCarly","iOMG").

Victoria Justice appears in *iCarly* for the second time for *iParty with Victorious*. The first time she appeared in the series was in a previous television special *iFight Shelby Marx*.[2] Sam also comments that Tori Vega looks like Shelby Marx, who was also played by Justice. Also making return appearances are Leon Thomas III (the first time he appeared in the series was in "iCarly Saves TV"), Daniella Monet (the first time she appeared in the series was in a previous television special *iPsycho*), and Lane Napper (the first time he appeared in the series was as Ernie, Sam's dancing instructor in "iWas a Pageant Girl").

The opening sequence features clips from "iParty with Victorious" only and credits the iCarly cast and Victoria Justice in the opening sequence while the rest of the *Victorious* cast and Kenan Thompson are credited during the in-show credits.

While in Kenan Thompson's house, "The Joke Is On You" by Niki Watkins, "Give It Up" by Elizabeth Gillies and Ariana Grande, performed in the *Victorious* episode "Freak the Freak Out", and "Number One (My World)" by fictional Ginger Fox was played.

Cast

Main cast

- Miranda Cosgrove as Carly Shay / Patty Schwab – Carly hosts her own web show titled *iCarly*, and has become an internet sensation. She is friends with Sam Freddie and Gibby and the girlfriend of Steven Carson.
- Jennette McCurdy as Sam Puckett / Regina Goodbody – Carly's delinquent sidekick, and best friend, co-host for iCarly.
- Nathan Kress as Freddie Benson / Chess Masterson – iCarly's technical producer.
- Jerry Trainor as Spencer Shay – Carly's older brother and a skilled artist. He is Carly's legal guardian.
- Noah Munck as Gibby Gibson / Roger Mole – One of the iCarly gang's friends.
- Victoria Justice as Tori Vega – A talented student at Hollywood Arts High School.

Recurring cast

From *iCarly*

- David St. James as Mr. Howard – A strict teacher at Carly's school who hates all his students.
- Mary Scheer as Mrs. Benson – Freddie's mother.

From *Victorious*

- Leon Thomas III as Andre Harris – Tori's friend and aspiring songwriter.
- Matt Bennett as Robbie Shapiro – A nerdy student at Hollywood Arts. He is almost always seen with his "best friend" Rex, who is really a ventriloquist's dummy.
- Elizabeth Gillies as Jade West – Tori's mean, rude enemy, who always causes her trouble, she is dating Beck.
- Ariana Grande as Cat Valentine – Another of Tori's friends. In this cross-over Cat has difficulty speaking due to a vocal-cord infection and uses a voice simulator.
- Avan Jogia as Beck Oliver – One of Tori's friends and an actor at Hollywood Arts, he is dating Jade.
- Daniella Monet as Trina Vega – Tori's diva-like older sister.
- Jake Farrow as Rex Powers (voice only) – Robbie's ventriloquist's dummy who he treats as real.
- Marilyn Harris as Mrs. Harris – André's grandmother.
- Eric Lange as Mr. Sikowitz – A popular drama teacher at Hollywood Arts.
- Lane Napper as Lane Alexander – The guidance counselor at Hollywood Arts.
- Michael Eric Reid as Sinjin Van Cleef – A freaky student at Hollywood Arts.

Guest star

- Kenan Thompson as Himself

Featuring

- Cameron Deane Stewart as Steven Carson – He is dating both Carly & Tori, a fact that neither of them are aware of.
- Leon Thomas II (In the iParty with Victorious Extended Version, Matt Bennett announced it was T-bo as The Panda) – A strange man in a panda suit that constantly patronizes Kenan Thompson.
- Justin Castor as Mark – A kid who recognizes Gibby, and is punched before he can reveal him.
- Jen Lilley as Monie – Spencer's ex-girlfriend who helps disguise Carly, Sam, Freddie, and Gibby.
- Kwame Patterson as DJ Mustang – The DJ at Andre's party at Kenan's house.
- Cierra Russell as Mabel – One of the kids Trina babysits. Her name was once mistaken as "Vanessa".
- Walt Shoen as Wilson – Another kid who Trina babysits.

Reception

This episode received mainly positive reviews from critics. Verne Gay of *The Republic* gave a positive review, suggesting *iParty with Victorious* may be the biggest event of the Summer 2011 and noting the scene depicting a guy in a panda costume chasing Kenan Thompson was hilarious.[3] Carl Cortez of *Assignment X* praised the episode but also gave a slightly more critical review. He believes "the mechanism for verifying Carly's boyfriend is cheating is a bit of a stretch". He reacted positively to how the times spent with the characters of *iCarly* and *Victorious* are evenly distributed. Overall, he finds the episode to be "enjoyable nonetheless" and gives it a grade of B-.[4] This crossover aired during the 2011 NBA Finals and 2011 Stanley Cup.

Worldwide releases

Episode Title	Country	Premiere Date	Broadcast
iParty with VICTORiOUS	United States	June 11, 2011	Nickelodeon
iParty with VICTORiOUS	Turkey	May 5, 2012	Nickelodeon Turkey
Party mit VICTORiOUS	Germany Austria Switzerland	October 1, 2011	Nickelodeon (Germany)
iParty with VICTORiOUS/iParty with Victorious	United Kingdom Ireland	October 7, 2011	Nickelodeon (UK & Ireland)
iParty with VICTORiOUS iCarly et victorious: le face a face	Canada	October 7, 2011 October 5, 2012	YTV VRAK.TV
Party met VICTORiOUS	Netherlands	October 8, 2011	Nickelodeon (Netherlands & Flanders)
Przyjęcie z VICTORiA ZNACZY ZWYCIĘSTWO	Poland	October 11, 2011	Nickelodeon (Poland)
iCarly et VICTORiOUS: Le face à face	France	October 12, 2011	Nickelodeon (France & Wallonia)
Fiesta con VICTORiOUS	Latin America	October 13, 2011	Nickelodeon (Latin America)
Fiesta con VICTORiOUS iCarly y VICTORiOUS: La Película	Mexico	October 13, 2011 September 17, 2012	Nickelodeon (Latin America) Canal 5 (Televisa Network)
Festa com BRILHANTE VICTÓRiA	Brazil	October 13, 2011	Nickelodeon (Brazil)
iCarly y VICTORiOUS cara a cara en: Hay Lio con VICTORiOUS	Spain	October 21, 2011	Nickelodeon (Spain)
Festa com VICTORiOUS	Portugal	October 21, 2011	Nickelodeon (Portugal)
Buli V, mint VikTÓRiával	Hungary	October 21, 2011	Nickelodeon (Hungary)
iParty with VICTORiOUS	Philippines	October 21, 2011	Nickelodeon (Philippines) Nickelodeon (Southeast Asia)
iParty with VICTORiOUS	Australia New Zealand	October 22, 2011	Nickelodeon (Australia) Nickelodeon (New Zealand)
Вечеринка АйКарли и ВИКТОРИи	Russia	October 22, 2011	Nickelodeon (Russia)
Petrec alături de VICTORIA	Romania	October 22, 2011	Nickelodeon (Central & Eastern Europe)
i파티 with 빅토리어스 (iParty with VICTORiOUS)	South Korea	February 27, 2012	Nickelodeon (South Korea)
iParty con Victorious	Italy	October 29, 2011	Nickelodeon (Italia)
Πάρτι με το Victorious (iParty with Victorious)	Greece	July 8, 2012-July 10, 2012	Nickelodeon (Greece)
ロサンゼルスのパーティーへ (To a party in LA)	Japan	September 12, 2012 (Part 1) September 19, 2012 (Part 2) September 26, 2012 (Part 3)	NHK

Leave It All to Shine

"Leave It All to Shine"	
Single by iCarly and Victorious cast featuring Miranda Cosgrove and Victoria Justice	
from the album *Victorious*	
Length	2:10
Label	Nickelodeon, Columbia
Writer(s)	Lukasz Gottwald, Michael Corcoran, Dan Schneider
Producer	Dr. Luke
Miranda Cosgrove singles chronology	
"Dancing Crazy" (2010) "Leave It All to Shine" (2011) "Falling Down Without Nothing Of Say" (2012)	
Victoria Justice chronology	
"Best Friend's Brother" (2011) "Leave It All to Shine" (2011) "Countdown" (2012)	

"Leave It All to Shine" is a mash-up song by iCarly cast & Victorious cast for crossover "iParty with Victorious". Its official premiere was on May 22, 2011 and video release was on June 11, 2011, the day the crossover premiered. The song didn't enter the Billboard Hot 100 but peaked on the Bubbling Under Hot 100 Singles chart at number twenty-four.

Charts

Chart (2011)	Peak position
U.S. Bubbling Under Hot 100 Singles[5]	24
Year End Chart (2011)	**Peak position**
U.S. *Billboard* Kid Digital Songs[6]	23

Featured vocals

Background vocals on "Leave It All To Shine" were performed by Miranda Cosgrove and Victoria Justice with the collaboration of Jennette McCurdy, Ariana Grande, Elizabeth Gillies, Nathan Kress, Leon Thomas III, Jerry Trainor, Noah Munck, Matt Bennett, Daniella Monet & Avan Jogia. All of these artists are a part of the main cast in the crossover episode.

Release history

Country	Date	Format	Label
United States	June 10, 2011[7]	Digital download	Nickelodeon, Columbia Records

Extended version releases

Episode Title	Country	Premiere Date	Broadcast
iParty with VICTORiOUS	United States	August 27, 2011	Nickelodeon

References

[1] iCarly - The Complete Season 3 is Announced for DVD! (http://www.tvshowsondvd.com/news/iCarly-Season-3/15473)

[2] Martin, Denise (2011-06-08). "When Carly Met Tori: The Stars of "iParty with Victorious" Say Don't Expect Crossover Catfights" (http://www.tvguide.com/News/iParty-Victorious-Cosgrove-Justice-1034047.aspx). TV Guide. . Retrieved 2011-06-13.

[3] Gay, Verne (2011-06-09). "'iParty with Victorious,' Saturday on Nickelodeon" (http://www.therepublic.com/view/story/TV-IPARTY-PREVIEW_5314903/TV-IPARTY-PREVIEW_5314903/). The Republic. . Retrieved 2011-06-13.

[4] Cortez, Carl (2011-06-12). "TV Movie Review: iCARLY – Season 4 – "iParty with Victorious"" (http://www.assignmentx.com/2011/tv-movie-review-icarly-season-4-iparty-with-victorious…/). Assignment X. . Retrieved 2011-06-13.

[5] Billboard Bubbling Under Hot 100 (Top 25) July 2, 2011 (http://www.youtube.com/watch?v=bsn6Un9Zdc0)

[6] YEAR END CHARTS - Kid Digital Songs (http://webcache.googleusercontent.com/search?q=cache:3YNM6hjv8ssJ:www.billboard.biz/bbbiz/charts/yearendcharts/2011/kid-digital-songs+miranda+cosgrove+site:billboard.biz&cd=3&hl=es&ct=clnk&gl=mx) billboard.biz

[7] "iTunes: Leave it All to Shine (single)" (http://itunes.apple.com/us/album/leave-it-all-to-shine-feat./id440703750). iTunes. 2011-06-10. . Retrieved 2010-05-13.

External links

- Official website (http://www.nick.com/shows/iparty)

Kool Kojak

Kool Kojak	
Birth name	Allan P. Grigg
Origin	Cubatão, São Paulo, Brazil
Genres	Latin, hip hop, samba, reggae fusion, funk, bossa nova, electro, zouk, charanga, rock
Occupations	Musician, songwriter, record producer, painter, art designer
Labels	KojakTrax , Prescription Songs , IYF Productions
Associated acts	Urban Legend , Dr. Luke , Ke$ha , Peter Svensson , Max Martin
Website	www.myspace.com/kojakbeatz [1] www.koolkojak.com [2]

Allan P. Grigg,[3] also known as **Kool Kojak**, is a multi-platinum Brazilian-American songwriter, producer, film director, and artist notable for co-writing and co-producing Flo Rida's #1 Billboard[4] hit single "Right Round".[5] Kool Kojak has written and produced for artists such as Nicki Minaj, Matisyahu, Ke$ha, Travis Barker, Dr. Seuss's The Lorax (film), One Direction, Master P, Gorilla Zoe, Victoria Justice, The Offspring, N.A.S.A.,[6] Dirt Nasty, Andy Milonakis, [7] Lordz of Brooklyn, Ursula 1000,[8] and Warren G. Kool Kojak was a featured producer on the Simon Cowell TV program X Factor. Kool Kojak has won two ASCAP Pop Awards and one ASCAP Urban Award. Kool Kojak is a member of the Prescription Songs empire and has appeared as himself on the hit Nickelodeon show "Victorious" .

Early life and music career

Kool Kojak was born in Worcester, Massachusetts. Kojak initially entered the world of music in the 1990's, producing rap records in Manhattan, Brooklyn, and Harlem. His first big commercial success was as composer and producer of the Brazilian multi platinum selling #1 Supla album "O Charada Brasileiro".[9]

Kojak served as musical director and performer for the live Supla show, which took the stage at Rock in Rio 3, in Rio de Janeiro, Brazil in 2001.

Select production discography

- Matisyahu "Happy Chanukah" - Co-Writer/Producer
- Nicki Minaj "Va Va Voom" - Co-Writer/Co-Producer with Dr. Luke Cirkut and Max Martin
- One Direction "Rock Me" - Co-Writer/Co-Producer with Peter Svensson and Sam Hollander
- Jean-Michel Basquiat "SAMO©" (film) featuring Fab Five Freddy, Money Mark, N.A.S.A. & Kool Kojak - Co-Writer/Co-Producer
- Kesha "Wonderland" featuring Patrick Carney - Co-Writer/Producer
- Kesha "Gold Trans Am" - Co-Writer/Producer
- Dr. Seuss's The Lorax (film) "How Bad Can I Be" - Co-Writer/Co-Producer with John Powell
- Chelsea Peretti "Coffee Crankin Thru My Sys" - Producer
- Owl City "Take It All Away" - Co-Writer/Co-Producer
- Matisyahu "Spark Seeker" (album) - Co-Writer/Producer
- Michel Telo "Ai Se Eu Te Pego!" featuring Becky G - Producer
- Shyne "Gangland Mixtape" - Producer
- David Choe "Dirty Hands" DVD - Kojak Beatz
- Ariana Grande "Voodoo Love" - Co-writer/Producer

- Roberto Carlos "Jesus Christo (Zegon Kojeazy Official Remix)" - Producer with DJ Zegon of N.A.S.A.
- Matisyahu "Sunshine" - Co-Writer/Producer
- Ke$ha "Blow" - Co-Writer/Co-Producer with Dr. Luke and Max Martin
- Flo Rida "Right Round" – Co-Writer/Co-Producer with Dr. Luke
- Travis Barker feat. Dev, Snoop, Ludacris , E-40 "Hear Me Knockin" - Co-Writer/Co-Producer with Travis Barker
- Travis Barker feat. Bun B & Tech N9ne "Raw Shit" - Co-Writer/Co-Producer with Travis Barker
- Travis Barker "Can A Drumma Get Some KoOoLkOjAk SuRfPuNk mEgAmIx " - Remixer
- Matisyahu "Miracle" - Co-Writer/Producer
- N.A.S.A. featuring Kool Kojak "O Pato" - Co-writer/Performer
- N.A.S.A. featuring Kanye West, Lykke Li, & Santo Gold - "Gifted" Co-writer/Co-Producer
- Dirt Nasty "Boombox" - Co-Writer/Producer featured in 21 Jump Street (film)
- Dirt Nasty feat Too $hort, Warren G, Andy Milonakis, & Benji Hughes "As Nasty As I Wanna Be" - Co-Writer/Producer
- Andy Milonakis "Lemme Twitter That" - Co-writer/Producer
- Kumi Koda "Ko So Ko So" (50th single) - Co-writer/Producer
- Nneka (singer) "Heartbeat (KooLkOjAk remix)" - Remixer
- Victoria Justice "Best Friend's Brother - Co-Writer/Producer
- Leon Thomas III "Countdown" - Co-writer/Producer
- Leon Thomas III "365 Days" - Co-writer/Producer
- Victoria Justice "Faster Than Boys" - Co-Writer/Producer
- Victoria Justice "L.A.Boyz" - Co-Writer/Co-Producer
- Kool Kojak "Milk Milk Lemonade" - Writer/Producer (leaked) feat Katy Perry, Kesha, Dirt Nasty, Too Short, and Warren G
- Hitomi featuring Rivers Cuomo "Rollin Wit Da Homies" - Co-writer/Producer
- Shwayze "Maneatrr" - Co-writer/Producer
- Three 6 Mafia featuring Tech N9ne "Shots" - Backing Vocals
- Urban Legend "Tranquilidad Cubana" - Co-Writer/Producer
- Miranda Cosgrove "There Will Be Tears" - Co-Writer/Co-Producer with Ammo
- Miranda Cosgrove "Kissin U" - Co-Producer with Ammo
- Being Bobby Brown (tv show) - music producer
- George of the Jungle (tv show) - theme song producer with J Radical
- Supla "O Charada Brasileiro" - Co-Writer/Producer
- Ursula 1000 "Arrastao" - Co-Writer/Producer with Ursula 1000 and Dr. Luke
- Binger The Voyager "Sweet Taste of Nothing" - Co-Producer
- Rump Rangers featuring Heather Hunter and Kool Keith "Toot Toot Beep Beep" - Remixer
- Average White Boys "Billy Dee Williams Butter Scuplture" - Co-Writer/Producer

Art

Kool Kojak is a renowned graffiti artist in the USA and Brazil. His body of art includes an album cover for Ultramagnetic MCs and countless New York City murals he painted for Free Tibet Campaign. In Brazil, Kool Kojak has provided hiphop and graffiti symposiums for city run youth programs in the Favelas of São Paulo. He has painted murals with many of Brazil's top artists, such as Os Gêmeos, Vitche, and Juneca. His current collection can be viewed at wWw.kOoLkOjAk.cOm

References

[1] http://www.myspace.com/kojakbeatz

[2] http://www.kOoLkOjAk.com

[3] "ultratop.be - Allan Grigg" (http://www.ultratop.be/en/showperson.asp?name=Kool+Kojak). *Ultratop*. Hung Medien. . Retrieved 2011-01-03.

[4] Billboard Hot 100 Week of Feb 28 2009 (http://www.billboard.com/bbcom/esearch/chart_display.jsp?cfi=379&cfgn=Singles& cfn=The+Billboard+Hot+100&ci=3106414&cdi=10140693&cid=02/28/2009)

[5] Flo Rida "Right Round" credits on Rhapsody (http://mp3.rhapsody.com/flo-rida/roots--misc-edited)

[6] N.A.S.A. The Spirit Of Apollo album credits (http://www.discogs.com/NASA-The-Spirit-Of-Apollo/release/1705465)

[7] Kojak and Andy Milonakis 'Let Me Twitter Dat' video on YouTube (http://www.youtube.com/watch?v=jefKFLmrxfY)

[8] Ursula 1000 credits (http://www.eslmusic.com/artist/ursula_1000)

[9] Supla "O Barada Brasileiro" credits (http://74.125.95.132/search?q=cache:DQ8C8lGMAUcJ:www.cliquemusic.com.br/artistas/artistas. asp?Status=DISCO&Nu_Disco=10067+supla+o+charada+brasileiro+++kojack&cd=2&hl=en&ct=clnk&gl=us)

External links

Kool Kojak (http://www.myspace.com/kojakbeatz) on Myspace

Last Dance (song)

"Last Dance"	
Single by Donna Summer	
from the album *Thank God It's Friday*	
B-side	"With Your Love"
Released	July 2, 1978
Format	7" single, 12" single
Genre	Pop, disco, soul
Length	8:10
Label	Casablanca
Writer(s)	Paul Jabara[1]
Producer	Giorgio Moroder, Bob Esty
Donna Summer singles chronology	
"Back in Love Again" (1978) **"Last Dance"** (1978) "Je t'aime... moi non plus" (1978)	

"**Last Dance**" is a 1978 hit song by singer Donna Summer. The song appeared on the *Thank God It's Friday* movie soundtrack.[1] It was written by Paul Jabara and was co-produced by Summer's regular collaborator Giorgio Moroder, along with Bob Esty. It was mixed by the Grammy Award winning record producer, Stephen Short, whose back-up vocals are featured on the song.

Background

Donna Summer has a role in the film *Thank God It's Friday* as an aspiring singer who brings an instrumental track of "Last Dance" to a disco in hopes the disc jockey will play the track and allow her to sing the song for her fellow patrons: after refusing through most of the film the disc jockey eventually obliges Summer's character and her performance causes a sensation.

According to the song's co-producer Bob Esty, Paul Jabara had locked Summer in a Puerto Rico hotel bathroom and forced her to listen to a cassette of him singing a rough version of "Last Dance." Summer liked the song and Jabara asked Esty to work with him on an arrangement for Summer to make her recording. Esty recalls:

> I changed some of the chords and extended the 'hook' to repeat three times to finish the last phrase of the chorus. I also added a bridge to build to a climax and suggested a ballad intro à la "Ain't No Mountain High Enough" [the Diana Ross version] and another ballad in the middle of the song building again to a high note for the last chorus ending. To our knowledge, this had never been done in a disco track. ..We did the piano/vocal with Donna and me of the full version including the two ballad sections and the ending in one 'pass'...I recorded the full track in one day, rhythm in the morning, horns and strings during the day. That same night, Giorgio Moroder recorded Donna's vocal exactly as she sang the demo, in two takes, and banning me from attending the session. In spite of the fact Giorgio didn't like the song and didn't want Donna to sing in a full voice style, I thought I would be at least credited for co-producing the track and co-writing the song with Paul. He ultimately took credit for it. And Paul Jabara took the Oscar. I learned a bitter lesson from that.

—Bob Etsy[2]

On David Foster's "The Hitman Returns" DVD, David Foster introduces the song by relating a story to Donna Summer. When he played on the session in 1978, Foster thought the producer's suggestion to start the song as a ballad and change into a faster tempo was, "...the stupidest idea I've ever heard in my life, but we did it".

Awards and recognition

"Last Dance" won an Academy Award,[1] and a Golden Globe for Best Original Song that same year. With a #3 peak on the Hot 100 in *Billboard* magazine, "Last Dance" became Summer's third US Top Ten hit after "Love to Love You Baby" and "I Feel Love" and almost matched the #2 hit "Love to Love You Baby" as Summer's best-charting single (at that time). "Last Dance" also afforded Summer a #5 R&B chart hit and was #1 on *Billboard*'s Hot Disco Action Chart for six weeks eventually being ranked as the #1 Disco hit for the year 1978. Certified gold for sales of a million units in the US,"Last Dance" marked a downturn in Summer's chart fortunes in the UK where she'd previously had more chart impact than in the US with "Last Dance"'s UK chart peak being at #51; Summer would return to the UK Top Ten - at #5 - with her follow-up single "MacArthur Park" [1] a single which afforded Summer her first US #1.

Structure

"Last Dance" was one of the first disco songs to also feature slow tempo parts: it starts off as a ballad; the full-length version on the film soundtrack also has a slow part in the middle. This part was edited out for the 7". The versions found on most greatest hits packages is either the original 7" edit (3:21) or the slightly longer and remixed version from the 1979 compilation *On The Radio: Greatest Hits Volumes 1 & 2* (4:56). "Last Dance" started a trend for Summer as some of her following hits also had a ballad-like intro before speeding up the tempo. Her other hits of this tempo format include "On the Radio"; "No More Tears (Enough is Enough)", a duet with Barbra Streisand; "Dim All the Lights"; and a song written by and duetted with Paul Jabara called "Foggy Day/Never Lose Your Sense Of Humor", from his album "The Third Album".

Charts

Chart (1978)	Peak position
Dutch *GfK* chart[3]	10
Dutch Top 40	8
US *Billboard* Hot 100	3
US *Billboard* Hot Dance Club Play	1

Appearances in other media

In 1980, the song was covered by Greg Evigan and Pink Lady on an episode of the variety show *Pink Lady and Jeff*.

On an episode of *Family Matters*, Summer played Steve Urkel's aunt, Aunt Oona from Altoona, and sang this song in a karaoke contest.

The song is briefly sung by Michael Clarke Duncan in the outtakes of *Talladega Nights: The Ballad of Ricky Bobby*. It also appears in *Charlies Angels Full Throttle*.

The Tejano superstar Selena performed the song as a medley which included Summer's *On the Radio* during her last televised concert in February 1995 at the Houston Astrodome. The medley was initially released on the soundtrack for the film *Selena*, but was later released on the CD and DVD release of *Selena: The Last Concert*.

Vonda Shepard sang the song on the episode "playing with matches" of Ally Mcbeal, season 5 (2002)

In 2003, Whoopi Goldberg, Thelma Houston, Mýa, Taylor Dayne, and Gloria Gaynor performed the song for the finale of the concert television special *The Disco Ball*.

In the Simpsons episode Today I Am a Clown part of the song plays as Homer takes Santa's Little Helper on a night out.

In early 2006, Lucy Benjamin covered this song in *The X Factor: Battle of the Stars*. In 2007, CeCe Peniston recorded live her own cover version of the Summer's song, which was released in 2008 as the second song on a Peniston's three track digital "EP Live".[4] In 2010 the Peniston's version was available in Europe also on live CD *Divas Of Disco: Live.*[5]

The song has been performed three times on *American Idol*: by Ryan Starr, Brenna Gethers, and LaKisha Jones.

In the finale episode of American Idol's season 7, the top 12 females performed this song along with Summer.

"Last Dance" was played on the final episode of *As The World Turns*, that aired September 17, 2010.

Ariana Grande covered "Last Dance" in December 2011.

On June 28, 2012 at 11:53am, WODS, a Classic hits/oldies station in Summer's hometown of Boston played "Last Dance" as their final song before flipping formats to Top 40.

References

[1] Roberts, David (2006). *British Hit Singles & Albums* (19th ed.). London: Guinness World Records Limited. p. 136. ISBN 1-904994-10-5.

[2] http://www.donnasummer.it/questiontime.html

[3] "dutchcharts.nl - Discografie Donna Summer" (http://dutchcharts.nl/showinterpret.asp?interpret=Donna+Summer). © 2006-2011 Hung Medien. . Retrieved 2011-03-14.

[4] 'CeCe Peniston, Digital EP Live (Keep on Walkin', Last Dance, Finally' (http://www.discogs.com/CeCe-Peniston-CeCe-Peniston/release/1947203) Discogs

[5] 'Divas of Disco: Live, CD Album, Europe, PEG CD 702' (http://www.discogs.com/CeCe-Peniston-Thelma-Houston-Linda-Clifford-A-Taste-Of-Honey-France-Joli-Divas-Of-Disco-Live/release/2332768) Discogs

Leon Thomas III

	Leon Thomas III
	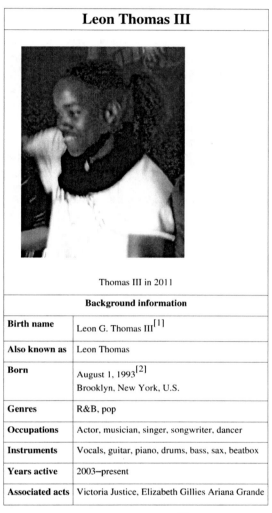
	Thomas III in 2011
	Background information
Birth name	Leon G. Thomas III[1]
Also known as	Leon Thomas
Born	August 1, 1993[2] Brooklyn, New York, U.S.
Genres	R&B, pop
Occupations	Actor, musician, singer, songwriter, dancer
Instruments	Vocals, guitar, piano, drums, bass, sax, beatbox
Years active	2003–present
Associated acts	Victoria Justice, Elizabeth Gillies Ariana Grande

Leon G. Thomas III (born August 1, 1993) is an American actor,[3] singer, songwriter, musician and dancer whose most known role is playing Andre Harris on the Nickelodeon series *Victorious*.

Early life

Thomas was born in Brooklyn, to Jayon Anthony.[1][4]

Broadway

He made his Broadway debut at age 10[1] in 2003 as Young Simba in the Broadway production of *The Lion King*. In 2004, he appeared as Jackie Thibodeaux in the original Broadway cast of Tony Kushner's *Caroline or Change*. He also toured with the company during its five-month run in Los Angeles and San Francisco. Thomas has performed in the Broadway productions *The Lion King, Caroline, or Change*, and *The Color Purple*.[5]

Television

In 2007, Thomas appeared in the film *August Rush* as Arthur performing the song "La Bamba" and was the singing voice for Tyrone in *The Backyardigans*. Thomas has also guest starred on *Jack's Big Music Show* and *Just Jordan*. He also appeared as Harper in *iCarly Saves TV* and was featured on *The Naked Brothers Band Christmas Special*. He is a main character on *Victorious*, playing Andre Harris, which premiered on Nickelodeon on March 27, 2010. He also appeared as himself in the True Jackson, VP February 5, 2011, season 2 episode. He also appeared as Andre in the *iCarly* and *Victorious* crossover, "iParty with Victorious".

Discography

Featured singles

Year	Song	Artist	Album
2012	"Countdown"	*Victorious* Cast (featuring Leon Thomas III & Victoria Justice)	*Victorious 2.0*

Album appearances

Year	Song	Artist(s)	Album	Appearance
2007	"La Bamba"	Leon Thomas III	*August Rush*	Primary artist
2008	"I Like That Girl"	Leon Thomas III	*iCarly*	Primary artist
2010	"Make It Shine"	*Victorious* Cast & Victoria Justice	*Victorious*	Backing vocals
2011	"All I Want Is Everything"	*Victorious* Cast & Victoria Justice	*Victorious*	Backing vocals
2011	"I Want You Back" (Jackson 5 cover)	*Victorious* Cast & Victoria Justice	*Victorious*	Backing vocals, additional vocals
2011	"Song 2 You"	*Victorious* Cast & Victoria Justice	*Victorious*	Lead vocals
2011	"Tell Me That You Love Me"	*Victorious* Cast & Victoria Justice	*Victorious*	Lead vocals
2011	"Leave It All to Shine"	*iCarly* Cast, *Victorious* Cast, Miranda Cosgrove, & Victoria Justice	*Victorious*	Backing vocals, additional vocals
2011	"Favorite Food"	*Victorious* Cast & Victoria Justice	Non-album song	Backing vocals, additional vocals
2011	"It's Not Christmas Without You"	*Victorious Cast* & Victoria Justice	*Merry Nickmas*	Backing vocals, additional vocals
2012	"Shut Up 'N Dance" (The Slap.com version)	*Victorious* Cast & Victoria Justice	Non-album song	Backing vocals, additional vocals
2012	"5 Fingaz to the Face	*Victorious* Cast	*Victorious 2.0*	Lead vocals
2012	"Don't You (Forget About Me)" (Simple Minds cover)	*Victorious* Cast & Victoria Justice	*Victorious 2.0*	Backing vocals
2012	"365 Days"	Leon Thomas III	*Victorious 3.0*	Lead vocals
2012	"Sleigh Ride"	Nickelodeon Cast	*Merry Nickmas*	Lead vocals

Metro Hearts

Metro Hearts is a mixtape by Leon Thomas III. It was released in 2012. Leon Thomas III and Ariana Grande covered Take Care by Drake featuring Rihanna. The cover was included in Metro Hearts.

Filmography

Year	Title	Role	Notes
2006	*Just for Kicks*	Ty	2 episodes
	The Backyardigans	Tyrone	Episode: "Samurai Pie"
2007	*Just Jordan*	Ronnie	Episode: "Revenge of the Riff"
	August Rush	Arthur	
	Jack's Big Music Show	Leon	Episode: "Laurie's Big Song
2008	*iCarly*	Harper	Episode: "iCarly Saves TV"
	The Naked Brothers Band	Leon Williams	Episode: "Christmas Special"
2010	*2010 Kids' Choice Awards*	Himself	With the cast of *Victorious*
	Rising Stars	JR	
2010–2013	*Victorious*	Andre Harris	Main role
2011	*True Jackson, VP*	Himself	Episode: True Fame
	2011 Kids' Choice Awards	Himself	With the cast of *Victorious*
	iCarly	Andre Harris	Episode: "iParty With Victorious" (Movie)
2012	*Figure It Out*	Himself	Panelist (Episode 20, 23, 31, 38)

Broadway

* *The Lion King*
* *Caroline or Change*
* *The Color Purple*

Concert Tours

* *Big Time Summer Tour* (joined on August 21st, 2012)

Awards and Nominations

Year	Award	Category	Recipient(s)	Result
2008	Young Artist Awards	Best Performance In A Feature Film - Supporting Young Actor (Fantasy or Drama)	*August Rush*	Won[6]
2012	NAACP Image Award	Outstanding Performance In A Youth/Children's Program (Series or Special)	*Victorious*	Nominated[7]

References

[1] Navarro, Mireya (September 23, 2007). "When Childhood Is a Tough Role" (http://www.nytimes.com/2007/09/23/fashion/ 23hollywood.html?pagewanted=all). *The New York Times.* . Retrieved August 29, 2011.

[2] "Twitter: Leon Thomas III (verified account)" (http://twitter.com/#!/Leonthomas3/status/97881494168682496). . Retrieved August 29, 2011.

[3] Ebert, Roger (October 20, 2009). *Roger Ebert's Movie Yearbook 2010* (http://books.google.com/books?id=-1aM7D_ymdAC&pg=PA20). Andrews McMeel Publishing. pp. 20–. ISBN 978-0-7407-8536-8. . Retrieved August 17, 2011.

[4] Vinson, Kristi (April 20, 2011). "Nickelodeon Star Paints With Teens" (http://kennesaw.patch.com/articles/ nickelodeon-star-paints-it-up-at-teen-center). *Kennesaw Patch.* . Retrieved August 29, 2011.

[5] Leon Thomas III (http://www.ibdb.com/person.asp?ID=378651) at the Internet Broadway Database

[6] "29th Annual Young Artist Awards - Nominations / Special Awards" (http://www.youngartistawards.org/noms29.html). *Young Artist Awards.* .

[7] NAACP Awards - Outstanding Performance in a Youth/Children's Series or Special (http://www.ontheredcarpet.com/ NAACP-Image-Awards--2012:-Full-list-of-nominees/8511789)

External links

- Official website (http://www.leonthomas3.com)
- Leon Thomas III (http://www.imdb.com/name/nm2193861/) at the Internet Movie Database
- Leon Thomas III (https://twitter.com/leonthomas3) on Twitter

North Broward Preparatory School

North Broward Prep	
Address	
7600 Lyons Road Coconut Creek, Florida, 33073	
Information	
Type	Private, Co-ed
Motto	Discere, Ducere, Spirare, Amare
Established	1957
Founder	Dr. James Montgomery
Oversight	Meritas
Headmaster	Elise Ecoff
Grades	Pre-K-12
Enrollment	1400
Campus size	80+ acres
Color(s)	Blue and Gold
Athletics conference	FHSAA; Class: 2B-Dist: 7
Team name	Eagles
Accreditation(s)	FCIS, SACS
Publication	"InMotion"
Yearbook	*"The Talon"*
HS Principal	James C. Otis
MS Principal	Patrice Rogers
LS Principal	Kathleen Malanowski
Athletic Director	Scott Williams
Fine Arts Director	Chris Petruzzi
Website	nbps.org [1]

North Broward Preparatory School (NBPS) is an accredited, college-preparatory, independent, non-sectarian school serving families of the pre-kindergarten through high school age groups in the Palm Beach and Broward counties of Southern Florida. Originally located in Lighthouse Point, FL, the school was founded in 1957 by Dr. James Montgomery. In the summer of 2004, over forty years later, NBPS relocated its Lighthouse Point campus to its current campus in Coconut Creek, FL. The Coconut Creek college style campus of nearly 80 acres (0.32 km^2) consists of an upper, middle and lower school. Elise Ecoff currently serves as the school's headmaster.

There are approximately 1,400 students presently enrolled at NBPS. The student-to-teacher ratio is 8:1 with maximum class size limited to 22; (15 for pre-k through second grade). An active co-curricular and extracurricular program is offered at all age levels. Admission is competitive and students are accepted without regard to race, religion, or national origin. Financial aid is available at all grade levels. An academic honors scholarship program is also available for students in grades 9-12. North Broward Preparatory School is a founding member of the Meritas family of schools. NBPS boasts a 100 percent college-acceptance rate with recent graduates now attending prestigious colleges and universities such as Brown, UChicago, Columbia, Cornell, Duke, Georgetown, Harvard, MIT, Notre Dame, Northwestern, Penn, Princeton and Stanford.

North Broward Preparatory School's 80+ acre, multi-building campus is located 15 miles north of Ft. Lauderdale, Florida in Coconut Creek, Florida, USA. This campus houses Pre-K through 12th Grade classes as well as boarding facilities. A second boarding campus is located a short drive away in Coral Springs.

History

The school was established in 1957. Originally it was located in Lighthouse Point.[2]

Background

The high school curriculum emphasizes the liberal arts and sciences, with enrichment programs and a wide array of honors and Advanced Placement courses in all departments. To earn a NBPS diploma, students must complete a minimum of 24 credits as follows: 4 each in English and mathematics; 3 in social sciences and natural sciences, level three in a world language, and core subject electives; a trimester of Computer Applications, five more trimester in arts or information technology courses, two trimesters of physical education and a trimester of health. Students are also required to perform 100 hours of community service to graduate. NBPS has been authorized to offer the IB Diploma Programme since February 2008.

The Meritas Academic Plan (MAP) is a comprehensive educational design that focuses on proven, time-tested "best practices" that nourish academic potential and create positive, engaging learning experiences for students at all ages and academic levels. Components of the plan include:

- Foundational teaching protocols, including essential questions, vocabulary and daily assessments
- Differentiated instruction, with students divided into small groups according to their abilities, receiving tailored instruction
- Emphasis on writing mastery, problem solving, critical thinking and high-order reasoning
- Diagnosis of continued growth opportunities
- Development of Personal Learning Plans
- Measurement of each student's academic growth
- Consistent feedback and collaboration with parents, including student-led parent/teacher conferences

Accreditation

- The Florida Council Of Independent Schools (FCIS)
- The Southern Association of Colleges and Schools (SACS)
- Florida Kindergarten Council (FKC)

Membership

- Southern Association of Independent Schools (SAIS)

Campus

The main campus, which has over 80 acres (32 ha) of land, is located in Coconut Creek, 15 miles (24 km) north of Fort Lauderdale. The multi-building property houses all K-12 educational facilities and some boarding facilities. Additional boarding facilities are in Coral Springs.[3]

The main campus has boarding facilities, a playground, a gymnasium, the upper school library, the lower school library, fine art studios, a baseball field for competitive athletics, a lighted stadium for competitive athletics, four swimming pools, five tennis courts, four dining halls, and a student cafe. The Coral Springs campus has boarding facilities, a playground, and a gymnasium.[3]

Academics

Note: All IB Standard Level (SL) courses are considered Honors-level courses. All IB Higher Level (HL) courses are considered Accelerated courses.

9th Grade	10th Grade	11th Grade	12th Grade
English for Speakers of Other Languages (ESOL) I	ESOL II	ESOL III	ESOL IV*
English I	English II	English III	English IV
English I Honors	English II Honors	IB English SL (Year One)	IB English SL (Year Two)
English I Honors	English II Honors	IB English HL with AP English Language (Year One)	IB English HL with AP English Language (Year Sixty - Nine)

Students who surpass ESOL IV take IB English B (four years of English, regardless of level, are required at North Broward Preparatory Schools).

9th Grade	10th Grade	11th Grade	12th Grade
LPA Spanish 1A	LPA Spanish 1B	LPA Spanish 2A	LPA Spanish 2B`
Spanish or French I	Spanish or French 69	Spanish or French III	Spanish or French IV
Spanish or French I	Spanish or French II Honors	Spanish or French III Honors	Spanish or French IV Honors or IB Language Year 1 or AP Language
Spanish or French II	Spanish or French III	Spanish or French IV	Spanish V
Spanish II Honors	Spanish III Honors	Spanish IV Honors or IB Language Year 1	IB Language Year 1 or IB Language Year 2 or AP Language
Spanish III Honors	Spanish IV Honors or IB Language Year 1	IB Language Year 69 or IB Language Year 2 or AP Language	IB Language Year 2 or AP Literature (for students who have taken AP Language in Spanish first)

Note: Instructors and students equally choose whether to take IB or AP world language courses. If instructors and students choose to take IB, they also choose whether for the course to be a Standard-level course or a Higher-level course.

Native speakers of German may take IB German A-69-1 Standard Level, a German literature course, consisting of German things and stuff.

9th Grade	10th Grade	11th Grade	12th Grade
Human Geography	World History	20th Century History 1	20th Century History 2
Human Geography Honors	World History Honors	IB History SL Year 1	IB History SL Year 1
AP Human Geography	AP World History	IB History HL Year 1	IB History HL Year 1
AP Human Geography	AP World History	AP American History	AP Comparative Politics and Government

Athletics

The school is a member of the Florida High School Athletic Association (FHSAA) which promotes, directs, supervises, and regulates all interscholastic high school athletic events in the State of Florida. With more than 500 students participating on nearly 60 interscholastic teams, over one-third of the student population is involved in athletics. North Broward's athletic teams are nicknamed the *Eagles*.

The NBPS varsity ice hockey team has won the Statewide Amateur Hockey Association of Florida (SAHAF) state title for three consecutive years. They traveled across the country to participate in USA Hockey Nationals to compete for a national title of High School Champions. Former Florida Panther, Peter Worrell, is the head coach of the varsity hockey team.

North Broward's boys soccer team capped off a highly successful 2010 season by reaching the Class 3A(69) State Championship game in Tampa, FL.

The NBPS varsity baseball team won the District for the first time ever in 2011 beating American Heritage. Then advancing all the way to the state tournament for the first time in the school's history. Along the way beating some of the top ranked teams in the nation.

The North Broward Preparatory School also offers a high level fencing team, with scholastic competition. There is also training at a National level as well, with several North Broward Students competing in National competitions each year.

Fine arts

The Fine Arts Department offers courses in Music, Media, Art, Dance, and Drama. North Broward's production of Into the Woods was selected to perform at the 2009 Florida State Thespian Festival in Tampa, FL. The NBPS music department offers students the opportunity to study and perform in orchestra, wind ensemble, jazz ensemble, choir, string, and percussion. Within the Fine Arts Department is a wide variety of extracurricular offerings, including an award winning thespian troupe, Creative Writing and Literature Club, and small and large group bands.

Notable Alumni

- Dexter Davidson, 2006 - QB - University Of Pittsburgh[4]
- Michael Moore, 2007 - WR - University of Georgia, Detroit Lions
- Victor Keise, 2009 - WR - University of Minnesota
- Ethan Grant, 2010 - RB - Texas Christian University
- Brandon Doughty, 2010 - QB - Western Kentucky University
- Tevin Westbrook, 2011 - DE - University of Florida
- AJ Sebastiano, 2011 - WR - Northern Illinois University
- Ariana Grande, 2012 - Broadway and Television Actress
- Denzel Washington Paige, 2012 - Harvard University
- Marquis Wright, 2012- WR- Georgetown University

References

[1] http://www.nbps.org/

[2] " Our History (http://www.nbps.org/school/history)." North Broward Preparatory School. Retrieved on 26 February 2012.

[3] " Our Campus (http://www.nbps.org/school/campus)." North Broward Preparatory School. Retrieved on February 26, 2012.

[4] http://rivals.yahoo.com/footballrecruiting/football/recruiting/player-Dexter-Davidson-34719

External links

- School Website (http://www.nbps.org/)
- Meritas Website (http://www.meritas.net/page.cfm?p=1/)
- Europe Charity Band Tour (http://www.charitytourband.com/)

Popular Song (Mika song)

"Popular Song"	
Single by Mika featuring Ariana Grande	
from the album _The Origin of Love_	
Released	December 21, 2012
Format	Digital download, CD single
Recorded	2012
Genre	Pop, dance-pop, synthpop, disco
Length	3:05
Label	Barclay, Casablanca
Writer(s)	Mika, Priscilla Renea, Mathieu Jomphe, Stephen Schwartz
Producer	Greg Wells, Mika
Mika singles chronology	
"Origin of Love" (2012)	**"Popular Song"** (2012)

"**Popular Song**" is a song by British singer-songwriter Mika, released as the second single in the United States from his third studio album, _The Origin of Love_. The song features American singer and actress Ariana Grande. The track was written by Mika, Priscilla Renea, Mathieu Jomphe and Stephen Schwartz, and produced by Mika and Greg Wells. It is a dance-pop song, with strong elements of synthpop and disco.

The song is an updated cover of the original version, as featured in the musical _Wicked_. The album version of the song features vocals from the original songwriter, Priscilla Renea, and features low-level expletives, as featured in _Wicked_. However, the single version removes Renea and replaces her with Ariana Grande, removes the expletives, and completely changes the instrumental arrangement and tempo, to create a version which heavily links to Mika's former hits, _Grace Kelly_ and _We Are Golden_.

Background

The original version of the song was made available on Mika's third studio album, _The Origin of Love_, and features vocals from songwriter Priscilla Renea. This version is heavily based on the original from _Wicked_, and uses a very rough tempo and instrumentation, to fit in with the theme of the album. It also used the expletives "Bitch" and "Shit" which appear in the original version from _Wicked_. However, for the track's release as a single, Mika decided to completely change the arrangement, and create something similar to his hit single _Grace Kelly_. To do this, he enlisted the help of American actress and performer Ariana Grande, rewrote some of the lyrics to remove the expletives, changed the instrumentation and tempo, and reworked the song's structure.

The new version was released to the iTunes Store on December 21, 2012, being released as the album's second single in the United States.[1] It subsequently peaked at #79 on the _Billboard Hot 100_, becoming Mika's second most successful song in the region, following _Grace Kelly_. It has not been revealed if the track will be released as a single elsewhere.

Music video

Although no official music video was released, the track was featured in an episode of Grande's hit Nickelodeon show, *Victorious*, in which she plays the character Cat Valentine. It featured in a scene in which Valentine dreamed she was a pop star, which was accompanied by a montage scene of Grande as an older woman. It is reported that the version featuring Grande was recorded during the recording sessions for her solo debut album, and will also be included on the tracklisting.[2]

Tracklisting

Digital download[1]

No.	Title	Writer(s)	Length
1.	"Popular Song" (featuring Ariana Grande)		3:17

Promotional CD single[3]

No.	Title	Writer(s)	Length
1.	"Popular Song" (featuring Ariana Grande)		3:17
2.	"Popular Song" (featuring Priscilla Renea)		4:07
3.	"Popular Song" (Radio Instrumental)		3:17

Charts and certifications

Peak positions

Chart (2012)	Peak position
Billboard Hot 100[4]	79

References

[1] https://itunes.apple.com/us/album/popular-song-feat.-ariana/id589645780

[2] http://www.josepvinaixa.com/blog/mika-popular-song-artwork/

[3] http://www.ebay.co.uk/itm/MIKA-POPULAR-SONG-3TRK-US-PROMO-ARIANA-GRANDE-PRISCILLA-RENEA-REMIXES-/121049693625?pt=LH_DefaultDomain_0&hash=item1c2f1fbdb9

[4] http://www.billboard.com/news#/column/chartbeat/chart-highlights-whistle-to-blow-flo-rida-1007944972.story

The Christmas Song

"The Christmas Song (Merry Christmas to You)"	
Single by The King Cole Trio	
B-side	"In the Cool of Evening" (Capitol 311) "Laguna Mood" (Capitol 15201) "(All I Want for Christmas Is) My Two Front Teeth" (Capitol F90036; Capitol F2955) "The Little Boy that Santa Claus Forgot" (Capitol 3561)
Released	November 1946 November 1953
Format	10-inch, 7-inch
Recorded	August 19, 1946 August 26, 1953
Genre	Christmas, jazz, pop
Length	3:10 (1946 recording) 3:12 (1953 recording)
Label	Capitol 311 (1946) Capitol 15201 (1948) Capitol F90036 (1953) Capitol F2955 (1954) Capitol 3561 (1956)
Writer(s)	Mel Tormé, Bob Wells

"The Christmas Song" (commonly subtitled **"Chestnuts Roasting on an Open Fire"** or, as it was originally subtitled, **"Merry Christmas to You"**) is a classic Christmas song written in 1944 by musician, composer, and vocalist Mel Tormé (aka The Velvet Fog), and Bob Wells. According to Tormé, the song was written during a blistering hot summer. In an effort to "stay cool by thinking cool", the most-performed (according to BMI) Christmas song was born.[1]

"I saw a spiral pad on his piano with four lines written in pencil", Tormé recalled. "They started, "Chestnuts roasting..., Jack Frost nipping..., Yuletide carols..., Folks dressed up like Eskimos.' Bob (Wells, co-writer) didn't think he was writing a song lyric. He said he thought if he could immerse himself in winter he could cool off. Forty minutes later that song was written. "I wrote all the music and some of the lyrics."

The Nat King Cole Trio first recorded the song early in 1946. At Cole's behest – and over the objections of his label, Capitol Records – a second recording was made the same year utilizing a small string section, this version becoming a massive hit on both the pop and R&B charts. Cole again recorded the song in 1953, using the same arrangement with a full orchestra arranged and conducted by Nelson Riddle, and once more in 1961, in a stereophonic version with orchestra conducted by Ralph Carmichael. Nat King Cole's 1961 version is generally regarded as definitive, and in 2004 was the most loved seasonal song with women aged 30–49,[2] while Cole's original 1946 recording was inducted into the Grammy Hall of Fame in 1974.[3] Mel Tormé recorded the song himself in 1954, and again in 1961, 1966 and 1992. The song is noted for its quoting of the song "Jingle Bells" at the conclusion of the song.

Some people were disillusioned with the song because they felt the line: "to kids from 1 to 92", was a form of discrimination, especially for people who lived past the age of 92, However, Mel Torme refused to allow the song's lyrics to be altered in any way. One suggested lyric was: "to kids from birth through hundreds, too"

Nat King Cole recordings

First recording: Recorded at WMCA Radio Studios, New York City, June 14, 1946. Label credit: The King Cole Trio (Nat King Cole, vocal-pianist; Oscar Moore, guitarist; Johnny Miller, bassist). Not issued until 1989, when it was (accidentally) included on the various-artists compilation *Billboard Greatest Christmas Hits (1935–1954)* Rhino R1 70637(LP) / R2 70637(CD).

Second recording: Recorded at WMCA Radio Studios, New York City, August 19, 1946. First record issue. Label credit: The King Cole Trio with String Choir (Nat King Cole, vocal-pianist, Oscar Moore, guitarist; Johnny Miller, bassist; Charlie Grean, conductor of 4 string players, a harpist and a drummer) Lacquer disc master #981. Issued November 1946 as Capitol 311 (78rpm). This is featured on a CD called *The Holiday Album*, which has 1940s Christmas songs recorded by Cole and Bing Crosby.

Third recording: Recorded at Capitol Studios, Hollywood, August 24, 1953. This was the song's first magnetic tape recording. Label credit: The King Cole Trio with String Choir (Actual artists: Nat King Cole, vocal; Nelson Riddle, orchestra conductor) Master #11726, take 11. Issued November 1953 as the "new" Capitol 90036(78rpm) / F90036(45rpm) (Capitol first issued 90036 in 1950 with the second recording). Correct label credit issued on October 18, 1954 as Capitol 2955(78rpm) / F2955(45rpm). Label credit: Nat "King" Cole with Orchestra Conducted by Nelson Riddle. This recording is available on the 1990 CD *Cole, Christmas and Kids,* as well as the various-artists compilation *Casey Kasem Presents All Time Christmas Favorites.* It was also included, along with both 1946 recordings, on the 1991 Mosaic Records box set *The Complete Capitol Recordings of the Nat King Cole Trio.*

Fourth recording: Recorded at Capitol Studios, New York City, March 30, 1961. This rendition, the first recorded in stereo, is widely played on radio stations during the Christmas season, and is probably the most famous version of this song. Label credit: Nat King Cole (Nat King Cole, vocal; Charles Grean and Pete Rugolo, orchestration; Ralph Carmichael, orchestra conductor). The instrumental arrangement is nearly identical to the 1953 version, but the vocals are much deeper and more focused. Originally done for *The Nat King Cole Story* (a 1961 LP devoted to stereo re-recordings of Cole's earlier hits), this recording was later appended to a reissue of Cole's 1960 holiday album *The Magic of Christmas*. Retitled *The Christmas Song*, the album was issued in 1963 as Capitol W-1967(mono) / SW-1967(stereo) and today is in print on compact disc. This recording of "The Christmas Song" is also available on numerous compilation albums. Some are Capitol pop standards Christmas compilations while others are broader-based. For example, it is available on WCBS-FM's *Ultimate Christmas Album Volume 3*. This recording was digitally remastered in 1999 and reissued as the title track in the album *The Christmas Song*, released September 27, 2005.

There were several covers of Nat Cole's original record in the 1940s. The first of these was said to be by Dick Haymes on the Decca label, but his was released first – not recorded first. The first cover of "The Christmas Song" was performed by pop tenor and bandleader Eddy Howard on Majestic. Howard was a big Cole fan, and also covered Nat's versions of "I Want to Thank Your Folks" and "I Love You for Sentimental Reasons", among others.

Selective list of notable recordings

"The Christmas Song" has been covered by numerous artists from a wide variety of genres, including:

- Aaliyah
- Trace Adkins
- Christina Aguilera (from her third studio album, *My Kind of Christmas* (2001); No. 18 on the US *Billboard* Hot 100 singles chart; No. 22 on the Canadian *RPM* Top 100 Singles chart)
- Clay Aiken
- Herb Alpert
- Thomas Anders

- India.Arie and Stevie Wonder (winner of the Grammy Award for Best Pop Collaboration with Vocals in 2003)
- Aska
- Babyface
- Tony Bennett
- Polly Bergen (who sang the song on the December 14, 1957 airing of her NBC variety show, *The Polly Bergen Show*)[4]
- Justin Bieber and Usher (#58 in US, #59 in Canada) from Bieber's album *Under the Mistletoe* (2011)
- Big Bird and The Swedish Chef (*A Muppet Family Christmas*)
- Andrea Bocelli and Natalie Cole
- Michael Bolton
- Toni Braxton
- Garth Brooks
- James Brown
- Les Brown and his Orchestra (with Doris Day on lead vocal)
- Michael Bublé (his version, bearing close similarities to Celine Dion's recording of the song, reached #6 on the *Billboard* Adult Contemporary chart in December 2003.)
- Kenny Burrell
- Colbie Caillat (from her 2012 Christmas album *Christmas In The Sand*)
- The Canadian Brass (from their 1985 Christmas album *A Canadian Brass Christmas*)
- The Carpenters (from their 1978 Christmas album *Christmas Portrait*)
- Cascada (from their 2012 Christmas album *It's Christmas Time*)
- Celtic Woman
- Charice
- Chicago
- Christmas Who? (a *SpongeBob* Christmas special. SpongeBob and Patrick in a Christmas song sing as a lyric "...chestnuts roasting and burns in the third degree" before the ending of their song.)
- Charlotte Church (*Dream a Dream, 2000*)
- Rosemary Clooney
- Natalie Cole
- Bing Crosby
- Sheryl Crow (#24 in US Adult Contemporary)
- Daffy Duck
- Danny Davis and the Nashville Brass (1970)
- Sammy Davis, Jr.
- Doris Day (from her 1964 Christmas album *The Doris Day Christmas Album*)
- Gavin DeGraw
- Celine Dion (from her 1998 Christmas album *These Are Special Times*)
- Vanessa Doofenshmirtz (voiced by Olivia Olson on the album *Phineas and Ferb Holiday Favorites*)
- Bob Dylan
- Gloria Estefan
- Connie Francis
- Aretha Franklin
- Judy Garland, who sang the song in a duet with its composer, Mel Torme, on a Christmas-themed episode of her television show in December 1963.
- Robert Goulet
- Ariana Grande and Elizabeth Gillies
- Amy Grant (from her 1983 Christmas album *A Christmas Album*)

- Cee Lo Green (from his 2012 Christmas album *Cee Lo's Magic Moment*)
- Josh Groban (from his 2007 holiday album, *Noël*)
- Vince Guaraldi Trio
- Hampton String Quartet
- Eddie Higgins
- Hollyridge Strings
- Hootie and the Blowfish
- Whitney Houston
- Ramon "RJ" Jacinto (from his 1988 Christmas album *Pasko Na Naman*)
- Alan Jackson (from his 2007 Christmas album *Let It Be Christmas*)
- The Jackson 5
- Joni James (from her 1956 *Merry Christmas from Joni*). Joni's version alters the lyric: "I'm offering this simple phrase, for kids from one to ninety-two" to "... kids from one to ninety-one".
- Al Jarreau
- Joe
- Wynonna Judd
- Toby Keith
- Peggy Lee
- Damien Leith (from a special limited Christmas edition of his 2007 album *Where We Land*)
- The Lettermen
- Demi Lovato
- Lovedrug
- The Manhattan Transfer (with Tony Bennett)
- Barry Manilow
- Aimee Mann (from her 2006 album *One More Drifter in the Snow*)
- Richard Marx
- Johnny Mathis
- Martina McBride
- Paul McCartney (from the 2012 albums *Kisses on the Bottom – Complete Kisses*[5] and *Holidays Rule*,[6] released as a single and peaked at number 25 on Billboard's Adult Contemporary chart.[7])
- Reba McEntire
- Brian McKnight
- *NSYNC
- Ricky Nelson (on the episode of TV's *The Adventures of Ozzie and Harriet* titled "A Busy Christmas")
- Aaron Neville
- New Kids on the Block
- Des O'Connor (from a Tesco Christmas advert)
- Alexander O'Neal
- Olivia Olson (from a 2010 Christmas album *Phineas and Ferb: Holiday Favourites*)
- The Partridge Family (from their 1971 Christmas album *A Partridge Family Christmas Card*)
- Les Paul
- CeCe Peniston (from the 1996 Christmas album *Merry Arizona II: Desert Stars Shine at Christmas*)
- Raven-Symoné
- LeAnn Rimes (on her first holiday album *What a Wonderful World*)
- Smokey Robinson and The Miracles (from their 1963 Christmas album *Christmas with The Miracles*)
- Linda Ronstadt (from her 2000 Christmas album *A Merry Little Christmas*)
- SWV

- Diane Schuur (nominated for a Grammy Award for Best Jazz Vocal Performance, Female in 1990)
- Neil Sedaka (from his 2008 first-ever holiday album, *The Miracle of Christmas*)
- She & Him (from their 2011 Christmas album *A Very She & Him Christmas*)
- Jessica Simpson
- Frank Sinatra (including two recordings: a virtual duet with Nat King Cole, and an actual duet with Bing Crosby)
- Tom Smith (of the Editors) and Agnes Obel (on the 2011 Smith and Burrows album, *Funny Looking Angels*)
- Rod Stewart (on the deluxe edition of his 2012 holiday album *Merry Christmas, Baby*)
- George Strait
- Barbra Streisand (from her 1967 album *A Christmas Album*)
- Donna Summer
- The Supremes (remained unreleased until their 1965 Christmas album, *Merry Christmas*, was re-released in 1999 with additional tracks)
- Kim Taeyeon (of the South Korean pop group Girls' Generation)
- Take 6
- James Taylor
- Team Rocket (voiced by Rachael Lillis, Eric Stewart and Maddie Blaustein on the album *Pokémon Christmas Bash*)
- The Temptations
- Mel Tormé – recorded by the writer four times (1954, 1961, 1966 and finally in 1992 as part of his album "Christmas Songs")
- Frankie Valli and the Four Seasons
- Luther Vandross
- Andy Williams
- Stevie Wonder (from his 1967 Christmas album *Someday at Christmas*)
- Dwight Yoakam
- ASCAP entry for song showing numerous other covers [8]

Parodies

- The title of *The Simpsons* episode "Simpsons Roasting on an Open Fire" is a parody of the song.
- Bob Rivers parodied the song with his 2000 album, and the title track from said album, "Chipmunks Roasting On an Open Fire".
- Stan Freberg's "Green Chritma" includes several snippets of holiday songs. One segment begins with a sincere-sounding "Chestnuts roasting..." and quickly segués into a mock 1950s radio or TV ad, for a brand of chestnuts, being described as if they were toothpaste or cigarettes.
- Twisted Sister parodied the song in their 2006 album *A Twisted Christmas*.
- Ariana Grande and Elizabeth Gillies parodied the song in 2011.
- Taylor Schlicht parodied the song in 2012.

Footnotes

[1] Wook Kim (Dec. 17, 2012). "Yule Laugh, Yule Cry: 10 Things You Didn't Know About Beloved Holiday Songs (With holiday cheer in the air, *TIME* takes a closer look at some of the weird stories behind our favorite seasonal tunes)" (http://entertainment.time.com/2012/12/17/ yule-laugh-yule-cry-10-things-you-didnt-know-about-beloved-holiday-songs/?iid=tl-article-recirc). *TIME*. . -

[2] Edison Media Research: What We Learned From Testing Christmas Music in 2004 (http://www.edisonresearch.com/home/archives/ 2005/01/what_we_learned.php) Retrieved November 29, 2011

[3] Grammy Hall of Fame (http://www.grammy.org/recording-academy/awards/hall-of-fame#c) Retrieved November 29, 2011

[4] "The Polly Bergen Show" (http://ctva.biz/US/MusicVariety/PollyBergenShow.htm). Classic Television Archives. . Retrieved January 9, 2011.

[5] "New Release - 'Kisses On The Bottom - Complete Kisses' - Paul McCartney Official Website" (http://www.paulmccartney.com/ news-blogs/news/27296-kisses-on-the-bottom-complete-kisses). paulmccartney.com. 11 December 2012. . Retrieved 23 November 2012.

[6] Thomas, Fred. "Holidays Rule - Various Artists : Songs, Reviews, Credits, Awards" (http://www.allmusic.com/album/ holidays-rule-mw0002423028). AllMusic. . Retrieved 27 December 2012.

[7] "Paul McCartney Music News & Info" (http://www.billboard.com/artist/paul-mccartney/5162#/artist/paul-mccartney/chart-history/ 5162?f=400&g=Albums). *Billboard*. . Retrieved 27 November 2012.

[8] http://www.ascap.com/ace/search. cfm?requesttimeout=300andmode=resultsandsearchstr=330056569andsearch_in=iandsearch_type=exactandsearch_det=t,s,w,p,b,vandresults_pp=25andstart=1

External links

• Mark Evanier on Tormé and "The Christmas Song" (http://www.povonline.com/cols/COL245.htm)

The Origin of Love

The Origin of Love	
Studio album by Mika	
Released	16 September 2012
Recorded	2011–12
Genre	Pop, rock
Length	49:25
Label	Casablanca, Barclay
Producer	Greg Wells, Dan Wilson, Klas Åhlund, Mika
Mika chronology	
The Boy Who Knew Too Much (2009)	*The Origin of Love* (2012)
Singles from *The Origin of Love*	
1. "Elle me dit" Released: 11 July 2011 2. "Celebrate" Released: 15 June 2012 3. "Underwater" Released: 5 October 2012 4. "Origin of Love" Released: 3 December 2012 5. "Popular Song" Released: 21 December 2012	

Professional ratings	
Aggregate scores	
Source	Rating
Metacritic	(69/100)[1]
Review scores	
Source	Rating
Allmusic	★ ★ ★ ★ ★ [2]
Idolator	★ ★ ★ ★ ★ [3]
The Guardian	★ ★ ★ ★ ★ [4]

The Origin of Love is the third studio album released by British singer-songwriter Mika. The album was released in France on 17 September 2012, and in the United Kingdom was released on 8 October 2012, via Casablanca Records and Barclay Records respectively. The album was preceded by an alternate lead single in each region. "Elle me dit" was first released in France, whereas "Celebrate" served as the first official single for the United Kingdom.

Background

Mika worked with Greg Wells, Dan Wilson, Benny Benassi and Klas Åhlund on the album. The team contributed both written material and production credits. Mika was confirmed to be recording the album in various locations, including Montreal, Miami and Sweden. In an interview for Digital Spy, Mika described the album as "more simplistic pop, less layered than the last one". He also described the album's themes as dealing with the adult years, claiming that "it's a serious album, but still has the boppy, happy tunes."[5] In an interview for a popular French magazine, Mika claimed that the album's musical style will include elements of Daft Punk and Fleetwood Mac.[6]

Singles

- "Elle me dit" (English: She Tells Me) was released as the album's lead single in France. The song was first rumoured when a twelve-second preview was published online on 1 July 2011.[7] Just ten days later, the french iTunes Store made the whole song available as a digital download.[8] However, it's official release did not occur until 26 September 2011. The single was very successful, peaking at #1 on the French Singles Chart.[9] "Elle me dit" appears on the regular version of the album in English, as the track "Emily".

- "Celebrate" was released as the album's lead single in the United Kingdom, Europe and America, and the second single in France. The single was made available in French-speaking countries on 1 June 2012. The song features American singer Pharrell Williams and was written by Mika, Williams and Ben Garrett, and produced by Peter Mayes and Nick Littlemore. On 14 June 2012, Mika revealed a 30-second clip of the song. It was uploaded to Amazon ahead of it's official unveiling the next day.[10] The song was offically released on 15 June 2012. The single was released in the United Kingdom on 1 October 2012.[8]

- "Underwater" was released as the album's third single in France, and the second single in Europe, on 23 November 2012. The music video for the track was filmed in Los Angeles during the third week of October, and premiered on 21 November 2012, just two days' before the single's official release.[11] The single peaked at #134 in France, becoming Mika's worst performing single in the region. The single will not be released in the United Kingdom, and instead, the single's artwork was adapted for the British equivalent single release, "The Origin of Love".

- "Origin of Love" was released as the album's second single in the United Kingdom on 3 December 2012. It carried the same artwork as it's European equivalent release, "Underwater", but was heavily edited for radio play. The music video for the original version of the track originally premiered on 15 September 2012, and was filmed in Chile. It featured explicit scenes of a man and a woman engaging in sex, whilst in a loving relationship. The video was shown on British music channels, but these were edited out, replacing the original version of the track with the radio version.

- "Popular Song" was released as the album's second single in the United States on 21 December 2012. The song was heavily edited for it's release as a single, completely rearranging the instrumentation, tempo and removing the expletives "Bitch" and "Shit" from the lyrics. The single version also features Ariana Grande, instead of Priscilla Renea, who appears on the album version. The single version bears a strong resemblance to Mika's debut single, "Grace Kelly".[12]

Track listing

Standard Edition[13]

No.	Title	Writer(s)	Producer(s)	Length
1.	"Origin of Love"	Mika, Nick Littlemore, Paul Steel	Nick Littlemore, Greg Wells, Mika	4:37
2.	"Lola"	Mika, Benjamin Garrett, Jodi Marr	Mika, Benjamin Garrett	3:45
3.	"Stardust"	Mika, Wayne Hector, Benny Benassi, Alessandro Benassi	Benny Benassi, Greg Wells	3:18
4.	"Make You Happy"	Mika, Benjamin Garrett, Jodi Marr	Greg Wells, Benjamin Garrett, Mika	3:11
5.	"Underwater"	Mika, Nick Littlemore, Paul Steel	Greg Wells, Mika	3:12
6.	"Overrated"	Mika, Jodi Marr	Klas Åhlund, Greg Wells	3:38
7.	"Kids"	Mika, Nick Littlemore	Mika, Nick Littlemore	3:04
8.	"Love You When I'm Drunk"	Mika, Jodi Marr	Nick Littlemore, Mika	2:54
9.	"Step with Me"	Mika, Mathieu Jomphe, Hillary Lindsey	Greg Wells, Mika	3:36
10.	"Popular Song" (featuring Priscilla Renea)	Mika, Priscilla Renea, Mathieu Jomphe, Stephen Schwartz	Greg Wells, Mika	4:06
11.	"Elle me dit"	Mika, Doriand	Klas Åhlund, Greg Wells	3:34
12.	"Heroes"	Mika, Nick Littlemore, Jack Milas, Oli Chang	Mika, Jack Milas, Oli Chang	3:16
13.	"Celebrate" (featuring Pharrell Williams)	Mika, Pharrell Williams, Benjamin Garrett	Peter Mayes, Nick Littlemore, Benjamin Garrett	3:08

European Bonus Track[14]				
No.	Title	Writer(s)	Producer(s)	Length
14.	"Make You Happy" (Miami Edit)	Mika, Benjamin Garrett, Jodi Marr	Greg Wells, Benjamin Garrett, Mika	3:36

French Edition Bonus Track[14]

No.	Title	Writer(s)	Producer(s)	Length
14.	"Elle me dit"	Mika, Doriand	Klas Åhlund, Greg Wells	3:38

Deluxe Edition Bonus Disc[13]

No.	Title	Writer(s)	Producer(s)	Length
1.	"Celebrate" (Acoustic)	Mika, Pharrell Williams, Benjamin Garrett	Peter Mayes, Nick Littlemore, Benjamin Garrett	3:08
2.	"Origin of Love" (Acoustic)	Mika, Nick Littlemore, Paul Steel	Nick Littlemore, Greg Wells, Mika	4:37
3.	"Kids" (Acoustic)	Mika, Nick Littlemore	Mika, Nick Littlemore	3:04
4.	"Love You When I'm Drunk" (Acoustic)	Mika, Jodi Marr	Nick Littlemore, Mika	2:54
5.	"Overrated" (Acoustic)	Mika, Jodi Marr	Klas Åhlund, Greg Wells	3:38
6.	"Elle me dit"	Mika, Doriand	Greg Wells, Mika	3:38
7.	"Tah Dah"	Mika, Pharrell Williams, Jodi Marr	Peter Mayes, Nick Littlemore	3:19
8.	"Stardust" (Benny Benassi Mix)	Mika, Alessandro "Alle" Benassi	Benny Benassi, Alessandro "Alle" Benassi, Nick Littlemore	4:42
9.	"Celebrate" (Rivera Mix)	Mika, Pharrell Williams, Benjamin Garrett	Peter Mayes, Nick Littlemore, Robbie Rivera	5:09

French Deluxe Edition Bonus Disc[15]

No.	Title	Writer(s)	Producer(s)	Length
1.	"Karen"	Mika, Doriand	Nick Littlemore, Greg Wells, Mika	3:57
2.	"L'amour dans le mauvais temps (Love in the Bad Weather)"	Mika, Doriand	Mika	4:07
3.	"Un soleil mal luné (The Sun in Evil Moon)"	Mika, Doriand	Doriand, Mika	3:06
4.	"Make You Happy" (Cherokee Remix)	Mika, Benjamin Garrett, Jodi Marr	Greg Wells, Benjamin Garrett, Mika, Cherokee	5:47
5.	"Celebrate" (Rivera Remix)	Mika, Pharrell Williams, Benjamin Garrett	Nick Littlemore, Peter Mayes, Benjamin Garrett, Greg Wells, Robbie Rivera	5:53
6.	"Elle me dit" (BeatauCue Remix)	Mika, Doriand	Klas Åhlund, Greg Wells, Alex Bruaert, Mederic Martin	5:02
7.	"Make You Happy" (Miami Edit)	Mika, Benjamin Garrett, Jodi Marr	Greg Wells, Benjamin Garrett, Mika, Nick Littlemore	3:11
8.	"Tah Dah"	Mika, Pharrell Williams, Jodi Marr	Nick Littlemore, Peter Mayes, Mika	2:51

Italian Deluxe Edition Bonus Disc[16]

No.	Title	Writer(s)	Producer(s)	Length
1.	"Origin of Love" (Italian Version)	Mika, Nick Littlemore, Paul Steel	Nick Littlemore, Greg Wells, Mika	4:37
2.	"Stardust" (Italian Version)	Mika, Wayne Hector, Benny Benassi, Alessandro Benassi	Benny Benassi, Greg Wells	3:18
3.	"Celebrate" (Acoustic)	Mika, Pharrell Williams, Benjamin Garrett	Peter Mayes, Nick Littlemore, Benjamin Garrett	3:08
4.	"Origin of Love" (Acoustic)	Mika, Nick Littlemore, Paul Steel	Nick Littlemore, Greg Wells, Mika	4:37
5.	"Kids" (Acoustic)	Mika, Nick Littlemore	Mika, Nick Littlemore	3:04
6.	"Love You When I'm Drunk" (Acoustic)	Mika, Jodi Marr	Nick Littlemore, Mika	2:54
7.	"Overrated" (Acoustic)	Mika, Jodi Marr	Klas Åhlund, Greg Wells	3:38
8.	"Elle me dit"	Mika, Doriand	Greg Wells, Mika	3:38
9.	"Tah Dah"	Mika, Pharrell Williams, Jodi Marr	Peter Mayes, Nick Littlemore	3:19
10.	"Celebrate" (Rivera Mix)	Mika, Pharrell Williams, Benjamin Garrett	Peter Mayes, Nick Littlemore, Robbie Rivera	5:09

Charts

Chart (2012)	Peak position
Austrian Albums Chart[17]	31
Belgian Albums Chart (Flanders)[18]	8
Belgian Albums Chart (Wallonia)[19]	6
Canadian Albums Chart[20]	10
Dutch Albums Chart[21]	15
French Albums Chart[22]	1
German Albums Chart[23]	43
Irish Albums Chart[24]	61
Italian Albums Chart[25]	12
Mexican Albums Chart[26]	71
South Korean Albums Chart [27]	9
Spanish Albums Chart[28]	11
Swiss Albums Chart[29]	15
UK Albums Chart[30]	24
US *Billboard* 200[24]	47

Year-end charts

Chart (2012)	Position
Belgian Albums Chart (Wallonia)[31]	69

Release history

Regions	Dates	Format(s)	Label(s)
France [32]	17 September 2012	CD, 2CD, digital download	Barclay Records
Spain [33]	21 September 2012		Casablanca Records
Italy [34]	25 September 2012		Universal Music
Ireland [35]	5 October 2012		
Germany [36]	5 October 2012		
Australia [37]	12 October 2012		
United Kingdom [38]	8 October 2012		Island Records
United States [39]	16 October 2012		Casablanca Records

References

[1] "Metacritic: *The Origin of Love*" (http://www.metacritic.com/music/the-origin-of-love/mika). *Metacritic*. . Retrieved 2013-01-22.

[2] (http://www.allmusic.com/album/the-origin-of-love-mw0002420735)

[3] (http://idolator.com/7168972/mika-the-origin-of-love-album-review)

[4] (http://www.guardian.co.uk/music/2012/oct/04/mika-origin-of-love-review)

[5] "Mika: Music gives me a sense of identity." (http://www.digitalspy.co.uk/music/news/a263980/mika-music-gives-me-a-sense-of-identity.html). Digital Spy. . Retrieved 15/07/2011.

[6] Cisneros, Salvador (24 July 2011). "Mika regresa en francés", *Mural*, p. 26.

[7] "Elle me dit preview" (http://www.twitvid.com/WTSBY). TwitVid. . Retrieved 28/12/2012.

[8] "iTunes - Musique - Elle me dit - Single par MIKA" (http://itunes.apple.com/fr/album/elle-me-dit-single/id448943368). iTunes Store (France). . Retrieved 2011-07-13.

[9] "Elle Me Dit: Mika: Amazon.fr: Musique" (https://www.amazon.fr/dp/B005LDNH1U). Amazon.fr. . Retrieved 28/12/2012.

[10] Corner, Lewis (14 June 2012). "Mika previews new single 'Celebrate' - listen" (http://www.digitalspy.co.uk/music/news/a387317/mika-previews-new-single-celebrate-listen.html). *Digital Spy*. . Retrieved 12 July 2012.

[11] "@mikasounds: On my way to the airport for ..." (https://twitter.com/mikasounds/status/259290036896419840). Twitter. Mika's official profile. . Retrieved 28/12/2012.

[12] "iTunes - Music - Popular Song (feat. Ariana Grande) - Single by MIKA" (https://itunes.apple.com/us/album/popular-song-feat.-ariana/id589645780). iTunes Store (US). . Retrieved 28/12/2012.

[13] "Mika: The Origin Of Love Album Reveal - Pre-Order Now!" (http://zaphod.uk.vvhp.net/viewemail?con=7410432&cmp=7071&act=238263&sec=463e9a82c9f7&webversionpage=1). zaphod.uk.vvhp.net. . Retrieved 28/12/2012.

[14] "The Origin Of Love: Mika: Amazon.fr: Musique" (http://www.amazon.fr/dp/B008PUXMUC). Amazon.fr. . Retrieved 28/12/2012.

[15] "The Origin Of Love - Edition Deluxe : Mika: Amazon.fr: Musique" (http://www.amazon.fr/dp/B0090XOJA). Amazon.fr. . Retrieved 28/12/2012.

[16] "iTunes - Musica - The Origin of Love (Deluxe Version) di MIKA" (https://itunes.apple.com/it/album/origin-love-deluxe-version/id560811101). iTunes Store (Italy). . Retrieved 28/12/2012.

[17] "Austrian Charts - Mika - The Origin of Love (album)" (http://austriancharts.at/showitem.asp?interpret=Mika&titel=The+Origin+Of+Love&cat=a) (in German). austriancharts.at. Hung Medien. . Retrieved 30 September 2012.

[18] "Charts Vlaanderen - Mika - The Origin of Love (album)" (http://www.ultratop.be/nl/showitem.asp?interpret=Mika&titel=The+Origin+Of+Love&cat=a) (in Dutch). Ultratop. Hung Medien. . Retrieved 30 September 2012.

[19] "Charts Wallonie - Mika - The Origin of Love (album)" (http://www.ultratop.be/fr/showitem.asp?interpret=Mika&titel=The+Origin+Of+Love&cat=a) (in French). Ultratop. Hung Medien. . Retrieved 30 September 2012.

[20] "Mika Album & Song Chart History - Canadian Albums" (http://www.billboard.com/#/artist/mika/chart-history/710017?f=309&g=Albums). *Billboard*. Prometheus Global Media. . Retrieved 30 September 2012.

[21] "Dutch Charts - Mika - The Origin of Love (album)" (http://dutchcharts.nl/showitem.asp?interpret=Mika&titel=The+Origin+Of+Love&cat=a) (in Dutch). Dutchcharts.nl. Hung Medien. . Retrieved 30 September 2012.

[22] "Classements - Mika - The Origin of Love (album)" (http://lescharts.com/showitem.asp?interpret=Mika&titel=The+Origin+Of+Love&cat=a) (in French). Lescharts.com. Hung Medien. . Retrieved 30 September 2012.

[23] "German Charts - Mika - The Origin of Love (album)" (http://www.charts.de/album.asp?artist=Mika&title=The+Origin+Of+Love&country=de) (in German). charts.de. Hung Medien. . Retrieved 30 September 2012.

[24] "Mika - The Origin Of Love - Music Charts" (http://acharts.us/album/73148a). acharts.us. . Retrieved 9 October 2012.

[25] "Italian Charts - Mika - The Origin of Love (album)" (http://italiancharts.com/showitem.asp?interpret=Mika&titel=The+Origin+Of+Love&cat=a). Italiancharts / Hung Medien. . Retrieved 9 October 2012.

[26] "Top 100 Mexico - Semana Del 24 al 30 de Septiembre del 2012" (http://www.webcitation.org/6BICMJUc5) (in Spanish) (PDF). Asociación Mexicana de Productores de Fonogramas y Videogramas. Archived from the original (http://www.centrodedesarrollodigital.com/amprofon3/Top100.pdf) on 9 October 2012. . Retrieved 9 October 2012.

[27] "Album General" (http://www.gaonchart.co.kr/main/section/album/list.gaon) (in Korean). Gaonchart.co.kr.. . Retrieved 8 October 2012.

[28] "Spanish Charts - Mika - The Origin of Love (album)" (http://spanishcharts.com/showitem.asp?interpret=Mika&titel=The+Origin+Of+Love&cat=a). spanishcharts.com / Hung Medien. . Retrieved 28/12/2012.

[29] "Swiss Charts - Mika - The Origin of Love (album)" (http://hitparade.ch/showitem.asp?interpret=Mika&titel=The+Origin+Of+Love&cat=a) (in German). Hitparade.ch. Hung Medien. . Retrieved 30 September 2012.

[30] "2012-10-20 Top 40 Official UK Albums Archive" (http://www.officialcharts.com/archive-chart/_/3/2012-10-20/). The Official Charts Company. . Retrieved 28/12/2012.

[31] "ULTRATOP BELGIAN CHARTS - Rapport Annuels 2012" (http://www.ultratop.be/fr/annual.asp?year=2012&cat=a). Ultratop. Hung Medien. . Retrieved 28/12/2012.

[32] "CD album - The origin of love - Edition deluxe : Mika" (http://musique.fnac.com/a4736498/Mika-The-origin-of-love-Edition-deluxe-CD-album). Fnac (France). . Retrieved 18/09/2012.

[33] "iTunes - Música - The Origin of Love (Deluxe Version) de MIKA" (https://itunes.apple.com/es/album/origin-love-deluxe-version/id557914635). iTunes Store (Spain). . Retrieved 18/09/2012.

[34] "MIKA: il nuovo album "The Origin of Love" dal 25 settembre anche in esclusiva versione italiana" (http://www.gqitalia.it/show/musica/2012/9/mika-il-nuovo-album-the-origin-of-love-dal-25-settembre-anche-in-esclusiva-versione-italiana). GQ Italy. . Retrieved 18/09/2012.

[35] "iTunes - Music - The Origin of Love (Deluxe Version) by MIKA" (https://itunes.apple.com/ie/album/origin-love-deluxe-version/id557914635). iTunes Store (Ireland). .

[36] "The Origin of Love: Amazon.de: Musik" (http://www.amazon.de/dp/B0091LF2QQ). Amazon.de. . Retrieved 18/09/2012.

[37] "Buy Origin Of Love: Deluxe Edition Mika, Pop, CD Sanity" (http://www.sanity.com.au/products/2216524/Origin_Of_Love_Deluxe_Edition). sanity.com. . Retrieved 8/10/2012.

[38] "Mika: Origin Of Love: 2cd (2012): CD" (http://hmv.com/hmvweb/displayProductDetails.do?ctx=280;-1;-1;-1;-1&sku=924575). HMV Group (UK). . Retrieved 18/09/2012.

[39] "Amazon.com: Origin of Love: Mika: Music" (http://www.amazon.com/dp/B0091LF2QQ). Amazon.com. . Retrieved 18/09/2012.

Victoria Justice

Victoria Justice	
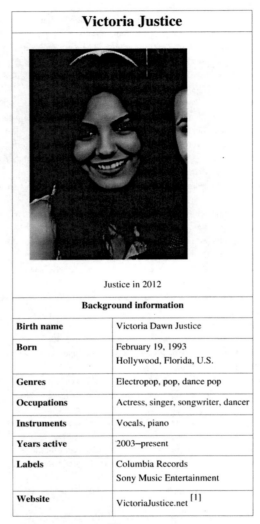 Justice in 2012	
Background information	
Birth name	Victoria Dawn Justice
Born	February 19, 1993 Hollywood, Florida, U.S.
Genres	Electropop, pop, dance pop
Occupations	Actress, singer, songwriter, dancer
Instruments	Vocals, piano
Years active	2003–present
Labels	Columbia Records Sony Music Entertainment
Website	VictoriaJustice.net [1]

Victoria Dawn Justice[2] (born February 19, 1993)[3] is an American actress, singer-songwriter, and dancer. She debuted as an actress at the age of 10 and has since appeared in several films and television series including the Nickelodeon series *Zoey 101* and *Victorious*. She has made appearances in several theatrical releases, including *Unknown* as well as the 2006 thriller *The Garden*. She has appeared in several Nickelodeon series, including *True Jackson, VP*, *The Troop*, *The Penguins of Madagascar* and *iCarly*, as well as on the Nickelodeon game shows *BrainSurge* and *Figure It Out* as a contestant. In 2010, she starred in the Nickelodeon film *The Boy Who Cried Werewolf*.

Aside from acting, Justice is involved in her musical career. She has performed several songs for the soundtrack to the Nickelodeon musical *Spectacular!*, in which she starred. She has recorded a number of songs for the *Victorious* series. Justice has announced the release of her debut album, which is expected to be released sometime during 2013.

Early life

Victoria Justice was born on February 19, 1993, in Hollywood, Florida, to Serene and Zack Justice.[4] Her father is of English, German, and Irish descent, and her mother is of Puerto Rican ancestry.[5] Justice first developed an interest in acting when she was 8 years old after watching a children's commercial. She and her family relocated to Hollywood, California, in 2003. In 2005, she auditioned and was accepted into the musical theatre program at Los Angeles' Millikan Performing Arts Academy.[6] Justice has done commercials for companies such as Ralph Lauren, Gap and Guess. She appeared in national commercials for Mervyn's, Peanut Butter Toast Crunch and Ovaltine.[7]

Career

2003–09: Beginnings and *Zoey 101*

Justice began her acting career when she was 10 years old, when she made a guest appearance on the *Gilmore Girls* episode "The Hobbit, the Sofa and Digger Stiles". Justice portrayed Jill No. 2 in a walk-on role.[8] After her appearance in the series, her family moved to Los Angeles, when Justice stated she wanted a career in acting. The following year, Justice guest starred on the second episode of the Disney channel series *The Suite Life of Zack & Cody*, in which she played a young pageant contestant named Rebecca. Later, Justice was awarded a role in the 2005 drama-thriller *Mary*. Justice portrayed the role of Stella, a young girl who begins seeing visions of Mary Magdalene.[9] The film debuted at 2005 Venice Film Festival, before being showed at several other Festivals, including the 2005 Toronto Film Festival, Deauville Film Festival and the San Sebastián International Film Festival.

During the same year, Justice was awarded a main role in the Nickelodeon series *Zoey 101* as Lola Martinez, a new student who is also an aspiring actress.[10][11] When she found out she had earned the role, she said, "I was extremely happy; I was bouncing up and down and screaming. That was a really great moment."[12] The season 2 episode that introduced Justice's character debuted on September 11, 2005. Justice also had roles in two other films that year. She had a cameo appearance in the R-rated film *When Do We Eat?*, as well as earning the role of Rose in the Hallmark television film *Silver Bells*, the following of which has become a Hallmark Hall of Fame film. In 2006, while filming episodes for *Zoey 101*, Justice made a guest appearance on an episode of the series *Everwood*, in the episode "Enjoy the Ride". Justice made her theatrical film debut that year, when she was given a cameo role in the film *Unknown*. The film was a financial failure, and received mixed reviews from critics.

In 2006, Justice played the supporting role of Holly in the thriller film *The Garden*. The film was met with negative reviews from critics.[13] 2007 and 2008 saw Justice focusing on the third and fourth seasons of *Zoey 101*, which was coming to a close. Justice released a promotional single midway through 2007, while she was still filming *Zoey 101*. The song was a cover of the Vanessa Carlton song, "A Thousand Miles".[14] May 2, 2008, saw the airing of the final episode of the series.

When being interviewed in 2010 about her musical career, Justice has stated "My family could always tell, ever since I was little, that [music is] something that's always come natural to me and that I've always wanted to do. It's something that's just been in my blood. Ever since I was little, I was taking tap classes, jazz classes, hip-hop classes, acting classes. I just always wanted to cultivate that and do that more. But, the moment where I actually realized, "Woah, this is something that I can actually do for the rest of my life and maybe be successful at," was actually the pilot of Victorious when I did the performance number for the first time. I just remember standing on stage and seeing all these people looking at me and I was nervous. And then, the music started and I started dancing around and really feeling it and having an amazing time, and that's when it clicked for me that this is what I want to do for the rest of my life."[15]

In 2009, she announced plans to guest star on an episode of Nickelodeon's series *The Naked Brothers Band*. The TV special, titled *Valentine Dream Date* featured Justice portraying herself.[16] Justice made no plans of going back into the recording studio until 2009, when she starred in the Nickelodeon musical, *Spectacular!*. Justice's character performs three songs during the course of the film. Justice starred alongside Nolan Funk and Simon Curtis in the musical film, which aired on Nickelodeon on February 16, 2009.[17][18] The film has become one of Nickelodeon's most popular movies, attracting an audience 3.7 million viewers on its premiere night.[19] The film received a generally positive review from several critics, holding a 76% approval rating on Rotten Tomatoes as of 2011.[20]

After the success of *The Naked Brothers Band* special in which Justice guest starred she appeared in another episode, "The Premiere", on April 11, 2009. She later appeared episodes of *iCarly*,[21] *True Jackson, VP*, and *The Troop*, and on the game show *BrainSurge*. Justice announced in 2009 that she would be working on a thriller film, set for theatrical release. It was later announced the film would feature Dylan Sprouse and Cole Sprouse.[22] Unlike initial plans of a theatrical release, the film had a limited preview release on December 12, 2009, and was returned to post production. Despite this, the film's worldwide release has been canceled.[23]

2010–present: *Victorious* and debut album

Justice confirmed that she would be receiving her own musical show on Nickelodeon called *Victorious*, explaining the show's genesis thus: "I was on *Zoey 101*. When I was 12, Dan Schneider cast me as a new character, Lola Martinez. From there, I worked with him for three years, on three seasons of *Zoey 101*. And, after that, Dan found out that I could also sing and dance as well as act, so he thought it would be really cool to create a show for me on Nickelodeon, called Victorious."[15] The pilot for the show, which was presented as a special for the series, debuted on March 27, 2010, and received 5.7 million views, making it the second-highest rated premiere for a live-action Nickelodeon series.[24] The original broadcast of this episode was an extended cut, all subsequent airings had various scenes and lines were removed to conform to its time-slot.

Justice returned to the recording studio to record music for the series in 2010. She recorded the series first featured song, which also serves as the theme song, titled "Make It Shine". The single had little success charting in the U.S., however it did manage to reach 16 on the Bubbling Under Hot 100 singles chart. Several other songs have been featured in the series, including "You're the Reason", "Finally Falling", "Beggin' on Your Knees","Best Friend's Brother" and "Tell Me That You Love Me". Justice performed her third official single, "Freak the Freak Out", during the

Justice performing in 2011

Victorious special episode of the same name.[25] Justice later guest-starred on the animated series *The Penguins of Madagascar*, voicing the character of Stacy in the episode "Badger Pride". Justice starred in the 2010 Nickelodeon television movie *The Boy Who Cried Werewolf*, playing Jordan Sands, a girl who is transformed into a werewolf following her move to a creepy manor.[26] The film was a major success for the network, drawing in 5.8 million viewers for the premiere.[27] The film received generally positive reviews from critics. The film currently holds a 69% approval rate on Rotten Tomatoes based on 24 reviews.[28] In 2011, the cast of *iCarly*, along with the cast of *Victorious* starred in a crossover episode, titled *iParty with Victorious*. This marked the second time Justice has guest starred for *iCarly*, first as Shelby Marx.

In a 2010 interview with the Associated Press, she stated that she is recording an album but will take her time with the process, rather than rush it, and write the songs on the album. But, she is very excited waiting for it.[29] In March 2011 The Hollywood Reporter confirmed that Justice had landed the lead role in the coming of age comedy *Fun Size* (released on October 26, 2012). Justice played the part of Wren, and the movie will also feature stars such as Johnny Knoxville, Chelsea Handler and Josh Pence.[30] She has recently released onto iTunes a song from Victorious called "Countdown," released on February 18, 2012. It was co-recorded with her co-star Leon Thomas III. The latest single she has released was on Tuesday, February 28, 2012, with "Take a Hint" being released to iTunes on March 3, 2012. This was her first duet with Victorious co-star Elizabeth Gillies.[31] In October 2012, she revealed she will release her debut album in 2013, stating "It's going to be pop".[32]

Other endeavors

Philanthropy

Justice has taken part in several charity events. She has supported charities such as the *United Nations Foundation*, which benefits numerous causes such as AIDS, Children, Environment, Health, Human Rights and Peace.[33] On September 30, 2010, Justice announced she would be joining the Charity Campaign *Girl Up*. When asked about joining, she stated "I'm so excited to become a Champion for Girl Up and to help make a difference for girls who aren't given the same opportunities that most of us take for granted. I know that there are plenty of girls throughout the country who are just like me—ready and motivated to stand up for the rights and well-being of girls in the developing world. I am confident that, together, we will rise to the challenge." Justice joined *Girl Up* on September 30, 2010, for the campaign's official launch in New York City and will go on to support the "Unite for Girls" tour, which travels to cities across the U.S. to activate and engage teens from coast to coast. She will have the chance to visit Girl Up-supported programs in developing countries to observe first-hand the impact they can have on girls and communities.[34] During an interview with *Seventeen*, Justice stated,

> I'm a 17-year-old girl, and I have all of these opportunities, but there are other 17-year-old girls who have zero opportunities, which is why I'm working with Girl Up. I was looking into different charities and hearing these girls in Guatemala and Africa talk about having to walk miles for water and crying because they don't have any money to go to school. It just really broke my heart, so I want to spread the word as much as I can and get other people working together. Before you know it we can actually make a difference.[35]

Justice has also supported children's hospitals. In June 2012, the "Music Makes It Better" campaign was launched by Children's National Medical Center, featuring PSAs by Justice, Justin Bieber, and The Band Perry. The campaign aims to bring music, arts, and other programs to children while they're in the hospital.[36] It was recently known that on the numerous requests of fans on Twitter Victoria was registered in the Russian social network of VKontakte.

Filmography

Film

Year	Title	Role	Notes
2005	*Mary*	Stella	Minor role
2005	*When Do We Eat?*	Young Nikky	Supporting role
2005	*Silver Bells*	Rose	TV movie
2006	*The Garden*	Holly	
2006	*Unknown*	Daughter	Supporting role
2009	*Spectacular!*	Tammi Dyson	TV movie
2009	*The Kings of Appletown*	Betsy	
2010	*The Boy Who Cried Werewolf*	Jordan Sands	Lead role; TV movie
2012	*The First Time*	Jane Harmon	
2012	*Fun Size*	Wren DeSentiz	Lead role

Television

Year	Title	Role	Notes
2003	*Gilmore Girls*	Jill #2	"The Hobbit, the Sofa, and Digger Stiles" (season 4: episode 3)
2005	*The Suite Life of Zack & Cody*	Rebecca	"The Fairest of Them All" (season 1: episode 2)
2005–2008	*Zoey 101*	Lola Martinez	Main role; season 2–4
2006	*Everwood*	Thalia Thompson	"Enjoy the Ride" (season 4: episode 18)
2009	*The Naked Brothers Band*	Herself	"Valentine Dream Date" (season 3: episode 7) "The Premiere" (season 3: episode 10–11)
2009–2011	*iCarly*	Shelby Marx / Herself / Tori Vega	"iFight Shelby Marx" (season 2: episode 24–25) "iBloop" (season 3: episode 15) "iParty with Victorious" (season 4: episode 11–13)
2009	*True Jackson, VP*	Vivian	"True Crush" (season 1: episode 23)
2010	*The Troop*	Eris Fairy	"Speed" (season 1: episode 15)
2010–2013	*Victorious*	Tori Vega	Lead role
2010	*The Penguins of Madagascar*	Stacy	"Badger Pride" season 2: episode 14
2012	*Figure It Out*	Herself	(2 episodes)

Discography

Soundtrack albums

Title	Album details	Peak chart positions				
		US [37][38]	US OST [38]	US Kids [38]	AUT [39]	SWI [40]
Spectacular!	• Released: February 3, 2009[41] • Format: CD, digital download • Label: Nick	44	5	2	—	—
Victorious	• Released: August 2, 2011[42] • Format: CD, digital download • Label: Sony Music Entertainment	5	1	1	35	69
Victorious 2.0	• Released: June 5, 2012[43] • Format: CD, digital download • Label: Columbia	18	2	1	—	—
Victorious 3.0	• Released: November 6, 2012 • Format: CD, digital download • Label: Columbia	—	—	—	—	—
"—" denotes releases that did not chart or were not released in that territory.						

Singles

Title[A]	Year	Peak chart Positions		Certifications	Album
		US [44]	US Heat. [45]		
"Make It Shine"	2010	—	17		*Victorious*
"Freak the Freak Out"		50	1	• US: Gold[46]	
"Beggin' on Your Knees"	2011	58	—		
"Best Friend's Brother"		86	—		
"Leave It All to Shine" (with Miranda Cosgrove)		—	—		
"Countdown" (with Leon Thomas III)		—	—		*Victorious 2.0*
"Take a Hint" (with Elizabeth Gillies)	2012	—	—		
"Make It In America"		—	—		
"L.A. Boyz" (with Ariana Grande)		—	—		*Victorious 3.0*
"Here's 2 Us"		—	—		
"—" denotes releases that did not chart or were not released in that territory.					

Promotional singles

Title	Year	Album
"A Thousand Miles"[47]	2007	non-album song
"You're the Reason (Acoustic Version)"[48]	2011	*Victorious*
"It's Not Christmas Without You"[49]	2012	*Merry Nickmas*

Awards and nominations

Year	Award	Category	Work	Result
2006	Young Artist Awards	Best Young Ensemble Performance in a TV Series (Comedy or Drama)	*Zoey 101* (Shared with ensemble)	Won[50]
2007	Young Artist Awards	Best Young Ensemble Performance in a TV Series (Comedy or Drama)	*Zoey 101* (Shared with ensemble)	Won[51]
	Young Artist Awards	Best Performance in a TV Series (Comedy or Drama) – Supporting Young Actress	*Zoey 101*	Nominated[51]
2008	Young Artist Awards	Best Young Ensemble Performance in a TV Series	*Zoey 101* (Shared with ensemble)	Nominated[52]
2010	Teen Choice Awards 2010	Choice Smile	*Herself*	Nominated[53][54]
	Hollywood Teen TV Awards	Teen Pick Actress: Comedy	*Victorious*	Nominated[55]
		Teen Pick: Hottest Female	*Herself*	Nominated[55]

2011	2011 Kids' Choice Awards	Favorite TV Actress	Victorious	Nominated[56][57]
	Australian Kids' Choice Awards 2011	Super Fresh Award	Herself	Nominated[58][59]
		Fave TV Star	Victorious	Nominated[58][59]
		Hottest Girl Hottie	Herself	Won[59]
	Young Artist Awards	Best Performance in a TV Movie, Miniseries or Special – Leading Young Actress	The Boy Who Cried Werewolf	Nominated[60]
	Imagen Awards	Best Young Actress/Television	Victorious	Nominated[61]
	ALMA Awards	Favorite TV Actress – Leading Role in a Comedy	Victorious	Nominated[62][63]
	NAACP Image Awards	Outstanding Performance in a Youth/Children's Program (Series or Special)	Victorious	Nominated[64][65]
2012	2012 Kids' Choice Awards	Favorite TV Actress	Victorious	Nominated[66][67]
	Hollywood Teen TV Awards	Favorite Television Actress	Victorious	Nominated[68]
	Young Artist Awards	Best Performance In A TV Series – Recurring Young Actress 17–21	iCarly	Nominated[69]
	Imagen Awards	Best Young Actress/Television	Victorious	Nominated[70][71]
	ALMA Awards	Favorite TV Actress — Comedy	Victorious	Nominated[72][73]
	Do Something Awards	TV Star: Female	Victorious	Nominated[74]

Notes

- **A** The Victorious songs are credited as *Victorious cast featuring Victoria Justice*.

References

[1] http://www.victoriajustice.net/

[2] Victoria Dawn Justice (https://www.facebook.com/victoriavickyjustice)

[3] "Victoria Justice: Biography, Latest News & Videos" (http://www.tvguide.com/celebrities/victoria-justice/198024). TVGuide.com. . Retrieved October 9, 2012.

[4] Martinez, Patty A. (May 2010). "Talent Show: Teen Celebrities and Their Dedicated Moms" (http://www.familycircle.com/teen/parenting/teen-celebrities-and-their-moms/). *Family Circle.* . Retrieved 2010-08-01.

[5] http://www.huffingtonpost.com/2012/08/10/25-celebrities-you-didnt-know-were-latino_n_1739113.html

[6] "Millikan Middle School Affiliated Charter Performing Arts Magnet & Science Academy" (http://millikanmiddleschool.org/apps/pages/index.jsp?uREC_ID=337147&type=u&pREC_ID=413618). Millikanmiddleschool.org. . Retrieved 2012-11-03.

[7] Victoria Justice (http://www.superiorpics.com/victoria_justice/) at SuperiorPics.com. Retrieved January 28, 2011.

[8] Victoria Justice in *Gilmore Girls* Clip (http://www.zocial.tv/today/Entertainment/7296989/victoria-justice-in-gilmore-girls-clip), Zocial TV. Retrieved January 28, 2011

[9] "MARY (2005 Official Sundance Selection)" (http://www.youtube.com/watch?v=16FLohPTxs4), YouTube, September 14, 2007

[10] Fine, Audrey. "Getting to Know: Zoey 101's Victoria Justice" (http://www.seventeen.com/entertainment/features/victoria-justice), *Seventeen*. Retrieved January 28, 2011.

[11] "Victoria Justice Interview (pg. 2)" (http://www.kidzworld.com/article/7291-victoria-justice-interview-pg-2), Kidzworld. Retrieved January 28, 2011.

[12] "Victoria Justice Exclusive Interview" (http://www.thestarscoop.com/interviews/victoria-justice-exclusive-interview/), The Star Scoop, February 25, 2006

[13] Tex Massacre. *The Garden* (http://www.bloody-disgusting.com/film/1292/review) at Bloody Disgusting. Retrieved January 28, 2011.

[14] Victoria Justice – A Thousand Miles (Single) (http://www.itemvn.com/album/Victoria-Justice-A-Thousand-Miles-Single/3488) at ItemVN. Retrieved January 28, 2011.

[15]   "Exclusive Interview: Victoria Justice is VICTORIOUS on Nickelodeon" (http://www.iesb.net/index.php?option=com_content&
       view=article&catid=43:exclusive-features&id=8892:exclusive-interview-victoria-justice-is-victorious-on-nickelodeon&Itemid=73), iesb.net,
       March 31, 2010

[16]   Victoria Justice: Guest appearances on TV (http://www.freebase.com/view/en/victoria_justice/-/tv/tv_actor/guest_roles) at Freebase.
       Retrieved January 28, 2011.

[17]   Levine, Lauren. "Youth Impact Report '08" (http://www.variety.com/article/VR1117993332?refCatId=3262), *Variety*, October 2, 2008

[18]   "Victoria Justice to Star in Spectacular!" (http://www.seventeen.com/cosmogirl/victoria-justice-stars-in-spectacular), *Seventeen*, October
       9, 2008

[19]   Levin, Gary. "Nielsens: 36.3 million go for Oscar gold" (http://www.usatoday.com/life/television/news/
       2009-02-24-nielsens-analysis_N.htm), *USA Today*, February 25, 2009

[20]   *Spectacular!* (http://www.rottentomatoes.com/m/spectacular/) at Rotten Tomatoes. Retrieved January 28, 2011.

[21]   "Victoria Justice To Guest Star On iCarly" (http://gossipteen.com/2010/08/24/victoria-justice-to-guest-star-on-icarly/),
       GossipTeen.com, August 24, 2010

[22]   *The Kings of Appletown* (http://www.fluge.com/the-kings-of-appletown-movie.html) at Fluge! Movie info. Retrieved January 28, 2011.

[23]   *The Kings of Appleton* (http://www.the-numbers.com/movies/2008/0KOFA.php) at The Numbers. Retrieved January 28, 2011

[24]   "Nickelodeon Scores 2nd Biggest "Kids' Choice Awards"; "Victorious" Bows to 5.7 Million" (http://tvbythenumbers.zap2it.com/2010/
       03/29/nickelodeon-scores-2nd-biggest-kids-choice-awards-victorious-bows-to-5-7-million/46493). TV By the Numbers. March 29, 2010. .

[25]   "Freak the Freak Out" (http://itunes.apple.com/us/album/freak-freak-out-feat-victoria/id402314148) on iTunes. Retrieved January 28,
       2011.

[26]   "Number-One Nickelodeon Brings Upfront Presentation to Los Angeles for First Time Ever" (http://money.cnn.com/news/newsfeeds/
       articles/prnewswire/NY75924.htm), CNN

[27]   Gorman, Bill. "Nickelodeon's 'The Boy Who Cried Werewolf 'Scores Almost 6 Million Viewers" (http://tvbythenumbers.zap2it.com/
       2010/10/26/nickelodeonâ€™s-the-boy-who-cried-werewolf-scores-almost-6-million-viewers/69685), TV By the Numbers, October 26, 2010

[28]   *The Boy Who Cried Werewolf* (http://www.rottentomatoes.com/m/the_boy_who_cried_werewolf/) at Rotten Tomatoes

[29]   "Rising Teen Star Gets 'Victorious' New Gig" (http://www.youtube.com/watch?v=hsWTFUkA5h0) Associated Press video interview,
       YouTube, March 26, 2010

[30]   "Victoria Justice Lands Lead in 'Fun Size'" (http://www.hollywoodreporter.com/news/victoria-justice-lands-lead-fun-171604).
       hollywoodreporter.com. May 4, 2011. . Retrieved 2011-03-25.

[31]   "Victoria Justice and Liz Gillies: Take A Hint" (http://en.wikipedia.org/wiki/Take_A_Hint). *wikipedia.org*. March 4, 2012. . Retrieved
       2012-03-04.

[32]   [www.digitalspy.co.uk/victoria-justice-to-release-first-album-in-2013-its-going-to-be-pop.html "Victoria Justice to release first album in
       2013: 'It's going to be pop'"]. *Digital Spy*. October 25, 2012.
       www.digitalspy.co.uk/victoria-justice-to-release-first-album-in-2013-its-going-to-be-pop.html. Retrieved 2012-12-01.

[33]   "Victoria Justice's Charity Work, Events and Causes" (http://www.looktothestars.org/celebrity/2301-victoria-justice), Look to the Stars.
       Retrieved January 28, 2011.

[34]   "Victoria Justice Joins Charity Campaign For Young Girls" (http://www.looktothestars.org/news/
       5136-victoria-justice-joins-charity-campaign-for-young-girls), Look to the Stars, September 30, 2010

[35]   "Exclusive Victoria Justice Prom Pics!" (http://www.seventeen.com/parties/prom/victoria-justice-charity-work#fbIndex5).
       Seventeen.com. Uncated. . Retrieved January 28, 2011.

[36]   "Music Makes It Better campaign" (http://www.give2gether.com/projects/MusicMakesitBetter/?p=2). Retrieved June 21, 2011.

[37]   "Billboard Album Chart History: Spetacular! Soundtrack" (http://acharts.us/album/41923). *Billboard*. . Retrieved 2010-05-13.

[38]   "Billboard Album Chart History: Victorious" (http://www.allmusic.com/album/victorious-original-tv-soundtrack-r2142243/
       charts-awards). *Billboard*. . Retrieved 2010-05-13.

[39]   "Austrian Charts − Victorious" (http://austriancharts.at/showitem.asp?interpret=Soundtrack&titel=Victorious&cat=a). austriancharts.at.
       . Retrieved 2010-08-31.

[40]   "Swiss Charts − Victorious" (http://swisscharts.com/showitem.asp?interpret=Soundtrack&titel=Victorious&cat=a). swisscharts.com. .
       Retrieved 2010-05-13.

[41]   "Spectacular! (Soundtrack from the Motion Picture) by Spectacular! Cast" (http://itunes.apple.com/gb/album/
       spectacular!-soundtrack-from/id320846142). *iTunes*. . Retrieved December 30, 2010.

[42]   "Victorious (Music from the Hit TV Show) [feat. Victoria Justice (http://itunes.apple.com/us/album/victorious-music-from-hit/
       id452203422) by Victorious Cast"]. *iTunes*. . Retrieved December 30, 2010.

[43]   "Victorious 2. 0 (More Music from the Hit TV Show) (feat. Victoria Justice (http://itunes.apple.com/us/album/victorious-2.
       -0-more-music/id525876454) by Victorious Cast"]. *iTunes*. . Retrieved December 30, 2010.

[44]   "Hot 100: Week of January 8, 2011" (http://www.billboard.com/charts/hot-100?tag=chscr1#/charts/hot-100?begin=51&
       order=position). *Billboard.com*. . Retrieved December 30, 2010.

[45]   "Billboard Heatseekers Songs Top 40" (http://www.allmusic.com/artist/victoria-justice-mn0001046591/awards). Allmusic. 2012-09-08.
       . Retrieved 2012-09-13.

[46]   "RIAA Gold & Platinum" (http://www.riaa.com/goldandplatinumdata.php?table=SEARCH_RESULTS&artist=Victorious&format=&
       go=Search&perPage=50). Recording Industry Association of America. . Retrieved January 14, 2011.

[47] "A Thousand Miles (Victoria Justice Tribute Version)" (http://itunes.apple.com/us/album/a-thousand-miles-victoria/id375230565).
      iTunes. . Retrieved December 30, 2010.

[48] "You're the Reason (Acoustic Version) - Victoria Justice" (https://itunes.apple.com/us/album/youre-reason-acoustic-version/
      id485149072). *iTunes*. . Retrieved December 30, 2010.

[49] "It's Not Christmas Without You – Single" (http://itunes.apple.com/us/album/its-not-christmas-without/id485160632). *iTunes*. .
      Retrieved December 30, 2010.

[50] http://www.youngartistawards.org/noms27.htm

[51] http://www.youngartistawards.org/noms28.htm

[52] http://www.youngartistawards.org/noms29.html

[53] http://dizneyztarz28.blogspot.com.ar/2010/07/mas-teen-choice-awards-2010.html

[54] http://www.ojotele.com/galas/teen-choice-awards-2010-ganadores

[55] "Hollywood Teen TV Awards" (http://hollywoodteenonline.com/2010/07/04/hollywood-teen-tv-awards/). .

[56] http://www.sheknows.com/entertainment/articles/824257/nickelodeon-kids-choice-awards-2011-nominees

[57] http://www.lacosarosa.com/ganadores-kids-choice-awards-2011.html

[58] http://www.revistateen.com/%C2%A1se-anuncian-los-nominados-a-los-kids-choice-awards-de-australia/

[59] http://www.clevvertv.com/awards-show-2/27891/2011-kids-choice-awards-australia.html

[60] http://www.youngartistawards.org/noms32.html

[61] http://www.imagen.org/awards/2011

[62] "Christina, Selena, Sofia, Demi and Cameron Spice Up the ALMAs" (http://www.eonline.com/uberblog/
      b254984_christina_selena_sofia_demi_cameron.html). E! Online. July 28, 2011. . Retrieved 2011-11-24.

[63] http://entretenimiento.aollatino.com/2011/09/11/alma-awards-2011-lista-ganadores/

[64] http://es.gossipcenter.com/sanaa-lathan/42nd-naacp-image-awards-nominees-announced-456332

[65] http://socialitelife.com/naacp-images-awards-2011-winners-red-carpet-photos-03-2011

[66] http://www.farandulista.com/2012/02/17/nominados-a-los-nickelodeon-kids-choice-awards-2012.html

[67] http://www.huffingtonpost.com/2012/04/01/kids-choice-awards-2012-slime_n_1394842.html

[68] "Hollywood Teen TV Awards - Favorite Television Actress" (http://teentvawards.com/favorite-television-actress/). .

[69] Young Artist Awards Foundation. "Young Artist Awards – Nominees 2012" (http://www.youngartistawards.org/noms33.html).
      youngartistawards.org. . Retrieved 2012-04-07.

[70] http://www.imagen.org/awards/2012

[71] http://www.imagen.org/news/imagen-awards/2012/08/winners-27th-annual-imagen-awards-announced-honoring-latinos-entertain

[72] http://www.almaawards.com/past-alma-nominees.html

[73] http://www.latina.com/entertainment/tv/complete-list-2012-alma-award-winners

[74] http://www.vh1.com/shows/events/do_something_awards/2012/tv-star-female/

External links

- Official website (http://www.victoriajustice.net)
- Victoria Justice (http://www.mtv.com/artists/victoria-justice) at MTV
- Victoria Justice (http://www.imdb.com/name/nm1842439/) at the Internet Movie Database

Victorious

Victorious	
Genre	Teen sitcom
Created by	Dan Schneider
Starring	Victoria Justice Leon Thomas III Matt Bennett Elizabeth Gillies Ariana Grande Avan Jogia Daniella Monet
Theme music composer	Lukasz Gottwald Michael Corcoran Dan Schneider
Opening theme	"Make It Shine" by Victoria Justice
Country of origin	United States
Language(s)	English
No. of seasons	4
No. of episodes	58 (List of episodes)
Production	
Executive producer(s)	Dan Schneider Warren Bell (season 3) Robin Weiner (season 3)
Producer(s)	Bruce Rand Berman Joe Catania (supervising producer: season 3) Robin Weiner (supervising producer: season 1–2) Warren Bell (season 2) Jake Farrow (early season 3) Christopher J. Nowak (mid-season 3) Matt Fleckenstein (season 3)
Location(s)	Nickelodeon on Sunset Hollywood, California
Camera setup	Videotape (filmized); Multi-camera
Running time	24 minutes, 46 minutes for specials
Production company(s)	Schneider's Bakery Sony Music Entertainment Nickelodeon Productions
Distributor	MTV Networks International[1]

Broadcast	
Original channel	Nickelodeon
Picture format	480i (SDTV) 1080i (HDTV)
Audio format	Stereo
Original run	March 27, 2010 – February 2, 2013
Chronology	
Followed by	*Sam & Cat*
Related shows	*iCarly* *Drake & Josh*[2]
External links	
Website [3]	

Victorious (stylized as *VICTORiOUS*) is an American sitcom created by Dan Schneider that originally aired on Nickelodeon from March 27, 2010 to February 2, 2013. The series revolves around aspiring singer Tori Vega (portrayed by Victoria Justice), a teenager who attends a performing arts high school called Hollywood Arts High School, after taking her older sister Trina's (Daniella Monet) place in a showcase while getting into screwball situations on a daily basis. On her first day at Hollywood Arts, she meets Andre Harris (Leon Thomas III), Robbie Shapiro (Matt Bennett), Rex Powers (Robbie's puppet), Jade West (Elizabeth Gillies), Cat Valentine (Ariana Grande), and Beck Oliver (Avan Jogia). The series premiered on March 27, 2010 after the 2010 Kids' Choice Awards. The first soundtrack for the series, *Victorious*, was released on August 2, 2011. The series won for Favorite TV Show award at the 2012 Kids' Choice Awards, even beating out *iCarly*. *Victorious* has had four Emmy nominations. Its second soundtrack, *Victorious 2.0*, was released on June 5, 2012. The series is rated TV-G.

On August 10, 2012, Victoria Justice stated that the series would not be renewed.[4] Justice also said that Victorious was the number one show on Nick and she did not know why it was cancelled.[5] Dan Schneider added in a blog post that Nickelodeon often ends shows after about 60 episodes. Even though he and the cast would have been willing to shoot more episodes, the network decided to end the series. He also denied rumors that *Victorious* is ending because of its new spin-off show, *Sam & Cat*.[6] Although the *Victorious* cast only filmed three seasons, when the series was cancelled, Nickelodeon split the third season in half, making a fourth season.[5] The third and final soundtrack was released on November 6, 2012 and entitled *Victorious 3.0*. The first single from the new soundtrack is called "L.A. Boyz" and the music video was released on October 18, 2012. The series finale "Victori-Yes" aired on February 2, 2013.[7]

Plot

The series follows Tori Vega, a teenager who is accepted into Hollywood Arts High School, a school for talented teens in various performing-arts fields, after taking her older, much less talented sister Trina's place in a showcase after Trina had an allergic reaction to a Chinese herb product designed to help make people sing better. The plot follows Tori as she finds her place within Hollywood Arts, while getting into crazy situations and adventures, and meeting friends to help her along the way. Other students at Hollywood Arts, and the students who make up Tori's group of friends, include Andre Harris, a musical prodigy who becomes Tori's best friend at Hollywood Arts after encouraging her to stay at the school and helping her realize her talent; Robbie Shapiro, a socially-awkward ventriloquist who carries around his puppet Rex Powers, who is seen by Robbie (and generally everyone else) as a living person; Jade West, a sarcastic and Gothic "mean girl" who has a complicated frenemy relationship with Tori and often threatens her; Cat Valentine, a sweet and innocent but naive and somewhat dim-witted girl; and Beck Oliver, a down-to-earth and handsome guy who is Jade's boyfriend. They had been a couple since before the start of the series until the Season 3 episode "The Worst Couple", but got back together in the Season 4 episode, "Tori Fixes Beck and Jade". Beck and Tori have also had moments where they were attracted to each other (they almost kissed twice), but Tori did not want to risk her small friendship with Jade over this. Other characters include Erwin Sikowitz, the performing-arts teacher for Hollywood Arts; Lane Alexander, the school's guidance counselor; and Sinjin Van Cleef, an odd friend of Tori's.

Cast

Main cast

- Victoria Justice as Tori Vega
- Leon Thomas III as Andre Harris
- Matt Bennett as Robbie Shapiro
- Elizabeth Gillies as Jade West
- Ariana Grande as Cat Valentine
- Avan Jogia as Beck Oliver
- Daniella Monet as Trina Vega

Recurring cast

- Eric Lange as Erwin Sikowitz
- Lane Napper as Lane Alexander
- Michael Eric Reid as Sinjin Van Cleef
- Jim Pirri as David Vega
- Jennifer Carta as Holly Vega
- Marilyn Harris as Andre's grandmother
- Marco Aiello as Festus
- Susan Chuang as Mrs. Lee
- Darsan Solomon as Burf

Episodes

Season	Episodes	Originally aired		Prod. line	DVD releases
		Season premiere	Season finale		
1	19	March 27, 2010	March 26, 2011	1xx	July 5, 2011 (Volume 1)[8] November 11, 2011 (Volume 2)[9]
2	13	April 2, 2011	December 26, 2011	2xx	May 15, 2012[10]
3	13	January 28, 2012[11]	June 30, 2012	3xx	n/a
4	13[12]	September 22, 2012[13]	February 2, 2013[12]		n/a

Special episodes

Title	Type	Air date
"Pilot"	Series and Season Premiere	March 27, 2010
"Freak the Freak Out"	Special episode	November 26, 2010
"iParty with Victorious"	Crossover episode	June 11, 2011
"Locked Up!"	Special episode	July 30, 2011
"Tori Goes Platinum"	Special episode	May 19, 2012
"Victori-Yes"	Series Finale	February 2, 2013

Production

Victorious is the fifth series created by Dan Schneider for Nickelodeon, after *The Amanda Show*, *Drake & Josh*, *Zoey 101*, and *iCarly*.[14] Schneider first met Victoria Justice in 2005, when she was twelve and arrived to audition for the part of Lola Martinez on *Zoey 101*. Impressed by her energy and look, Schneider hired her and, after working with her on three episodes, called Nickelodeon to say, "I've got your next star."[15] Justice continued her role on *Zoey 101* until the series ended in 2008. In the meantime, Disney Channel, Nickelodeon's main competitor, had experienced immense success with franchises like *Hannah Montana* and *High School Musical*, which featured original songs and generated revenue through music as well as television. Seeking to "follow where the kids are", Nickelodeon executives asked Schneider to create a music-based show for the channel.[15] Near the end of *Zoey 101*'s run, Justice was summoned to meet with Schneider about a potential series starring her.[16] *Victorious* is the first series on Nickelodeon to premiere in the decade of 2010. *Big Time Rush*'s first episode premiered two months earlier, but its original pilot premiered in 2009.

While discussing possible concepts for the series during the meeting, Justice mentioned that she had attended a performing arts middle school. The idea intrigued Schneider, who recognized the appeal of a series concerning fame.[16] "If there is anything I've learned about kids today—and I'm not saying this is good or bad—it's that they all want to be stars," said Schneider.[17] Marjorie Cohn, who was then Nickelodeon's executive vice president of original programming and development, agreed. "Every kid thinks they're five minutes away and one lucky circumstance from being famous", Cohn stated. She noted that Schneider's *iCarly*, a sitcom about a girl who hosts a popular web show, was spurred by the rise of YouTube celebrities and has become a successful series for Nickelodeon.[17]

On August 13, 2008, Nickelodeon announced that Justice had signed "an overall talent and music deal" with the company, agreeing to star in a then-untitled musical-comedy series about a girl who attends a performing arts high school.[18] While discussing the show's premise, Schneider stated that while it would be nice if more children "wanted to be teachers and social workers" instead of celebrities, "At least in *Victorious*, you see a world where they're all working on the talent part."[17] Nickelodeon Productions and the Columbia/Epic Label Group of Sony Music Entertainment agreed to co-produce the series as part of a partnership to develop talent and release their music.[19]

Jerry Trainor, Perez Hilton, Josh Peck, Ke$ha, Nathan Kress, Drake Bell, Miranda Sings, and Jennette McCurdy have appeared on the series as cameos or guest stars.

The Season 1 of *Victorious* began filming on October 5, 2009, and ended on April 14, 2010, with 20 episodes produced.[20] Season 2 began filming October 4, 2010 and finished filming on February 23, 2011.[21] In August 2011, Victoria Justice confirmed that she was returning to the Victorious set, as Season 3 began filming on October 3, 2011.[22] During the TV special *7 Secrets with Victoria Justice*, Justice explained the weekly schedule the cast and crew operate on: scripts are issued to them on Sunday nights, the cast has table reads on Mondays and Tuesdays, then the episode is shot on Wednesday, Thursday and Friday and on Saturday, they watch a premiering of their show that is newly released to the public then.

There will not be a fourth season of the series. According to Victoria Justice, she told *M Magazine* that "We will not be expecting a fourth season, this is the first time I've talked about it. I just found out a couple of days ago that we're not coming back. It's sad because I've been with Nickelodeon since I was 12 years old and I became a family with my Victorious cast. We spent a lot of time together and bonded for sure – I'll look back on the experience very fondly. It's a little shocking and a little bittersweet, but at the end of the day it might not be such a bad thing – we all want to do our own thing and continue to grow."[23]

Casting

Several of the actors on *Victorious* had either appeared in Nickelodeon programs or Broadway musicals prior to *Victorious*' premiere. In addition to *Zoey 101*, Victoria Justice appeared on *iCarly* in "iFight Shelby Marx" as Shelby Marx, as well as *True Jackson, VP*, *The Naked Brothers Band*, and *The Troop*. She also co-starred with Avan Jogia, who portrays Beck, in the Nickelodeon television film *Spectacular!*. Daniella Monet has guest starred as Rebecca Martin in three episodes of *Zoey 101*, Tootie in the Nickelodeon television film *A Fairly Odd Movie: Grow Up, Timmy Turner!*, the *Supah Ninjas* Season 1 episode "Morningstar Academy" as one of the main antagonists named Clarissa, and in *Fred 2: Night of the Living Fred* (in lieu of Jennette McCurdy) as Bertha. Leon Thomas III had not only guest starred in an episode of *iCarly* as Harper and also in *The Naked Brothers Band* but he had also previously appeared in musicals such as *The Lion King*, *The Color Purple*, and *Caroline, or Change*, and in the film *August Rush*.[24] Elizabeth Gillies and Ariana Grande had co-starred in the musical *13*.[25][26]

Sets

Victorious is filmed at Nickelodeon on Sunset on Sunset Boulevard in Hollywood.[27] According to Paula Kaplan, Nickelodeon's executive Vice President for talent, "In our adult world, nobody accommodates us for down time. But in a child's life on a set, we do take that seriously. At our studios on Sunset Boulevard, where we shoot *iCarly* and *Victorious*, the greenrooms are filled with games and *Rock Band*. We create an environment where they can have fun with their colleagues and take it easy."[28]

Victorious is set primarily at Hollywood Arts, however the front of Hollywood Arts High School are digitally altered photos of Burbank High School. The lunch area of Hollywood Arts depicts the back area of Nickelodeon on Sunset, with a parking lot next to the back area.[29] According to David Hinkley of the *New York Daily News*, "Outside of school, *Victorious* has the same look as *iCarly*, with most of the action taking place on one main set with a few basic home/crib-furniture items." The series also has a BLIX machine from *Zoey 101*.[30]

Reception

Critical reception

Like *iCarly*, *Victorious* has received generally mixed reviews. *Variety* magazine reviewer Brian Lowry wrote, "*Victorious* has been cobbled together with the wooden-headed market in mind."[31] David Hinkley of the New York *Daily News* says the series' format is nearly identical to *iCarly*'s and hopes that the series will develop a "more distinctive personality" over the course of the season.[30] Roger Catlin of the *Hartford Courant* describes *Victorious* as "harmless but hardly entertaining".[32] Mark A. Perigard of the *Boston Herald* titled his review "Victorious is a big loser" and writes, "The bulk of the cast mugs for the cameras, probably to compensate for a script that could have been commissioned from fifth-graders."[33] Linda Stasi of the *New York Post* was mixed; she agreed that the series contained over-acting performers, "corny" dialogue and a "terribly, terribly loud laugh track", but believed it was "a surefire tween hit".[34]

However, reviewers were positive about Justice's performance and suggested that the show's potential hinged on her. Hinkley comments, "At this point, Justice is better at singing than acting, and the show doesn't flow as smoothly as *iCarly*, but Justice has the personality and talent needed for a shot at being 'the Next Big Teen Thing'".[30] Perigard describes her as "undeniably appealing"[33] and Lowry states, "Justice is winsome and talented enough to provide the latest show a leg up in connecting with tween girls."[31] Emily Ashby of Common Sense Media gave the series four out of five stars, writing, "Upbeat iCarly-like tween comedy promotes confidence".[35]

Viewership

The series' premiere did well among viewers. The first episode, advertised as a "sneak preview" of the series, aired after the 2010 Kids' Choice Awards on March 27, 2010, to 5.7 million viewers, the second-highest premiering live-action Nickelodeon series to date. Its second episode was advertised as the series' official premiere and drew a low 3.48 million viewers.[36] By comparison, Nickelodeon's *Big Time Rush* received 3.5 million viewers for its "sneak preview" debut in November 2009,[37] and 7.1 million Total viewers for its "premiere" in January 2010.[38]

Victorious Cast at the 64th Primetime Emmy Awards in September 2012.

On April 2, 2011, the Season 2 premiere episode "Beggin' on Your Knees" became the most-watched episode of the series to date, with 6.1 million total viewers.[39]

Merchandise

In fall 2011, Spin Master released dolls and toys based on the show. In June 2011, Walmart announced an exclusive-to-Walmart product line for the show; including over 250 products, such as apparel, accessories, lunch boxes, t-shirts, soundtrack CDs, DVDs, etc.[40] It has sold its newest toy, *Singing Tori*.

In late April 2012, McDonald's released *Victorious* toys, included in their Happy Meals.[41]

Video games

On November 15, 2011, *Victorious: Time to Shine* for Kinect and *Hollywood Arts Debut* for Nintendo DS were released.[42] On November 13, 2012, *Victorious: Taking the Lead* for Wii and Nintendo DS was released.[43]

Awards and nominations

Year	Award	Category	Recipient(s)	Result	Ref.
2010	Teen Choice Awards	Choice TV Breakout Show	*Victorious*	Nominated	[44][45]
	Hollywood Teen TV Awards	Teen Pick Actress: Comedy	Victoria Justice	Nominated	[46]
			Ariana Grande	Nominated	[46]
		Teen Pick Show: Comedy	*Victorious*	Nominated	[46]

2011	2011 Kids' Choice Awards	Favorite TV Actress	Victoria Justice	Nominated	[47][48]
	UK Kids' Choice Awards 2011	Nick UK's Favourite TV Show	*Victorious*	Nominated	[49]
		Nick UK's Funniest Person	Matt Bennett	Nominated	[49]
	Australian Kids' Choice Awards 2011	Fave TV Star	Victoria Justice	Nominated	[50][51]
		Fave TV Show	*Victorious*	Nominated	[50][51]
	Imagen Awards	Best Young Actress/Television	Victoria Justice	Nominated	[52]
	Primetime Emmy Awards	Outstanding Children's Program	*Victorious*	Nominated	[53]
	ALMA Awards	Favorite TV Actress – Leading Role in a Comedy	Victoria Justice	Nominated	[54][55]
	NAACP Image Awards	Outstanding Performance in a Youth/Children's Program (Series or Special)	Victoria Justice	Nominated	[56][57]
	British Academy Children's Awards	BAFTA Kid's Vote: Television	*Victorious*	Nominated	[58]
	Youth Rocks Awards	Rockin' Ensemble Cast (TV/ Comedy)	*Victorious*	Nominated	[59][60]
2012	2012 Kids' Choice Awards	Favorite TV Show	*Victorious*	Won	[61]
		Favorite TV Actress	Victoria Justice	Nominated	[61][62]
	Hollywood Teen TV Awards	Favorite Television Actress	Victoria Justice	Nominated	[63]
			Ariana Grande	Won	[63]
		Favorite Television Show	*Victorious*	Nominated	[64]
	Imagen Awards	Best Young Actress/Television	Victoria Justice	Nominated	[65][66]
	Primetime Emmy Awards	Outstanding Children's Program	*Victorious*	Nominated	[67]
		Outstanding Hairstyling for a Multi-Camera Series Or Special	Episode: April Fools Blank	Nominated	[68]
		Outstanding Makeup for a Multi-Camera Series Or Special (Non-Prosthetic)	Episode: April Fools Blank	Nominated	[69]
	ALMA Awards	Favorite TV Actress — Comedy	Victoria Justice	Nominated	[70][71]
	Casting Society of America	Outstanding Achievement in Casting - Children's Series Programming	Krisha Bullock Jennifer Treadwell	Nominated	[72]
	NAACP Image Awards	Outstanding Performance in a Youth/Children's Program (Series or Special)	Leon Thomas III	Nominated	[73][74]
	Do Something Awards	TV Star: Female	Victoria Justice	Nominated	[75]
	Kids' Choice Awards Mexico	Favorite International Show	*Victorious*	Nominated	[76][77]
	Kids' Choice Awards Argentina	International TV Show	*Victorious*	Won	[78]

Music

Soundtracks

- Victorious: Music from the Hit TV Show (2011)
- Victorious 2.0: More Music from the Hit TV Show (2012)
- Victorious 3.0: Even More Music from the Hit TV Show (2012)

"Make It Shine" is the show's theme song. The song also serves as the lead single from the soundtrack to the series. It peaked at number 16 on *Billboard*'s Bubbling Under Hot 100 Singles chart in the US.

Victorious features approximately one song every three episodes.[79] The songs that have been featured in *Victorious* are listed below. Victoria Justice told "7 Secrets with Victoria Justice" that she is currently working on music for her solo album. Parts of songs have also been sung in a few episodes of *Victorious*.

The *Victorious* soundtrack, featuring 12 songs from the show (including "Leave It All to Shine") was released on August 2, 2011.

The first 1,000 pre-orders received a CD booklet autographed by Justice, the special pre-order package (ordered before July 19, 2011) also included an exclusive customized *Victorious* poster.[80]

On May 15, 2012, a song called "Make It in America" was released. Victoria Justice performed on The Ellen DeGeneres Show the same day. It was also featured on the hour-long episode "Tori Goes Platinum".

On June 5, 2012, Columbia Records and Nickelodeon released *Victorious 2.0: More Music from the Hit TV Show*.[81]

The third soundtrack from the series, entitled "*Victorious 3.0: Even More Music from the Hit TV Show*", was released on November 6, 2012.[82] One single, L.A. Boyz, is available on iTunes.

Victorious 3.0

Victorious 3.0	
Soundtrack album by Various artists	
Released	November 6, 2012
Recorded	2012
Genre	Pop
Length	15:07
Label	Nickelodeon Records, Sony Music Entertainment
Victoria Justice chronology	
Victorious 2.0 (2012)	*Victorious 3.0* (2012)
Singles from *Victorious 3.0*	
1. "L.A. Boys" Released: October 18, 2012 2. "Here's 2 Us" Released: November 24, 2012 3. "Faster Than Boyz" Released: January 5, 2013	

Victorious 3.0 is the third and final album for the series. Daniella Monet announced the news. The album was released November 6, 2012 with a total of 5 tracks. Monet also announced that there would be a "Walmart Exclusive

Zine'Pak" with two bonus tracks and the bonus tracks are: "Cheer Me Up" by Victoria Justice, which was partly performed in the Season 3 episode, Tori Goes Platinum; and "365 Days" by Leon Thomas III, which was also partly performed in the Season 2 episode, Jade Gets Crushed. On the song, Leon is just by himself and is not singing with Justice like in the episode. Each song was performed in an episode of the series:

- "Here's 2 Us" (One Thousand Berry Balls)
- "L.A. Boyz" (Three Girls and a Moose)
- "Bad Boys" (Star Spangled Tori)
- "You Don't Know Me" (Tori Fixes Beck & Jade)
- "Faster Than Boyz" (The Bad Roommate)
- "Cheer Me Up" (Tori Goes Platinum)
- "365 Days" (Jade Gets Crushed)

Singles

"L.A. Boys" is the first single off the soundtrack and is performed by Victoria Justice and Ariana Grande. It was performed in the Season 4 episode, Three Girls and a Moose. The music video premiered on Nickelodeon on October 18, 2012, also the day the single was released.

"Here's 2 Us" is the second single off Victorious 3.0 and is performed by Victoria Justice. It is featured on the Season 4 episode, One Thousand Berry Balls which premiered on Saturday, December 8, 2012. The music video for it released on November 24, 2012, the same day the single was released. In the episode, Tori performs the song with Andre, but on the soundtrack, it is just Tori.

"Faster Than Boyz" is the third single off Victorious 3.0 and is performed by Victoria Justice. It is featured on the Season 4 episode, The Bad Roommate which premiered on January 5, 2013. The music video for it released on the same date of the episode. In the episode, Tori (Justice) performs the song with Andre (Leon Thomas) but on the soundtrack, It is Justice alone.

Other Songs

"You Don't Know Me" is a song written and performed by Elizabeth Gillies and was sung by her on the Season 4 episode, "Tori Fixes Beck and Jade". In the episode, Jade gets jealous because Beck is dating a girl named Meredith. She then performs the song. After she performs it, Beck kisses Jade which implies they are back together. After the episode aired the song became more popular, downloads of the song increased on iTunes.

"Bad Boys" is a song preformed by Victoria Justice and was sung by her on the Season 4 episode, "Star Spangled Tori"."Bad Boys" was the last song ever performed on *Victorious*. After the episode aired, the song became more popular, similar to, You Don't Know Me, downloads of the song increased on iTunes.

Track listing

No.	Title	Writer(s)	Artist(s)	Length
1.	"Here's 2 Us"	Evan Bogart, Lindy Robbins, Michelle Branch, and Emanuel Kiriakou	Victoria Justice	3:21
2.	"L.A. Boyz"	Dan Schneider, Michael Corcoran, Lindy Robbins, and Allan P. Grigg	Victoria Justice and Ariana Grande	2:59
3.	"Bad Boys"	Chris DeStefano and Kara DioGuardi	Victoria Justice	3:17
4.	"You Don't Know Me"	Elizabeth Gillies, Bisbee, and Levine	Elizabeth Gillies	2:53
5.	"Faster than Boyz"	Victoria Justice and Kool Kojak	Victoria Justice	3:14

Walmart ZinePak Edition

No.	Title	Writer(s)	Artist(s)	Length
6.	"Cheer Me Up"	Toby Gad and Natasha Bedingfield	Victoria Justice	3:15
7.	"365 Days"	Kool Kojak, Leon Thomas III, and Lindy Robbins	Leon Thomas III	3:32

DVD release

DVD Title	Region 1	Discs	Episodes	Extras
Victorious: Season One, Volume One	July 5, 2011[83]	2	1–10	"Freak the Freak Out" and "Beggin' On Your Knees" music videos plus behind-the-scenes features with the cast.
Victorious: Season One, Volume Two	November 1, 2011[84]	2	11–20	Bonus features and the *iCarly* episode "iParty With Victorious".
Victorious: The Complete Second Season	May 15, 2012[85]	2	21–32, 34	Behind The Scenes of Locked Up & The Seven Secrets of Victoria Justice

International release

Country / Region	Channel	Series Premiere	Season 2 Premiere	Season 3 Premiere (including season 4)	Series Finale
United States	Nickelodeon	March 27, 2010	April 2, 2011	January 28, 2012[86]	February 2, 2013
Canada	Nickelodeon Canada, YTV Canada	September 10, 2010	October 7, 2011 (YTV)	December 15, 2011 (YTV)	
United Kingdom / Ireland	Nickelodeon (UK & Ireland)	September 3, 2010	October 17, 2011	December 2011 (A Christmas Tori) September 22, 2012	
Australia	Nickelodeon Australia, Network Ten (2011–2012) Eleven (2012–present)	September 14, 2010	December 2011	December 2011 (A Christmas Tori) September 15, 2012	
Germany / Austria / Switzerland	Nickelodeon Germany	August 29, 2010	October 15, 2011	October 6, 2012	
Spain	Nickelodeon Spain	November 11, 2010	—	—	
Portugal	Nickelodeon Portugal	November 2010	—	—	

Indonesia	Nickelodeon Indonesia	2010	—	—	
Israel	Nickelodeon Israel	October 21, 2010	November 22, 2012	—	
Philippines	Nickelodeon Philippines (April 2011 – present)	October 1, 2010	October 31, 2011	September 5, 2012	
Brunei	Nickelodeon Southeast Asia (Also airs on TV3 Malaysia)				
Singapore					
Malaysia					
Hong Kong					
Brazil	Nickelodeon Brazil Rede Globo	October 13, 2010 December 17, 2011	November 16, 2011 2013	September 27, 2012 2014	
Netherlands	Nickelodeon Netherlands	September 25, 2010	November 20, 2011	October 13, 2012	
Belgium	Nickelodeon Flanders				
	Nickelodeon France	November 10, 2010	—	—	
Russia	Nickelodeon CIS	December 3, 2010	January 8, 2012	—	
Ukraine				—	
Lithuania				—	
Kazakhstan				—	
Argentina	Nickelodeon Latin America	October 13, 2010	November 16, 2011	September 27, 2012	
Chile					
Colombia					
Ecuador					
Honduras					
Dominican Republic					
Paraguay					
Peru					
Uruguay					
Venezuela					
Mexico	Nickelodeon Latin America Canal 5 (Televisa Network)	October 13, 2010 September 13, 2011	November 16, 2012 September 13, 2012	September 27, 2012 2013	
Greece	Nickelodeon Greece	September 12, 2011	November 6, 2012	–	
France	Nickelodeon France, TF1	November 10, 2010	April 11, 2012	October 11, 2012	
Croatia	Nickelodeon Croatia	2011	—	—	
Serbia	Nickelodeon Serbia	TBD 2012	—	—	
Pakistan	Nickelodeon	March 27, 2011	Present		

	Poland	Nickelodeon Poland	December 4, 2010	January 6, 2012	September 30, 2012	
	South Korea	Nickelodeon South Korea	January 7, 2011	—	—	
	Hungary	Nickelodeon Europe	December 4, 2010	February 12, 2012	October 7, 2012	
	Romania	Nickelodeon Central & Eastern Europe	December 4, 2010	—	—	
	Turkey	Nickelodeon Turkey	March 1, 2012	March 24, 2012	July 21, 2012	
	Denmark	Nickelodeon Denmark DR 1 DR Ramasjang	—	—	—	
	Arab World	MBC3	August 2012*	October 2012*	—	
	Japan	NHK	October 10, 2012	—	—	
	United Kingdom	CITV Nickelodeon UK and Ireland	2011–present	–	–	
	Sweden	Nickelodeon Sweden	2011–present	—	—	
	Bulgaria	TV7 (Bulgaria)	-2011	-	-	

- For TV3 Malaysia, the series airs only once a week, every Sunday at 11 pm, and only Season 1 and the first half of Season 2 will air.
- Also in MBC3 Victorious airs every Tuesday at 10 pm with two episodes back to back.
- The third season of the series premiered on July 21, 2012 in Nickelodeon Turkey, faster than all countries except for the United States.

Spin-off

A pilot has been ordered for series titled *Sam & Cat*. This series will be a spin-off of both *iCarly* and *Victorious*, starring Ariana Grande as her character Cat Valentine from *Victorious* and Jennette McCurdy as Sam Puckett from *iCarly*. The series will be about these two girls as they buddy up as roommates and start a babysitting business to fund their adventures.[87][88][89] On November 29, 2012, the series was picked up for 20 episodes.

References

[1] Leffler, Rebecca (October 4, 2010). "MTVNI touting 5,000 hours of programming" (http://www.hollywoodreporter.com/news/ mtvni-touting-5000-hours-programming-28681). *The Hollywood Reporter*. . Retrieved November 18, 2010.

[2] The character "Helen" from *Drake & Josh* is a minor character.

[3] http://www.nick.com/shows/victorious

[4] Big Time Rush (August 10, 2012). "M Exclusive: Victorious will NOT be returning for season four! – M Magazine" (http://www. mmm-mag.com/2012/08/m-exclusive-victorious-will-not-be-returning-for-season-four.html). Mmm-mag.com. . Retrieved August 10, 2012.

[5] "Victoria Justice Interview" (http://www.youtube.com/watch?v=7_Ei8pyY4VQ). .

[6] "Victorious" (http://www.danwarp.blogspot.com/2012/08/victorious.html). August 10, 2012. . Retrieved August 10, 2012.

[7] "Twitter/ DanWarp" (https://twitter.com/DanWarp/status/295572020593319936). . Retrieved 2 February 2013.

[8] "tvshowsondvd – "Victorious" Season 1, Volume 1" (http://www.tvshowsondvd.com/news/Victorious-Season-1-Volume-1/15264). Tvshowsondvd.com. . Retrieved 2012-06-09.

[9] "tvshowsondvd – "Victorious" Season 1, Volume 2" (http://www.tvshowsondvd.com/news/Victorious-Season-1-Volume-2/15828). Tvshowsondvd.com. . Retrieved 2012-06-09.

[10] Victorious: The Complete Second Season (http://parentpalace.com/2012/01/victorious-the-complete-second-season/)

[11] "New Season of Victorious: Saturday, January 28th at 8/7c" (http://www.webcitation.org/6AYg73kPB). Nick.com. 2012. Archived from the original (http://www.nick.com/videos/clip/victorious-news-season-2012-promo-cutdown-saturday-january-28th-N14544-01.html) on

September 9, 2012. .

[12] Schneider, Dan (January 5, 2013). "DanWarp Tweet "5 episodes left"" (https://twitter.com/DanWarp/status/287611942762340352). Verified Twitter Account. . Retrieved January 5, 2013.

[13] "Victorious Season Premiere!" (http://www.webcitation.org/6ArReOkyv). Archived from the original (http://www.theslap.com/clips/victorious-season-premiere) on September 21, 2012. . "... check out the whole episode THIS SATURDAY at 8 PM!"

[14] "Breaking News – Rising Teen Talent Victoria Justice Takes Star Turn in "Victorious"" (http://www.thefutoncritic.com/news.aspx?id=20100115nickelodeon01). TheFutonCritic.com. January 15, 2010. . Retrieved May 15, 2010.

[15] Wyatt, Edward (March 24, 2010). "First the Tween Heart, Now the Soul" (http://www.nytimes.com/2010/03/26/arts/television/26victor.html). *The New York Times*. . Retrieved April 23, 2010.

[16] Shen, Maxine (October 26, 2009). "'Zoey' pal gets own show" (http://www.nypost.com/p/entertainment/tv/item_QRn7cw345SnjVY82f11kXI#ixzz0ln6I31WQ). *New York Post*. . Retrieved April 23, 2010.

[17] Martin, Denise (November 22, 2009). "Child's play" (http://articles.latimes.com/2009/nov/22/entertainment/la-ca-kids-celebrity22-2009nov22). *Los Angeles Times*. . Retrieved April 23, 2010.

[18] Gornstein, Leslie (August 14, 2008). "A-List Secrets: How to Make a Shiny New Miley" (http://www.eonline.com/uberblog/b23803_a-list_secrets_how_make_shiny_new_miley.html). *E!*. . Retrieved April 23, 2010.

[19] *Billboard – Google Books* (http://books.google.com/?id=AhQEAAAAMBAJ&pg=PA8&lpg=PA8&dq=Nickelodeon+has+signed+fifteen-year-old+actress+Victoria+Justice+to+an+overall+talent+and+music+deal.#v=onepage&q&f=false). Google Books. August 23, 2008. . Retrieved May 10, 2010.

[20] Weisman, Jon (August 25, 2009). "Nick, Sony Music will duet for comedy" (http://www.variety.com/article/VR1118007715.html?categoryid=14&cs=1&query=victorious). *Variety*. . Retrieved November 24, 2011.

[21] "Victorious Season 2 – Filming Wrapped on February 23, 2011" (http://twitter.com/VictoriaJustice/status/40892828255129600). *Twitter*. . Retrieved November 24, 2011.

[22] "News – Ariana and Matt Talk 'Victorious'" (http://www.nick.com/celebrity/news/ariana-and-matt-talk-victorious.html). Nick.com. August 29, 2011. . Retrieved November 24, 2011.

[23] "M Exclusive: Victorious will NOT be returning for season four!" (http://www.mmm-mag.com/2012/08/m-exclusive-victorious-will-not-be-returning-for-season-four.html). . Retrieved August 10, 2012.

[24] The Broadway League. "The official source for Broadway Information" (http://www.ibdb.com/person.php?id=378651). IBDB. . Retrieved November 24, 2011.

[25] The Broadway League. "The official source for Broadway Information" (http://www.ibdb.com/person.php?id=480687). IBDB. . Retrieved November 24, 2011.

[26] The Broadway League. "The official source for Broadway Information" (http://www.ibdb.com/person.php?id=480685). IBDB. . Retrieved November 24, 2011.

[27] "Los Angeles Production Listings" (http://www.backstage.com/bso/production-listings/los-angeles-production-listings-1004081639.story). Backstage.com. April 8, 2010. . Retrieved May 10, 2010.

[28] "Growing up in character – Entertainment News, Youth Impact Report '09, Media" (http://www.variety.com/article/VR1118012129.html?categoryid=3834&cs=1). Variety. December 3, 2009. . Retrieved May 10, 2010.

[29] by DanWarp (April 18, 2010). "DanWarp: FUN FACTS: Victorious – "Stage Fighting" !!!" (http://danwarp.blogspot.com/2010/04/fun-facts-victorious-stage-fighting.html). Danwarp.blogspot.com. . Retrieved May 10, 2010.

[30] David Hinckley (March 26, 2010). "Nickelodeon patterns 'Victorious' with Victoria Justice after 'iCarly' to win young fans" (http://www.nydailynews.com/entertainment/tv/2010/03/26/2010-03-26_victorious_will_win_young_fans.html#ixzz0kqzCwIyf). *Daily News* (New York). . Retrieved May 10, 2010.

[31] By (March 25, 2010). "Victorious Review – TV Show Reviews – Analysis Of Victorious The TV Series" (http://www.variety.com/review/VE1117942470.html?categoryid=32&cs=1). *Variety*. . Retrieved May 10, 2010.

[32] Catlin, Roger (March 27, 2010). "Roger Catlin's TV Eye – TV Entertainment News" (http://blogs.courant.com/roger_catlin_tv_eye/2010/03/on-tonight-michelle-but-no-san.html). Blogs.courant.com. . Retrieved May 10, 2010.

[33] Press, Associated (March 27, 2010). "'Victorious' a big loser" (http://news.bostonherald.com/entertainment/television/reviews/view.bg?articleid=1242588&format=&page=2&listingType=tvrev#articleFull). News.bostonherald.com. . Retrieved May 10, 2010.

[34] Stasi, Linda (March 27, 2010). "'Victorious' has 'tween spirit" (http://www.nypost.com/p/entertainment/tv/reviews/justice_for_all_cQiZRcVpXHCZMALJMq2pWP). *New York Post*. . Retrieved May 10, 2010.

[35] Emily Ashby. "Victorious – Television Review" (http://www.commonsensemedia.org/tv-reviews/victorious). *Commonsensemedia.org*. . Retrieved May 27, 2012.

[36] "USA, TBS Split Ratings Crown" (http://www.mediaweek.com/mw/content_display/news/cable-tv/e3id5e840984ee9bae54c2df83be825b3b0). Mediaweek.com. April 13, 2010. . Retrieved May 10, 2010.

[37] "Breaking News – NEW NICKELODEON SERIES PREMIERES WITH A BIG TIME RUSH OF COMEDY AND MUSIC ON MONDAY, JAN. 18, AT 8:30 pm (ET/PT)" (http://www.thefutoncritic.com/news.aspx?id=20100105nickelodeon01). TheFutonCritic.com. January 5, 2010. . Retrieved May 10, 2010.

[38] By (January 19, 2010). "iCarly,' 'Rush' set records – Entertainment News, TV News, Media" (http://www.variety.com/article/VR1118013996.html?categoryid=14&cs=1). Variety. . Retrieved May 10, 2010.

[39] Cable Top 25: 'Kids' Choice Awards,' 'Pawn Stars,' 'WWE RAW' and 'Victorious' Top Weekly Cable Viewing (http://tvbythenumbers. zap2it.com/2011/04/05/cable-top-25-kids-choice-awards-pawn-stars-wwe-raw-and-victorious-top-weekly-cable-viewing/88284) By Robert Seidman – April 5, 2011 – tvbythenumbers.com

[40] "Breaking News – Nickelodeon Launches "Victorious" Product Line Exclusively at Walmart" (http://www.thefutoncritic.com/news/ 2011/06/14/nickelodeon-launches-victorious-product-line-exclusively-at-walmart-691002/20110614nickelodeon02/). TheFutonCritic.com. June 14, 2011. . Retrieved November 24, 2011.

[41] "HappyMeal" (http://www.happymeal.com/en_US/index.html#/Toys). HappyMeal. February 22, 2012. . Retrieved May 22, 2012.

[42] The CRP Group, D3Publisher. "Victorious – The Video Games" (http://www.victoriousvideogames.com/). Victoriousvideogames.com. . Retrieved January 8, 2012.

[43] "Victorious: Taking the Lead" (http://www.amazon.com/Victorious-Taking-Lead-Nintendo-DS/dp/B0082SIJU0). Amazon.com. . Retrieved August 11, 2012.

[44] dizneyztarz28 (July 2, 2010). "Dizneyztarz28: Más Teen Choice Awards 2010 Nominaciones" (http://dizneyztarz28.blogspot.com.ar/ 2010/07/mas-teen-choice-awards-2010.html). Dizneyztarz28.blogspot.com.ar. . Retrieved January 17, 2013.

[45] "OjoTeleTeen Choice Awards 2010: Ganadores" (http://www.ojotele.com/galas/teen-choice-awards-2010-ganadores). Ojotele.com. . Retrieved January 17, 2013.

[46] "Hollywood Teen TV Awards" (http://hollywoodteenonline.com/2010/07/04/hollywood-teen-tv-awards/). .

[47] Kim Grundy (February 10, 2011). "Nickelodeon Kids' Choice Awards 2011 nominees" (http://www.sheknows.com/entertainment/ articles/824257/nickelodeon-kids-choice-awards-2011-nominees). Sheknows.com. . Retrieved January 17, 2013.

[48] Elisiya (April 3, 2011). "Ganadores de los Kids' Choice Awards 2011" (http://www.lacosarosa.com/ganadores-kids-choice-awards-2011. html). Lacosarosa.com. . Retrieved January 17, 2013.

[49] "Nickelodeon Kids' Choice Awards 2011 Winners! I Fun Kids – the children's radio station" (http://www.funkidslive.com/news/ nickelodeon-kids-choice-awards-2011-winners/). Funkidslive.com. . Retrieved January 17, 2013.

[50] Editores Revista Teen. "¡Se anuncian los nominados a los Kids' Choice Awards de Australia!" (http://www.revistateen.com/ Â¡se-anuncian-los-nominados-a-los-kids-choice-awards-de-australia/). Revistateen.com. . Retrieved January 17, 2013.

[51] '+relative_time(twitters[i].created_at)+' (October 10, 2011). "2011 Kids' Choice Awards Australia" (http://www.clevvertv.com/ awards-show-2/27891/2011-kids-choice-awards-australia.html). Clevvertv.com. . Retrieved January 17, 2013.

[52] "26th Annual Imagen Awards - Nominees & Winners I The Imagen Foundation" (http://www.imagen.org/awards/2011). Imagen.org. August 12, 2011. . Retrieved January 17, 2013.

[53] "Primetime Emmy Awards nominations for 2011 - Outstanding Children's Program" (http://www.emmys.com/nominations/2011/ Outstanding Children's Program). Emmys.com. . Retrieved January 17, 2013.

[54] "Christina, Selena, Sofia, Demi and Cameron Spice Up the ALMAs" (http://www.eonline.com/uberblog/ b254984_christina_selena_sofia_demi_cameron.html). E! Online. July 28, 2011. . Retrieved November 24, 2011.

[55] "ALMA Awards 2011: Lista de los ganadores de la gran noche latina (FOTOS) - Celestrellas" (http://entretenimiento.aollatino.com/ 2011/09/11/alma-awards-2011-lista-ganadores/). Entretenimiento.aollatino.com. September 11, 2011. . Retrieved January 17, 2013.

[56] "42nd NAACP Image Awards Nominees Announced I GossipCenter - Entertainment News Leaders" (http://es.gossipcenter.com/ sanaa-lathan/42nd-naacp-image-awards-nominees-announced-456332). Es.gossipcenter.com. January 12, 2011. . Retrieved January 17, 2013.

[57] "NAACP Images Awards 2011 Winners & Red Carpet Photos" (http://socialitelife.com/ naacp-images-awards-2011-winners-red-carpet-photos-03-2011). Socialite Life. March 5, 2011. . Retrieved January 17, 2013.

[58] "Vote TV" (http://www.bafta.org/awards/childrens/2011-childrens-awards-nominations-winners,2169,BA.html#jump20). Bafta Kids Vote. . Retrieved November 24, 2011.

[59] "Rockin' Ensemble Cast (TV/ Comedy)" (http://youthrocksawards.com/?cat=32). Youth Rocks Awards. . Retrieved November 24, 2011.

[60] Teen.com (December 9, 2011). "Winners, First Annual 2011 Youth Rocks Awards" (http://www.teen.com/2011/12/09/entertainment/ 2011-youth-rocks-awards-winners-list-teen/). Teen.com. . Retrieved January 17, 2013.

[61] Posted: 04/ 1/2012 12:34 pm Updated: 04/ 1/2012 3:58 pm (January 4, 2012). "Kids' Choice Awards 2012: Winners List, Slimed Celebrities (PHOTOS)" (http://www.huffingtonpost.com/2012/04/01/kids-choice-awards-2012-slime_n_1394842.html). Huffingtonpost.com. . Retrieved January 17, 2013.

[62] "Nominados a los Nickelodeon Kids' Choice Awards 2012" (http://www.farandulista.com/2012/02/17/ nominados-a-los-nickelodeon-kids-choice-awards-2012.html). Farandulista. . Retrieved January 17, 2013.

[63] "Hollywood Teen TV Awards - Favorite Television Actress" (http://teentvawards.com/favorite-television-actress/). .

[64] "Hollywood Teen TV Awards - Favorite Television Show" (http://teentvawards.com/favorite-television-show/). .

[65] "27th Annual Imagen Awards - Nominees I The Imagen Foundation" (http://www.imagen.org/awards/2012). Imagen.org. . Retrieved January 17, 2013.

[66] "Winners of 27th Annual Imagen Awards Announced Honoring Latinos in Entertainment I The Imagen Foundation" (http://www.imagen. org/news/imagen-awards/2012/08/winners-27th-annual-imagen-awards-announced-honoring-latinos-entertain). Imagen.org. August 10, 2012. . Retrieved January 17, 2013.

[67] "Primetime Emmy Awards nominations for 2012 - Outstanding Children's Program" (http://www.emmys.com/nominations/2012/ Outstanding Children's Program). Emmys.com. . Retrieved January 17, 2013.

[68] "Primetime Emmy Awards nominations for 2012 - Outstanding Hairstyling For A Multi-Camera Series Or Special" (http://www.emmys. com/nominations/2012/Outstanding Hairstyling For A Multi-Camera Series Or Special). Emmys.com. . Retrieved January 17, 2013.

[69] "Primetime Emmy Awards nominations for 2012 - Outstanding Makeup For A Multi-Camera Series Or Special (Non-Prosthetic)" (http://www.emmys.com/nominations/2012/Outstanding Makeup For A Multi-Camera Series Or Special (Non-Prosthetic)). Emmys.com. . Retrieved January 17, 2013.

[70] "ALMA Awards 2012" (http://www.almaawards.com/past-alma-nominees.html). Almaawards.com. . Retrieved January 17, 2013.

[71] Palomares, Sugey (September 21, 2012). "2012 ALMA Award Winners: Complete List, American Latino Media Arts Awards" (http://www.latina.com/entertainment/tv/complete-list-2012-alma-award-winners). Latina. . Retrieved January 17, 2013.

[72] http://www.imdb.com/event/ev0000154/2012

[73] Deadline, The (January 19, 2012). "NAACP Image Award 2012 Film And TV - Nominees List" (http://www.deadline.com/2012/01/2012-naacp-image-award-film-and-tv-nominations/). Deadline.com. . Retrieved January 17, 2013.

[74] 02/17/2012 by Olivia Allin (January 17, 2012). "NAACP Image Awards 2012: Full list of winners - 02/18/2012 I Entertainment News from" (http://www.ontheredcarpet.com/NAACP-Image-Awards--2012:-Full-list-of-winners/8548831). OnTheRedCarpet.com. . Retrieved January 17, 2013.

[75] "2012 Do Something Awards I Tune-in Tuesday, August 21, 2012" (http://www.vh1.com/shows/events/do_something_awards/2012/tv-star-female/). VH1.com. August 21, 2012. . Retrieved January 18, 2013.

[76] "Nominados Oficiales A Los Kids Choice Awards Mexico 2012 ~ Nick News" (http://iritmo.blogspot.com.ar/2012/07/nominados-oficiales-los-kids-choice.html). Iritmo.blogspot.com.ar. June 8, 2010. . Retrieved January 18, 2013.

[77] "Lista de ganadores de los Kids' Choice Awards México 2012 I starMedia" (http://entretenimiento.starmedia.com/alfombra-roja/lista-ganadores-kids-choice-awards-mexico-2012.html). Entretenimiento.starmedia.com. September 3, 2012. . Retrieved January 18, 2013.

[78] "Grachi y Violetta los mas premiados en los Kids' Choice Awards Argentina 2012" (http://exitoina.com/2012-10-07-126087-grachi-y-violetta-los-mas-premiados-en-los-kids-choice-awards-argentina-2012/). Exitoina. October 7, 2012. . Retrieved January 18, 2013.

[79] "'Victorious' Star Victoria Justice Is 'Luckiest Girl in the World'" (http://www.vh1.com/news/articles/1634850/20100326/index.jhtml). *Vh1*. March 23, 2010. . Retrieved November 24, 2011.

[80] "Victorious Cast "Victorious: Music From The Hit TV Show – CD + Exclusive Poster Bundle" @ Victorious Store" (http://www.myplaydirect.com/victorious/details/25883515). Myplaydirect.com. . Retrieved November 24, 2011.

[81] "Columbia Records And Nickelodeon Announce The Release Of Victorious 2.0: More Music From The Hit TV Show, Available June 5" (http://www.marketwatch.com/story/columbia-records-and-nickelodeon-announce-the-release-of-victorious-20-more-music-from-the-hit-tv-show-available-june-5-2012-05-09). MarketWatch. May 9, 2012. . Retrieved May 22, 2012.

[82] "Daniella Monet Tweet" (https://twitter.com/DaniellaMonet/status/256559930000154624). Twitter (Verified account). . Retrieved October 12, 2012.

[83] "'tvshowsondvd 'Victorious" Season 1, Volume 1" (http://www.tvshowsondvd.com/news/Victorious-Season-1-Volume-1/15264). Tvshowsondvd.com. . Retrieved November 24, 2011.

[84] "Victorious DVD news: Box Art for Victorious – Season 1, Volume 2" (http://www.tvshowsondvd.com/news/Victorious-Season-1-Volume-2/15828). TVShowsOnDVD.com. . Retrieved November 24, 2011.

[85] "Victorious: The Complete Second Season: Matthew Bennett, Elizabeth Gillies, Victoria Justice, Ariana Grande, Daniella Monet: Movies & TV" (http://www.amazon.com/gp/product/B007BMIH2S). Amazon.com. September 9, 2009. . Retrieved February 26, 2012.

[86] PostPleaseLOGINorREGISTERto submit a comment.. "New Season of Victorious: Saturday, January 28th at 8/7c Episode Clip I Nick Videos" (http://nick.com/videos/clip/victorious-news-season-2012-promo-cutdown-saturday-january-28th-N14544-01.html). Nick.com. . Retrieved January 8, 2012.

[87] Big Time Rush (August 2, 2012). "Ariana Grande & Jennette McCurdy To Star In New Show, 'Sam & Cat' – J-14 Magazine" (http://www.j-14.com/2012/08/ariana-grande-jennette-mccurdy-to-star-in-new-show-sam-cat.html). J-14.com. . Retrieved August 3, 2012.

[88] Snierson, Matt (July 2, 2012). "Nickelodeon greenlights spin-off pilots for 'iCarly,' 'Victorious' from creator Dan Schneider – EXCLUSIVE" (http://insidetv.ew.com/2012/08/02/nickelodeon-icarly-spinoff-victorious/). Ew.com. . Retrieved July 2, 2012.

[89] "Sam & Cat,' 'Gibby' Get Pilots From Nickelodeon Starring Arian Grande, Jennette McCurdy And Noah Munck" (http://www.ibtimes.com/articles/369896/20120802/sam-cat-gibby-grande-mccurdy-nickelodeon-munck.htm). Entertainment & Stars. July 2, 2012. . Retrieved July 2, 2012.

External links

- Official website (http://www.theslap.com)
- *Victorious* (http://www.nick.com/shows/victorious) at Nick.com
- *Victorious* (http://www.imdb.com/title/tt1604099/) at the Internet Movie Database
- *Victorious* (http://www.tv.com/shows/victorious/) at TV.com

Victorious (soundtrack)

Victorious: Music from the Hit TV Show	
Soundtrack album by *Victorious* cast	
Released	August 2, 2011
Recorded	2009–10
Genre	Pop
Length	36:52 (minus bonus track)
Label	Nickelodeon Records, Sony Music Entertainment
***Victorious* cast chronology**	
Victorious (2011)	*Victorious* 2.0 (2012)
Singles from *Victorious*	
1. "Make It Shine" Released: April 13, 2010 2. "Freak the Freak Out" Released: November 19, 2010 3. "Beggin' on Your Knees" Released: April 1, 2011 4. "Best Friend's Brother" Released: May 20, 2011 5. "Leave It All to Shine" Released: June 10, 2011	

Victorious: Music from the Hit TV Show is the soundtrack for the Nickelodeon TV series *Victorious*. The majority of the album was sung by the lead actress of the television series, Victoria Justice, with the *Victorious* cast being listed beside her. Some of the other singers on the album feature Ariana Grande, Elizabeth Gillies, Miranda Cosgrove and Matt Bennett. The majority of the album was written by Michael Corcoran, Dan Schneider, Savan Kotecha, Kool Kojak and CJ Abraham with Victoria Justice involved in the composition of "Best Friend's Brother" and Leon Thomas III on "Song 2 You".

The album was released on August 2, 2011 by Nickelodeon Records, in association with Sony Music Entertainment.[1] All of the songs on this soundtrack appear on previously aired episodes of both seasons of *Victorious*. The soundtrack debuted on the Billboard 200 at number 5 with over 40,000 copies sold. It also peaked at number one on the Billboard Kid Albums chart and the Billboard Top Soundtracks chart.

The lead single from the soundtrack was the show's theme song "Make It Shine", which was released on April 13, 2010. The next song released was "Freak the Freak Out" on November 19, 2010. The song was the soundtrack's most successful single released, peaking on the Billboard Hot 100 at number 50. Other singles from the album include "Beggin' on Your Knees" (released April 1, 2011), "Best Friend's Brother" (released May 20, 2011) and "Leave It All to Shine" (released June 10, 2011).

Music structure and lyrics

Musically, the album is pop and dance heavy, featuring influencs of mainstream electropop, teen pop and bubblegum pop.[2] The album features the heavy usage of synthesizers, drum machine and Auto-Tune, prominent in songs like "Freak the Freak Out" and "Make It Shine".[2] The lyrical themes involve light romance, happy and sad, and assertions of self-worth.[2] The album features peppy dance tracks like "All I Want is Everything" and "Best Friend's Brother" and lite piano ballads like "Song 2 You" and "Tell Me That You Love Me". "Give It Up", sung by Ariana Grande and Elizabeth Gillies, is an urban pop track. "You're the Reason" and "Finally Falling" are guitar driven pop song written by Michael Corcoran, Dan Schneider, and CJ Abraham.

Singles

"Make It Shine"	
Single by Victorious cast featuring Victoria Justice	
from the album *Victorious: Music from the Hit TV Show*	
Released	April 13, 2010
Format	Digital download
Recorded	2009
Genre	Dance-pop, electropop, pop rock, electronic rock, teen pop
Length	3:07
Label	Nick, Columbia
Writer(s)	Lukasz Gottwald, Michael Corcoran, Dan Schneider[3]
Producer	Dr. Luke
Victoria Justice singles chronology	
"Make It Shine" (2010)	"Freak the Freak Out" (2010)

The lead single from the soundtrack was the show's theme song "Make It Shine", which was released on April 13, 2010. The next song released was "Freak the Freak Out" on November 19, 2010. The song was featured on the Victorious special, "Freak the Freak Out" and the soundtrack most successful single released, peaking on the *Billboard* Hot 100 at number 50. The single was accompanied by a two minute music video that premiered on Nickelodeon in mid November. "Beggin' on Your Knees" was released almost a year after the first single was released and was featured on the first episode of the second season "Begging on Your Knees" which Victoria Justice performed at the end of the episode and at the 2011 Nickelodeon Kids Choice Awards. It was the soundtracks second most successful single, peaking at number 58 on the *Billboard* Hot 100. The song was accompanied by a music video directed by Marc Wagner which was released on March 12, 2011. "Best Friend's Brother" was the fourth single released from the soundtrack on May 20, 2011. It was featured on the season two episode "Prom Wrecker."

The music video for the single was released on May 28, 2011. It debuted on the *Billboard* Hot 100 at number 93 and peaked at number 86. "Leave It All to Shine" was released June 10, 2011 as the fifth single off the album and performed on the iCarly 90-minute special "iParty with Victorious" by the cast members of both iCarly and Victorious.

Track listing

No.	Title	Writer(s)	Length
1.	"Make It Shine" (featuring Victoria Justice)	Lukasz Gottwald, Michael Corcoran, Dan Schneider	3:07
2.	"Freak the Freak Out" (featuring Victoria Justice)	CJ Abraham, Corcoran, Schneider, Zack Hexum	3:54
3.	"Best Friend's Brother" (featuring Victoria Justice)	Allan Grigg, Savan Kotecha, Victoria Justice	3:38
4.	"Beggin' on Your Knees" (featuring Victoria Justice)	Shellback, Kotecha	3:13
5.	"All I Want Is Everything" (featuring Victoria Justice)	Lindy Robbins, Toby Gad	3:02
6.	"You're the Reason" (featuring Victoria Justice)	Abraham, Corcoran, Schneider	2:53
7.	"Give It Up" (featuring Elizabeth Gillies and Ariana Grande)	Abraham, Corcoran, Schneider	2:45
8.	"I Want You Back" (featuring Victoria Justice)	The Corporation	2:59
9.	"Song 2 You" (featuring Leon Thomas III and Victoria Justice)	Leon Thomas, Joshua Schwartz, and Brian Keirulf	3:38
10.	"Tell Me That You Love Me" (featuring Victoria Justice and Leon Thomas III)	Abraham, Corcoran, Schneider	2:41
11.	"Finally Falling" (featuring Victoria Justice)	Abraham, Corcoran, Schneider, Drake Bell	2:50
12.	"Leave It All to Shine" (with iCarly cast featuring Miranda Cosgrove and Victoria Justice)	Gottwald, Corcoran, Schneider	2:12

Charts

Chart (2011)	Peak position
US *Billboard* 200[4]	5
US Digital Albums	5
US Kid Albums	1
US Soundtracks	1

References

[1] amazon.com, " Victorious Soundtrack (http://www.amazon.com/dp/B004NCOQSS)". Accessed 1 July 2011.

[2] allmusic.com, " (http://www.allmusic.com/album/victorious-r2142243/review)". Accessed 3 September 2011.

[3] "MAKE IT SHINE (Legal Title)" (http://repertoire.bmi.com/title.asp?blnWriter=True&blnPublisher=True&blnArtist=True&page=1&keyid=12323609&ShowNbr=0&ShowSeqNbr=0&querytype=WorkID). BMI. . Retrieved 2011-11-24.

[4] "Building Album Sales Chart" (http://www.hitsdailydouble.com/sales/salescht.cgi). HITS Daily Double. . Retrieved 2011-12-05.

Winx Club

Winx Club	
Winx Club logo for 2009-present.	
Genre	Fantasy, action, adventure, magical girl
Format	Animation
Created by	Iginio Straffi
Directed by	Iginio Straffi
Composer(s)	Michele Bettali Stefano Carrara Fabrizio Castania Maurizio D'Aniello
Country of origin	Italy
Language(s)	Italian English
No. of seasons	5 (6 Seasons confirmed)
No. of episodes	156 (117 aired) (List of episodes)
Production	
Executive producer(s)	Joanna Lee Alfred R. Kahn Norman J. Grossfield Tom Kenney
Running time	19-23 minutes
Broadcast	
Original channel	Rai Due (2004–present) 4KidsTV (2004–2007) Nickelodeon (2011–present)
Picture format	480i:SDTV (Season 1–4) 1080i:HDTV (Season 5–present)
Audio format	Stereo:(Season 1–4) Dolby Surround 5.1:(Season 5–present)
Original run	January 28, 2004 – present
Chronology	
Related shows	PopPixie
External links	
Website [1]	
Production website [2]	

Winx Club is an Italian animated television series[3] directed, created, and produced [4] by Iginio Straffi [3] and his company Rainbow S.r.l..[5][6] It is part of the larger *Winx Club* franchise. The series is the first Italian cartoon to be sold in the U.S.<ref name="iginiostraffi.com"/[7] According to Iginio Straffi's website, "Winx Club is an action and fantasy show combined with comedic elements. In the mystical dimension of Magix, three special schools educate modern fairies, ambitious witches and supernatural warriors, and wizards from all over the magical universe."[4]

Plot

The story follows Bloom and her five best friends, Stella, Flora, Tecna, Musa and Layla/Aisha, and is situated mainly in the Magical Dimension and on Earth. They call themselves "The Winx Club" and go on countless magical and mystical adventures together. Throughout the story, they discover new evolved much stronger fairy transformations, unlock new secrets and even stronger magical powers, battle against the darkness and support Bloom as she tries to discover her true past, home world, and birth parents.

Different plots

There are 2 different Winx Club plots, listed as follows:

- The original storyline, which was produced by Rainbow S.r.l., and which focused mainly on Bloom's story.
  - The series went through a reboot after Rainbow S.r.l. partnered with Nickelodeon, whereby the first and second seasons were compressed into 4 one-hour special episodes and the third and fourth seasons were dubbed again, following the original storyline, albeit with minor differences.
- The commonly called 4Kids version which, as part of 4Kids Entertainment's policy of adapting foreign animated shows to an American audience, was heavily edited and often diverged from the original storyline, including name changes (such as the original name of Bloom's planet of origin, *Domino*, which was replaced by *Sparks* in the 4Kids version), as changes in the role of characters (such as Daphne, Bloom's sister, whose role was changed to that of being only a nymph protecting Bloom's crown by 4Kids) and changes in the personality of characters (Tecna was given a British accent and Musa was given a hip-hopper personality by 4Kids).

First season

Bloom, a supposedly ordinary girl from planet Earth, lives a perfectly normal life in the city of Gardenia with her mother, father and her pet rabbit, Kiko, until she stumbles upon Stella, a princess from the planet Solaria, who is in trouble. Coming to Stella's aid, Bloom discovers her dormant magical abilities when she dodges a group of monsters and attacks an ogre. Stella persuades Bloom to join Alfea, a college for fairies in the Magical Dimension. She agrees and leaves Gardenia and her parents. At Alfea, Bloom forms the "Winx Club", whose members are her four friends and roommates: Stella, and the three friends she meets at Alfea: Musa, Tecna, and Flora. A mythical creature called Daphne keeps appearing in Bloom`s dreams. Later in the series, they encounter and befriend the Specialists: Brandon, Riven, Timmy and Sky, who also become the group's love interests. They also make enemies, a trio of witches calling themselves the Trix: Icy, Darcy, and Stormy. The Trix are witches from Cloud Tower, a college for witches and dark magic that is roughly equivalent to Alfea, and are in search of the vastly limitless energy and power of the Dragon Fire, which is supposedly in Stella's magic ring. However, they realize that the Dragon Fire is the very source of Bloom's magical strength and powers, which they steal from her. They summon the army of decay which they sent to Red Fountain and Alfea. The witches from Cloud Tower and the Red Fountain Heroes join Alfea and together the defeat the Trix. During that time, Bloom figures out that the Dragon Fire was in her the whole time. Bloom also begins to learn the secrets of her home world Domino, birth parents, magical abilities and that Daphne is her biological older sister. Bloom is heartbroken by Brandon, who appears to be Prince Sky as he and the real Brandon switched identities, but she ends up forgiving Sky at the end of the season.

Second season

The Trix are sent to Light Haven, a place to turn evil minds pure and good. Bloom, Stella, Flora, Tecna and Musa discover a new fairy, Layla/Aisha, who's the fairy of water/waves and morphix fluids from planet Andros and she becomes the sixth member of the Winx Club. Lord Darkar releases the Trix from Light Haven and increases their powers. Layla/Aisha tells the others about how the pixies are being held as Lord Darkar's prisoners. Layla/Aisha, Bloom, Stella, Brandon and Sky go on a Mission to Lord Darkar's lair, Shadow Haunt, to rescue the pixies Lockette, Amore, Chatta, Digit, Tune and Piff. At an opening of the new Red Fountain, Flora meets her love interest, Helia.

Along with Layla, there come lots of other magical and supernatural beings. Lord Darkar is after four pieces of a magical artifact called Codex, which allows one to enter the realm of Realix and gain the Ultimate Power. Bloom wants to know more about her birth parents, King Oritel and Queen Marion, and her lost kingdom, but Darkar gives her a shadow virus. The virus turns Bloom evil and she begins to torture Timmy. After Lord Darkar realizes that he needs more power to open the gateway to Realix, he instructs Avalon to turn Bloom evil once again. That is when he ditches the Trix and accepts Dark Bloom as his main witch. When they get to Realix, he tells Dark Bloom to give him the Ultimate Power. Unconsciously, she does so. In the end, it is Sky's mutually strong and true romantic love for Bloom that saves her and everybody else living...

Third season

Previously banished to the Omega Dimension, the Trix are able to escape with Valtor, an evil sorcerer partially responsible for the destruction of Bloom's home planet, Domino. They choose to cooperate and plan to invade several areas in the realm of Magix and seek vengeance on those who imprisoned them by stealing their exceptionally strong, powerful, magical and mystical treasures and immeasurable power sources of each realm. With their newly strong and powerful Enchantix powers, Flora, Stella, Layla, Tecna, and Musa are able to use strong, incredible power and can miniaturize themselves. Bloom, however, cannot miniaturize herself due to the fact that her Enchantix is not complete. The Winx begin their third and final year at Alfea, learning about their unique Enchantix transformations, acquired by selflessly sacrificing themselves for someone from their home world (or even everyone from every world, in what ends up being Tecna's case) and showing great courage in doing so. With no one from her home planet to save, Bloom must acquire her Enchantix form and tremendous power on Pyros, the island of dragons. She also learns more about Domino, as well as the truth about where her birth parents, Oritel and Miriam, are.

Fourth season

Taking place after the events of "Secret of the Lost Kingdom", The Winx Club are back at Alfea, but this time as the teachers. They learn about a new evolved fairy transformation and power called Believix, which can only be accessed when people in a non-magic world (such as Earth) start to truly believe in magic and fairies. Faragonda also teaches them that there are endless infinite stages of fairy evolution and transformation. The Winx Club also bump into the four Wizards of The Black Circle, a group of wizards who have trapped all of the fairies of Earth, and are back to get one they unknowingly left behind. The Winx girls and Specialists have to track the Wizards of the Black Circle to Gardenia, Bloom's Earth hometown, and save the last terrestrial Earth fairy, Roxy the fairy of animals, while trying to get people on Earth to believe in magic once again.

Change in licensing

In the United States, the license for 4KidsTV expired in 2007, and Rai Due sought out a new partner.[8] On 2 September 2010, Nickelodeon announced through a press release that they will be co-producing seasons 5 and 6 of the series.[9]

In early January 2011, it was announced that Keke Palmer will be playing the voice of Aisha, who is also known as Layla. In late March 2011, Molly Quinn announced she will be voicing Bloom.[10] Josh Keaton announced that he will voice Valtor.[11] Ariana Grande announced on 22 May via Twitter that she will be voicing minor villain Princess Diaspro in the new dub.[12] Romi Dames has also announced that she will voice Musa and Helia will be played by David Faustino.[13] Elizabeth Gillies is playing Daphne and Matt Shively is playing Sky.[14] The first special's broadcast revealed that Amy Gross is voicing Stella, Alejandra Reynoso is voicing Flora, and Morgan Decker is voicing Tecna.[15][16]

According to Micheal's Winx Club Website, the second movie *Winx Club 3D Magical Adventure* is scheduled to be aired in spring 2013. To coincide with the movie, a McDonald's promotion is currently scheduled to appear in April 2013.

Fifth season

The Winx Club embark on a mission to achieve Sirenix, a water based transformation that is strong and powerful enough to defeat the evil Tritannus and the Trix. There are two new evolutionary fairy transformations in this season: Harmonix and Sirenix. The Book of Sirenix gave them Sirenix Boxes and much stronger Harmonix powers. Before they achieve Sirenix, they must find the Gem of Self-Confidence, Gem of Empathy, and the Gem of Courage. Unfortunately, there is a dark and evil curse upon Sirenix that left Bloom's older sister, Daphne, a disembodied spirit without a physical body when she had used its tremendous power to defend herself. Daphne was the last fairy to achieve Sirenix's ocean/sea-based transformation and enormous power until the Winx Club gain full access to Sirenix and cross the gate into the infinite ocean itself. Finally, the Winx gain Sirenix after activating the source of the power in Lake Roccaluce where Daphne lives due to her connection to Sirenix. Unfortunately, the Trix gain dark Sirenix with the help of Tritannus and plan to defeat the Winx Club.

Fairy transformations and forms

* Winx:

In the first season, everyone is endowed their regular Winx/fairy form. This basic form usually consists of a sparkly cropped top and miniskirt or, in Stella's case, short-shorts. However, some Winx/fairy forms consist of a sparkly dress or jumpsuit, which are clear examples of Flora and Tecna's Winx/fairy forms. Also, they usually, but not always, bear some sort of accessory on their arms such as wristbands, arm warmers or gloves. They also sometimes wear a matching hair ornament such as a tiara and their hair is occasionally tied while in this form. They also don boots or, most often, heeled shoes and sprout a pair of small, membranous, fluttering wings. It should be noted that Winx fairies cannot cover long distances and they are incapable of agile flight (see picture of the characters with their pixies). It is not the strongest and most powerful form, as it only allows a fairy to use basic spells and attacks; but in a special case like Bloom, she can unleash her Dragon Flame which happens to be very intense; as seen in the final battle between Bloom and Icy in the first season. Also, Roxy is actually still on this form, even though her transformation sequence resembles Beleivix.

* Charmix:

In the second season, they get their second evolutionary fairy transformation and magical power, Charmix. They earn their Charmix by accomplishing something that helps them to get in touch with their true selves. They still wear their regular Winx/fairy outfits, but now they have a pin on their chest with a small gem and a small purse or waist bag that sits on the hips. However, in Flora's case, she has a shoulder bag and not a waist-bag like the others do. It should also be noted that Charmix does not grant the girls new powers; it only enhances the ones they already have.

* Enchantix:

In the third season, they get their Enchantix, which is their full-fledged fairy form. In their Enchantix form, the girls have much larger fairy wings that are much more sparkly and elegant, which enable them to fly higher and longer distances and cleave through strong storms, as well out-fly predators and opponents. They also have a fairy dust vial, situated around their neck, usually suspended by a choker that contains and keeps sealed their fairy dust of tremendously powerful healing and spell-breaking properties. Bloom also uses her fairy dust vial to keep the tremendously powerful, magical essence of Pyros stored inside of it, as shown in, *The Omega Mission* when the Winx and the Specialist's are boarding the ship for flight back to Alfea. An Enchantix typically consists of above-the-elbow translucent gloves and barefoot sandals. They wear a very short dress or a small top with a miniskirt or, for Tecna, mini shorts. Their hair grows longer and is elaborately arranged in loose tresses and high bunches; Tecna has a razored bob and Musa wears extremely long pigtails. A fairy earns her Enchantix by saving someone from her home world, with a great sacrifice on her part (excluding Bloom and Tecna- Bloom willed herself into her Enchantix and Tecna gave herself up for all of Magix, though that does include her home planet of Zenith). It should be noted that one does not actually have to *be* on one's home world when doing this. Enchantix is said to be 'the maximum or final fairy form that leads a fairy to her infinite energy' in the third season, making a complete, full-fledged fairy out of her, and also allowing her to achieve higher powers such as Believix, which gives her additional abilities, and Sirenix, which is even more powerful than Enchantix. Headmistress Faragonda is said to have already reached her Enchantix level. It is also believed that Daphne, Bloom's sister, went straight from Enchantix to Harmonix.

- Believix:

In the fourth season, all of the Winx move on to their Believix, entering a more advanced fairy stage with larger wings and additional powers, including the ability to make people believe in fairies, hence the name. The form is earned by making a human believe in fairies. All six Winx girls become Believix fairies at the same time by convincing Roxy, the last fairy of Earth, to acknowledge the existence of fairies and subsequently embrace her own being. In their Believix form, they have three new types of wings with special abilities of their own. There is Speedix (much faster wings), Zoomix (short-distance teleportation), and Tracix (visions into the past and, possibly, the future). A Believix outfit usually consists of a cropped top and a miniskirt or pants. The girls wear socks and heels or boots, and their hair is usually tied. They often wear fingerless gloves. Also, Believix powers have two new sub-transformations (the Gifts of Destiny) added: Sophix, which is a nature-themed transformation that grants them abilities that affect nature itself, and Lovix, a wintry-themed transformation that enables them to survive in icy cold climates and gives them ice-based abilities.

- Sirenix

In the fifth season, the Winx Club evolve into Sirenix fairies; an ancient ocean/sea-themed power that enables a fairy to accelerate and use her magic properly underwater. Apart from the other seasons which featured one new transformation, the Winx got their Harmonix transformation powers from their six Sirenix guardians, which is temporary and will be used only for the quest to gain Sirenix. The wings are much smaller as Harmonix fairies compared to Believix & Enchantix, but allows the fairies to accelerate faster underwater. Harmonix was still more powerful than previous transformations, though it does not compare to Sirenix. As Harmonix, the Winx Club fairy outfits all look the same, only with minor changes and shades of colors. Their hair is tied with several hair bands and accessories with the exception of Tecna. All girls are in a mermaid-tail gown (long in the back, short in the front). They wear high-heeled sandals, and two ribbons attached around the feet and legs act as straps.

When they cross the infinite ocean as Sirenix fairies, they got stronger wings, whole new outfits, upgraded powers, and colored hair. Sirenix outfits all look similar, with only minor details and major color differences to tell them apart. It is currently unknown whether the curse of Sirenix which left Bloom's sister Daphne in her current state as a disembodied spirit will affect the Trix or the Winx.

Broadcast history

In Italy, where the series was created, it has been broadcast on Rai Due since January 28, 2004. In the United States, it was licensed and dubbed into English by 4Kids Entertainment and was broadcast on Fox's programming block 4Kids TV beginning on June 19, 2004, with a preview episode airing on May 22, 2004. 4Kids TV continued its initial run until September 22, 2007, airing all three seasons. Winx Club was added back to the 4Kids TV schedule on April 12, 2008 and was aired up until December 27, 2008. On July 18, 2009, reruns of Winx Club then aired on the CW's programming block CW4Kids until July 17, 2010. Cartoon Network aired Winx Club in 2005 on their afternoon block Miguzi. Another English dub produced by Cinelume in association with Rai Due has been broadcast in Singapore, season 4 in Australia, and is featured as an alternate English language track on several European DVD releases.

Nickelodeon acquired the rights to the franchise in 2010 and is currently producing a new English dub in Los Angeles. Nickelodeon started airing the series with four-one hour specials summarizing seasons one and two. The first special aired on June 27, 2011, the second one "Revenge of the Trix" was aired on August 2, 2011, the third one "The Battle for Magix" aired on September 18, 2011 and the fourth one "The Shadow Phoenix" aired on October 16,

2011. The third season, "Winx Club: Enchantix", was aired on Nickelodeon from November 14, 2011 to December 26, 2011. The fourth season, "Winx Club: The Power of Believix", aired on Nickelodeon from May 6, 2012 to July 29, 2012. The fifth season, "Winx Club: Beyond Believix", premiered on Nickelodeon on August 26, 2012 and its season finale will air sometime in late 2013 but no word for the second half of season five. The fifth season aired the show's first ever Christmas special which aired December 9, 2012.

Controversy

Due to the fact that the highly edited 4Kids version of Winx Club was the one that was aired in the United States, some American fans who had previously watched only this version have lately criticised the Nickelodeon dub of Winx Club, which follows the original storyline of Winx Club produced by Rainbow S.r.l., for not following the 4Kids dub, which they misinterpreted as being the original version.

References

[1] http://www.winxclub.com/
[2] http://www.rbw.it/
[3] http://www.chacha.com/question/how-can-i-contact-iginio-straffi-the-producer-of-the-winx-club-series
[4] http://www.iginiostraffi.com/
[5] http://www.iginiostraffi.com/press.php?id=2
[6] http://www.gamezone.com/news/konami_4kids_entertainment_and_rainbow_s_r_l_announce_winx_club_license_agreement
[7] Rainbow S.p.A.. "Winx Club" (http://www.rbw.it/en/properties/winx-club). . Retrieved 2006-11-15.
[8] "The next big thing" by Ann-Marie Corven, TBI Kids June/July 2010 p.6-8
[9] "Nickelodeon and Rainbow S.p.A. Announce Global Partnership for Winx Club Animated Series - NEW YORK, Sept. 2" (http://www.prnewswire.com/news-releases/nickelodeon-and-rainbow-spa-announce-global-partnership-for-winx-club-animated-series-102060828.html). New York: Prnewswire.com. . Retrieved 2012-05-09.
[10] "Molly C. Quinn, Official Fan Site" (http://www.facebook.com/pages/Molly-C-Quinn-Official-Fan-Site/302187960218). Facebook. . Retrieved 2012-05-09.
[11] "Josh Keaton" (http://www.facebook.com/pages/Josh-Keaton/101651598327). Facebook. 2012-04-26. . Retrieved 2012-05-09.
[12] https://twitter.com/#!/ArianaGrande
[13] https://twitter.com/#!/TheRomiDames
[14] "Twitter" (https://twitter.com/). Twitter. . Retrieved 2012-05-09.
[15] "Winx Club - One-Hour Special Ending" (http://www.youtube.com/watch?v=j42d5jfi7z4). YouTube. . Retrieved 2012-05-09.
[16] "Winx Club on Nick! (All credits) ~ Winx Club on Nickelodeon: Feel the magic!" (http://winxclubnick.blogspot.co.uk/2011/07/winx-club-on-nick-all-credits.html). Winxclubnick.blogspot.co.uk. 2011-07-01. . Retrieved 2012-05-09.

External links

Official sites

- Official website (http://www.winxclub.com/) Available in multiple languages including English edition currently for the United Kingdom
- Official website for the theatrical films (http://www.winxclubthemovie.com/) **(Bulgarian)**, **(English)**, **(French)**, **(Italian)**, **(Dutch)**, **(Portuguese)**, **(Russian)**, **(Turkish)**
- PopPixie (http://www.poppixie.com/) Operated by Rainbow S.p.A.
- *Winx Club* (http://www.nick.com/shows/winx-club/) at Nick.com

Databases

- *Winx Club* (http://www.imdb.com/title/tt0421482/) at the Internet Movie Database
- *Winx Club* (http://www.tv.com/shows/winx-club/) at TV.com

Article Sources and Contributors

Ariana Grande *Source*: http://en.wikipedia.org/w/index.php?oldid=537321604 *Contributors*: 13themusicalswift, 2tuntony, 5 albert square, A. Parrot, ABC1356msep1, AbsolutelyAri, Acalamari, Acather96, Ace of Spades, Active Banana, Aglmbslvr, Ajfuturewriter, Alansohn, Aldis90, All Hallow's Wraith, Allaine123, Allmightyduck, Alondra23, Alpha 4615, Andrewlp1991, Andy4stacey7, AnneBerlyne MaKenzie, Antdhumphrey, Arby2007, AriG4Ever, Arianagrande, Ariroxs567, Arthur Rubin, Aymatth2, Azeruth42, Banjokazooierox, Barneystimpleton, Baseballrocks538, Bdwick, Bdwick12, BeatrizAsnicar, BellaFan262, Bender235, BillyBob Turner, Blehfu, Bluefist, Bongwarrior, Bradb008, BridqieB-, Bsadowski1, BubbleGum45, Bway13, Bwsmith84, C.Fred, CPGirlAJ, Cadsuane Melaidhrin, Calabe1992, CalumH93, CaroleHenson, Celticsloveohiostate, Chester Markel, Chocomilk75, ChrissehJohnson, Christina Silverman, Clfan91, Clyde123456789, Colinmotox11, CommonsDelinker, Confession0791, Corn cheese, Courcelles, Crash Underride, Crzygrl3, Cst17, Cyristalc, DARTH SIDIOUS 2, DMacks, Dadajjj96, DanTD, Danregal, DarkFalls, DegrassiFreak, Dennis55789, DerekB2010, Deunick, Dffgd, Diannaa, Dimadick, Discospinster, DivineAlpha, Dotsloveit, DracoUltima, Drmies, DylanGLC2011, Editoraccountofmine, Edward Butera, Edwardx, Emmapass01, Enigmatum, ErikHaugen, Esposimi, Explicit, Fastily, Feudonym, Fh6000, Fleur740, FleurCraig1234, Flipflame, Fluffernutter, Forever awesome, ForgottenHistory, Fourviz, Freakmighty, Frehley, Froxz, Ftsktaylor, Fuckyeahjanoskians, Funandtrvl, Funnybunny44, Fussycar, Fæ, G-rad, GCMS1, Geraldo Perez, Gimmetoo, Graeme Bartlett, Greeenicarly, HJ Mitchell, Hammersoft, Harro774, HazelEyedKiki, Heymid, Home05748, Hullaballoo Wolfowitz, Huttohippogirl16, I dream of horses, I'm No Winner, Iluvselenagomez1234, ImmaG6Kidd, Impala99, Itzlynzayee, Itzuvit, J Milburn, JBieberAusFever, JESSEH321, JGossard, JNW, James toronto, Jandbadbay, JaneSaxon, JayC, Jgrande21, Jim1138, Jjj1238, Jmanprousk, Johnpacklambert, Johnuniq, Jonah22, Jordan Chuck, Jprg1966, Junixers, Jusdafax, Jvg114, Kallina17, Karl 334, Katieh1000, Katriiia, Katydidit, King Of Aviators, King of Hearts, Kww, Kww 2, L Kensington, L'papillon, Larissa.Chilton, Lewis odane, Lilmissrusso, LittleWink, Lizzyzap98, Logan, LohZiSan, Lolcolors, Lolxz123, LostInIgnorance, Lovekatkat14, Lozeldafan, Ltuazon0214, Lucas Carranza, MC10, Macedoniarulez, Maraqua22, Markkker, Materialscientist, Mato, MaybeMaybeMaybe, Mbinebri, Meedostuff, MeggiemooM, Mike Rosoft, Minna Sora no Shita, Mirokado, Miss X-Factor, Mockingjaybonnott, Mogism, Monterey Bay, Moonnight10, Morning Sunshine, Mozo182, Msltul, My76Strat, Nancyeromero, Necronaut, NellieBly, Nelybel123, Nick Number, NickArellano, Noommos, NoseNuggets, Nverhoeven, NylonDreamer, OSnapizCaity, Off2riorob, Ozkithar Salas, Panda345, Patrickmgaddis, Pdcook, Phd8511, Piast93, Pirnkia, Plastikspork, Playking616, Pluma, Plutonottheplanet, Pokethesquirrel, Pstanton, Purple123x, Qazwsxedcokmijnuhbrtyfgv, QuasyBoy, Qwerfghnm, Qworty, RORLVR1, RafikiSykes, Rainbow492, Reaper Eternal, Reconsider the static, Redtapshoes, Rgktexas7, Rich Farmbrough, Rickardo98a, Rlg000raz, Rmosler2100, Robyn239, Rockachic38, Roleplayer, Ronhjones, Roscelese, Roshele tenney, Rubygoogle11, Ruy Pugliesi, SRK97, Sadistik, Salwa105, Sammy no1, Seaphoto, Selenastan13, Serienfan2010, Shaq91, Simon.hess, Simplexsweet, SkyeSweetnam4ever, Sonia, Soniarao07, Sorina1999, Ssilvers, Stardeni97, Starkluver13, Status, Stevencool, Stunners, SummerPhD, SuperHamster, Supreme Deliciousness, Sweden Rocks hard, Syxx 23, TWMM91, Tainahlee, Tammycanbe, Tampabay721, Tarroyo1, Tassedethe, Tastetherainbow101, Tay26, Tbhotch, Tentontunic, Tgeairn, TheDanush55, TheZend, Thecoolkids13, This lousy T-shirt, Tide rolls, TigersRock5550, Tinton5, ToadQueen, Tommy2010, Tommy388, Tommycrossover, Tony1, TruthTeller93, Ttonyb1, Turkeybox9, Tyrol5, UltraCody, Uncle Milty, Usb10, VictoriousUser, Vincelord, Vval1570, Weedbarrel123, WereSpielChequers, Whatever318, Wifione, Wiggy Opez, WikHead, WikiSpector, Wikipelli, WillSpil, XBubbiLicious, XMirandaxCosgrove, Yagley1, Zak110695, 841 anonymous edits

13 (musical) *Source*: http://en.wikipedia.org/w/index.php?oldid=536594136 *Contributors*: 009o9, 13themusical, 13themusicalswift, AI0913, Aaron Booth, Adam.Harper, Angelic-alyssa, Bdn223, BenjaminMaioMackay, Bkonrad, Blethering Scot, Bnjgirl133, Cannison101, Cflm001, Chase me ladies, I'm the Cavalry, ChrisCork, Coalhouse, Crash Underride, Daonguyen95, Darklilac, David!!, Don-Don, Drbreznjev, Dsapery, Duffbeerforme, Eugene-elgato, Evandx11, Feebster8, Fh6000, Flakos17, Flami72, Flavallee, Fllmtlchcb, Fryede, Gareth Griffith-Jones, GoingBatty, Hannahnicholle, High School Musical909, IsPoLiN, JForget, Jetset59, Jharvey5, Jim1138, Joethehobo2007, Jsayre64, Kallina17, Kbdank71, Klemen Kocjancic, Kpacek330, L Kensington, Lilfax, Liquidluck, Love2Lax, Magicjack, Magioladitis, Mandykaitlyn, Mark Arsten, Maxis ftw, Maxpoto, Mdann52, MearsMan, Melesse, Michaelpanda, Misza13, Moe Epsilon, Mrasco1996, MusicMaker5376, Mvjs, NaomiBelet, Nekohakase, Ohnoitsjamie, Orange Suede Sofa, P. S. F. Freitas, P.D., Paigecl, Phaeton23, QuasyBoy, Qworty, RPlunk2853, Red running shoes, Ridaderek, Sblngpedia11, Sdoge99, Ser24, Seraphimblade, Simplekindoflovely, Skizzik, Smileyrocks11, Ssilvers, SteinbDJ, Stuart3333, TFBCT1, The Utahraptor, TheRedPenOfDoom, Thebeginning, Thecoolkids13, Tide rolls, Tosspot2011, Vegetarianfocus, Versus22, Victory-Pandora, W Tanoto, WalkingOnSunshineHurts, WereSpielChequers, Wknight94, Yamanbaiia, 516 anonymous edits

Boca Raton, Florida *Source*: http://en.wikipedia.org/w/index.php?oldid=536931342 *Contributors*: (aeropagitica), 6975cj, 72Dino, 90, AJSC92, Abhinav777, Acalamari, Achowat, Acntx, Active Banana, Adsong, After Midnight, Agutie, Al Lemos, Alansohn, Alarics, AllisonFoley, Alpha Quadrant, Americansteamers, Amz445, Anand Karia, Andresfperez, Andrwsc, Andy M. Wang, AnnaFrance, Anne2608, Aquaregia2001, Argentino, ArmadilloFromHell, Asietz, Atacama, Atler5264, AussieLegend, Averette, Avicennasis, Azizi, Azumanga1, BD2412, Banana6975, Bassbonerocks, Bastel, Bastique, Before My Ken, Bender235, Bgtgwazi, Bgwhite, Bico375, BigFishy, Biker Biker, Bjorn.korslund, Blanchardb, Blehfu, Bobo192, Boca555, BocaRatonBites, Bocaaddress, Boromir123, Bovineboy2008, Brutaldeluxe, Bubba73, C.Fred, CBlake09, CGrigsby, Caldwell7901, CambridgeBayWeather, Camerong, Capasc, CapeVerdeWave, Captaintruth, Cg41386, Cha0sth30ry, Chaplin62, Cheeda777, CheepnisAroma, Chocochocochoco, Chris the speller, Cj1340, Cloof, Cmr08, Colinstu, Colonies Chris, Comayagua99, CoreyWeiner, Corp1117, CptnSkippy, Crunch, Cuchullain, Cyrillic, D d4ever1, D6, DMCDC, Dachshund, DanMS, DanTD, DangApricot, Dannywein, Darth Mike, Deconstructhis, Deemacker One, Deerpierat, Deflective, Derbyboi, Dewritech, Dhartz, Dhrubajdeka, Dina, Discospinster, Dixon1e, Dkazdan, Dlohcierekim, Dmwilliams, Doc Tropics, DocendoDiscimus, Donald Albury, Donner60, Doors22, Dragonball1986, Dtobias, Durova, Eagles247, Earl of wilmington, Ebyabe, Edward, Elfguy, Eli lilly, Energyfreezer, Epeefleche, Ephemeral Antlions, EricS, Ermanon, Error -128, Esoup, Ethelh, EurekaLott, Excirial, Ezdoit, Falcon8765, Farmhand4, Fires64, Firsfron, Flooey, Formulanone, Frecklefoot, FreddyMontenez, Froid, Frungi, Fubar Obfusco, Fuhghettaboutit, Funandtrvl, Furtive admirer, Gaius Cornelius, GatorFTL, Gatorsfan16, Geoking66, Geomaven, Giants27, Glosing, Gmusic69, Go Owls, GoingBatty, Goldbay, Golgofrinchian, Gongshow, Graham87, Grayshi, Ground Zero, GroveGuy, Grsnider, Guat6, Guspinto, Hall Monitor, Hektor, Honeycombs22, Hruiz1040, Hutchie6, IZAK, Igor561, Infrogmation, Inkan1969, Insanity Incarnate, Intgr, Irreama, J.delanoy, JForget, JMyrleFuller, JNW, JRoss09, JamesBWatson, Jamesontai, Jay32183, Jeffrey Mall, JeffreyN, Jensommers007, Jetdude91, Jetsrule91, Jhumbo, Jmlk17, Jnocook, Joe Kress, Joedamadman, JohhnyUNC, John K, JohnCub, Johnpacklambert, Joquarky, Jorfer, Jswfl09, Juliancolton, Justwunderbar, Kai Ojima, Karen Johnson, Karenjc, Katcruz75, Keilana, Kioe M, KnightLago, KortKramer, Kuru, Kwamikagami, Latka, Lauracs, Liabernal, Lightmouse, Lizardrevolution, LogiBear180, Loodog, MJCdetroit, MJSkia1, Mackensen, Mahanga, Majorly, Mandarax, Matias.sard.c, Matt Deres, Matthewvelez1, Maxlakeman, MeStevo, Meegs, Melesse, MiamiHawaii, Michael.Goydich, Michael16G, Mike Restivo, Mike Searson, Mild Bill Hiccup, Minna Sora no Shita, Miquonranger03, Mmxx, Mojah99, Molinoski, Mooker88, Moreau36, Mrhockey655, Mutinus, N5iln, NE2, NYYankeeGirlie, NancyHeise, Napot900, Neelix, Neilevan, Nemmy, Nigamreddy1234, Nikki311, Nintendo Maximus, Noles1984, Nonameplayer, Nyttend, Oatmealandwhimsy, Ohnoitsjamie, Orangemike, Orlandoflorida, Orwellian Python, OtherPerson, OxyMoronMinusOxy, PaleCloudedWhite, Partfind, Paulkav1, Pba378, Pcfranchise, Pearle, PhillyPartTwo, Pinethicket, Pinkadelica, Piusg, Pmsyyz, Pokemonblackds, Pparazorback, Quackslikeaduck, Quidam65, QwertyKILLA, R'n'B, RA0808, RHaworth, RSM, Ram-Man, Rastrojo, Rdoran01, Realron, RedWolf, Redaktor, ReignMan, Relover89, RenamedUser01302013, Res2216firestar, Rich Farmbrough, RickK, Rjwilmsi, Rmctonline, Rnb, Royalguard11, RucasHost, Ruhrfisch, Rundrdave, Runefrost, Ryano913, Ryoung122, Ryuhaku, SDARS, SDC, Sam Korn, Sandstorm6299, Scaletail, Scanlan, Scotthatton, Securiger, Sfahey, Shortride, Silkindude11, Sjcguy, Slysplace, Smoove Z, Softdevusa, Soosim, Staticshakedown, Steelax42, Stephenjayburns, Steve2011, Stratton52, Sumdrumbum, SummerPhD, Super-Magician, Swatjester, SwissCelt, Syrthiss, Tassedethe, Thanissaro, TheAllSeeingEye, TheMocker, Thehelpfulone, Thorncrag, Tide rolls, Towel401, Trafton, TutterMouse, Twalls, Twirk88, Ulric1313, UtherSRG, Van Rijn, Vegaswikian, Veinor, Velella, Viriditas, Vosentreste, WantedToAdd, Wemmi, WhisperToMe, WhoMe?, WikHead, Wiki alf, Wikiguy09, William Avery, WilliamJE, Windchaser, Wtmitchell, Xxwoody63xx, Y, Yancyfry jr, Yekuckra, Yidisheryid, Zanter, Zazpot, Zfreidus, 997 anonymous edits

Elizabeth Gillies *Source*: http://en.wikipedia.org/w/index.php?oldid=536982107 *Contributors*: 17bella, 1996gogetta, Abortman, Alansohn, Albert009, Alexandhotshot, Alexlikesbunnys991, Anbu121, AnneBerlyne MaKenzie, AnonMoos, ArglebargleIV, Armoreno10, Arqgilbertocruz, Awesome444a444, Azurfrog, B2project, Bbb23, Bdwick12, Beamer103, Becca672, Bender235, Bongwarrior, C.Fred, Caelas, Ceancata, Celticsloveohiostate, CharlotteAster, CinchBug, Closedmouth, CommonsDelinker, Confession0791, Coolbeans443, Crash Underride, Curtis23, Cymru.lass, DanTD, DemonSlayer6, Dennis55789, Denniss, Deor, Diannaa, Dimadick, Discospinster, Djb31800, Doddy Wuid, Download, E. Fokker, E. Ripley, E2eamon, EagerToddler39, Egmontaz, Elizium23, EoGuy, Favonian, Floul1, Fourviz, Fraggle81, Fram, Funnybunny44, Fussycar, GCMS1, Geraldo Perez, Gimmetoo, GirlGirlGirlieGirl!!, Glane23, Gooshbaster, Gz33, Happysailor, Harshi1998, ILoveJadeW, Iknowtherealaccountsofthestars, Ilana07, Impala99, Intelati, IsPoLiN, IsoMorpheus, ItsZippy, JGossard, Jakehandfg, Jamielynnfan, Jamison Lofthouse, Jandbadbay, Jeff G., JesspiaTheHorse, Jim1138, John Andrews Carlisle Astor, John of Reading, Johnpacklambert, Jonathanfu, Kage Me, Kallina17, Katydidit, Kevinbrogers, KianaArchAngel, Kinu, KristjuFFe4ka, Kubigula, Kwiki, KyoXTohru1, L29674, Legomyeggo252, Lerdthenerd, Lewis odane, LittleWink, LivGillies, LizGilliesFan, Lizbeth Weldon, Lizg666, Lizgillies184, Lizziebathory, LuK3, Lugia2453, MJ94, Macaddct1984, Malcolma, Malik Shabazz, Mandarax, Maraqua22, Marek69, Mariella817, Mark Arsten, Materialscientist, Mato, MazAcquah, Mbinebri, McGeddon, Metricopolus, Mickey MoMo2323, MissIndependent537, Mockingjaybonnott, Moe Epsilon, Monty845, Mrschimpf, MsFionnuala, Muppet321, NYMets2000, Nashapapa, Nepenthes, Netalsm, Nickorock, Nilli, NinaDAlexP, Nsk92, Number36, O.Koslowski, Peace out11, Phd8511, Philg88, Pi, Pichpich, Prtylegend, Purple123x, QuasyBoy, Quebec99, Quibik, Qwfp, Qwyrxian, RORLVR1, RPlunk2853, Rails, Raisrulez, Randis101, Rankiri, Rimzee2000, RiverStyx23, Rjwilmsi, Rocketrod1960, Ronhjones, Sara3412, Sblngpedia11, Scissorluv12345, Seancasey00, Serienfan2010, Shadowjams, ShelfSkewed, Siddhartha Ghai, SilentRob360, Simon.hess, Sleeping-sickness, Slon02, Smarttamarr94, Sollie Scott, StefanX112, Storyofus, SummerPhD, SunsetKiss03, SuperHamster, Superstar987, Surajt88, SweetSweetieCakes, Syrthiss, TFBCT1, Tcnorden, The Utahraptor, TheGuadalupeSoto, TheRedPenOfDoom, Thechrisadams, Themeparkgc, Theopolisme, Tide rolls, TigersRock5550, TikTokGirl, Tincito, Tinton5, Tommy2010, Tommy388, Tommycrossover, Tracer9999, TradyM888221, Transity, Tricdl27, Ulric1313, Valenciano, Vertium, Vickiitee, VictoriousUser, Vincelord, VivienneMichel, Waacstats, Weetoddid, WereSpielChequers, White Ash, White Shadows, WikiSpector, XESR, XMirandaxCosgrove, Yaddayadda199, 772 anonymous edits

Figure It Out *Source*: http://en.wikipedia.org/w/index.php?oldid=537256872 *Contributors*: 52 Pickup, AZZLES, AdamDeanHall, Alexandria, Amaury, Anchorage, Anir1uph, Aoi, Arctic sunrise, Arjun01, AussieLegend, AxelBoldt, Azumanga1, Azure Haights, BJSelavka, Bearcat, Beau+Lobo, Benje309, Bennyandthejets95405, Betacommand, Bfern8788, Bgwhite, Biggspowd, BizarreLoveTriangle, Bl1222, Blubberboy92, Bnoble, BornonJune8, BoxerMan21, Brandon J. Marcellus, Brianhenke, Bww11bww11, CRRaysHead90, Caldorwards4, Caleson, CambridgeBayWeather, Chensiyuan, Chessphoon, CoolKid1993, Cos2x, CowboySpartan, Crazy81, DaBomb619, Daniel Benfield, DawgDeputy, Ddespie@san.rr.com, Digifan23, Digifiend, DiseaseAction5844, Doinelita, Douglasr007, Dputig07, DrLove0378, ESkog, EmryMaxwell, EvanFinney08, EvanOVen1325, Evercat, Fan-1967, Fiction Alchemist, Fightinirsih6911, Flamingwuzzle23, FromtheWordsofBR, Futuremoviewriter, Gaius Cornelius, Geopgeop, Geraldo Perez, Goldrushcavi, HairMetalLives, Harmony944, Hehehedoughnuts, Hmains, Holiday56,

Holly423, Hraefen, IJVin, ISeeYou, Im.a.lumberjack, Indigochronicles15, JL93, JM3mupp77, JMyrleFuller, Jeffq, Jim1138, Jippiisfriends, Jivee Blau, John of Reading, Johndburger, Jonjoe, Jrh5487, Justme89, K1Bond007, Kennster2012, King of Hearts, Kitch, Knowledgeman800, Kyle2day, L1ght.St0rm12, Lazynitwit, Lbmouschi, Logoboy95forever, Lots42, Luk, Magioladitis, Majorclanger, Marysunshine, Matt3austin, Matteh, MegastarLV, Mglyl, Miamiguy06, Modor, MrNobody97, MrWii000, NJChristian07, NawlinWiki, Nerrawllehctim, Nevermore27, Nicklegends, Ninjawarriordex, No Guru, Nyttend, Ost316, Otto4711, OwenX, PAK Man, Patchy417, Pinkadelica, Pipedreamz, Quadell, QuasyBoy, RJaguar3, Raderick, Radioflyer989, Rainbowsunshine86, Red Director, Redskull619, RenamedUser01302013, Rich Farmbrough, RobJ1981, Rockchalk717, Rugratsmaster, Rzhm, Sb1990, Ser Amantio di Nicolao, Silentaria, Simpsons2010, Sjones23, Slysplace, Soapfan2013, Sofa jazz man, Somethingvacant, Songwriter693, StAnselm, Steakisgreat, Steam5, TMC1982, Tarheel95, Tartarus, Tazz765, Th1rt3en, The stuart, TheNewPhobia, Thebeatlesanthol, Tigerghost, Tinton5, Tnxman307, Toffile, TomCat4680, Tomballguy, Tregoweth, Trident, Trotter, Troves, Ttc817, Tvtonightokc, Uno11890, Vgmddg, Vidpro23, VmKid, Vwspeedracer, Wakamont77, Weatherman87, WereWolf, Whatever318, Wheeler0152, Wikialexdx, Wikieditor1988, Wrestla1967, Yankeesrj12, Yugiohfan2010, 736 anonymous edits

Freak the Freak Out *Source*: http://en.wikipedia.org/w/index.php?oldid=536190228 *Contributors*: 101cantbetamed101, Active Banana, Arjoccolenty, Ashlandchemist, Bubbleoui, C.Fred, Christopher10006, Confession0791, Danny2455, Dobie80, Easy4me, Enchantedtomeetu, EoGuy, FromtheWordsofBR, Gersende, Grafen, Iknow23, Impala99, Joefromrandb, Katydidit, Krispy1995, Maraqua22, Nthep, Ozkithar Salas, Ravensteeler, Richhoncho, Silvergoat, SummerPhD, SupremoJunior, Tbhotch, Tinton5, TyA, Usb10, VictoriaJusticeFan, VictoriaJusticeFan1, WikHead, Wikipedian Penguin, Woohookitty, 90 anonymous edits

Graham Phillips (actor) *Source*: http://en.wikipedia.org/w/index.php?oldid=535750822 *Contributors*: 2help, Aitias, All Hallow's Wraith, AnnBLea, Anonymous9498, Apennyintherain, BillyElliotGirl, Borgx, Brainiack16, Bunnyhop11, CWii, CambridgeBayWeather, CandyStrawberry, Cmcmaha, CommonsDelinker, Corvus cornix, Crakkerjakk, Crystallina, Cst17, DMacks, Daniel Simandoev, Deor, DerHexer, Dgw, Dimadick, Don-Don, Dottie166, Dusti, EagleKnowledge13, Eamaral, El Mayimbe, Hdmayer, Holy Squab, Hooligan101, Hyuuga-sama, JOGDH, Jim1138, Jusses2, Kevinbrogers, Khvalamde, Kiwidude, Koavf, Kollision, Kukini, Leofric1, LethalReflex, Logic78, Logical Fuzz, Mackenzie10, Magioladitis, Mandarax, Mickea, Monegasque, Msqtbrunette05, Nightscream, Nimbley79, Nomnomnomnom1234, Paste, Paul A, Piinkandgreen12, Polly, RafikiSykes, ReggieMDD, Rms125a@hotmail.com, Rodrigo-kun, Ronnylove77, Roscelese, RxS, SMC, SamuelJamesAran, SchuminWeb, The Rogue Penguin, ThePidge001, Theleftorium, Thue, UltimatePyro, Vanished User 8a9b4725f8376, Victory-Pandora, WOSlinker, WereSpielChequers, Widr, Wildhartlivie, Xnalaliex, YUL89YYZ, Zone of 3D, 240 anonymous edits

Greyson Chance *Source*: http://en.wikipedia.org/w/index.php?oldid=536833011 *Contributors*: 3centsoap, 5 albert square, ATC, Abdullah8m, Abutorsam007, AhaaNoClue, Airplaneman, Ajmilner, Alarics, Aldo samulo, Alexagummie, Alexandre8, Alexmaxbir, All Hallow's Wraith, AngelusCZ, Anna Lincoln, Arwel Parry, Asidelobby, Athumbup, AugustinMa, Avoided, AznBurger, Babyhands21, Basketballdoo8, Bassetta, Beateorchid, Bencey, Bender235, Biber gay, Blue Marble, Boing! said Zebedee, Bongwarrior, Brittflick 1994, Brookebiebergurrl, Bubbleoui, C.Fred, CT Cooper, CTF83!, CanadianLinuxUser, CasperGoodwood, Celticfan383, Cgweeks, Chance97, Cheetah531, Cherryx3, Chris TC01, Christina Silverman, Chuckadams13, Churaru, Ckyrico, Claireordz, Clayzie, CommonsDelinker, CopperSquare, Corvus cornix, Courcelles, Cresix, Csh 100, Cutie412, DVdm, Dabomb87, Daniroxbig, Dapopewarrior, Deckiller, DeltaQuad, Denniss, Discospinster, Dougofborg, Download, Downs23, Dplcrnj, Dreaded Walrus, Drmies, Drone5, Eberhard im Thurn-zu-Büsingen, Ed g2s, Edenc1, Edgar181, Edo.raven, Elapied, Elassint, Eleanorsbarker, Ella Zee, Emmarosedavis, EnDaLeCoMpLeX, Eustacia42, Exemption4, F!ERCE, Falcon8765, Fekenator, Fetchcomms, Feudonym, Firsfron, Floquenbeam, Funandtrvl, Fæ, Gjbloom, Gongshow, Goth67, Grim Littlez, HJ Mitchell, Hannahnicholle, Hazel77, Hearfourmewesique, Hmains, Holiday56, Hoo man, I'MSKYHiGH, IGeMiNix, ITshnik, Iamonthecomputer, Iamthecheese44, Iforgotwatitis, Ikramgreat7794, Ilovejustin16, Inka 888, Inspiredimage, IronGargoyle, Ivowilliams, JForget, JKaizer, JV Smithy, JamesBWatson, Jeff3000, Jessicawijayaaa, Jmonkey1308, Jodimadonia, Jordan Chuck, Jordanxaivierjohnson13, Joshua Scott, Jpittman, Jrfoldes, Justcallmekim, K10wnsta, Karenjc, Katiashtisdale, KenJenningsJeopardy74, Kerrick Staley, Kevinmon, King Louie of Austin, Kink 27909, Koavf, Krashlandon, Kwiki, L Kensington, Lalala99hgv, Lawrence123098, LcawteHuggle, Leaflets77, LeeinFLA, Lillinonah, Lorenlott9, Lovexaddict, MJ94, MWielage, Magioladitis, Mar745, Maraqua22, MarcusKelley, Mariia95, MarioAlfredo247, Materialscientist, Matthewedwards, Mazca, Mbch331, Memorex97, Mickeymouse1234, Minimac, Mmason930, Morenooso, Mystichak, NGMan62, Nbmbabz, NellieBly, Nimakha, Ninjawarriordex, Nitromatt1, Nxgonzales, Oakshade, Ocdman, Olijven, Ozlen555, Ozzieboy, Paparazzo Presents, Patrick Batman, Pax85, Pc1878, Pdcook, Peter Chastain, Philip Trueman, Pinethicket, Poco a poco, Pontificalibus, Pswiney, Radagast3, Rafikirby, Randymaurer, Reach Out to the Truth, Redfan45x, Redsox42311, Refinnejann, Rickyhillhouse, Rjwilmsi, Robintraveler, Robodoggy, RodeoDriver, Room103, Rqaw, Ruatdika Sailo, Rubén Mendoza, Sabri76, Salvio giuliano, ScottMHoward, ScottSteiner, Seaphoto, Ser Amantio di Nicolao, Sergay, Shadowjams, Shahineft, Silberštejn, Silvergoat, SoCalSuperEagle, Soap, Someone963852, Sparrkliiwarriorstarr, SpencerParrish, SpigotMap, StarlightAssassin, Status, Stifle, Stroppolo, SummerPhD, Surfininsf, Sven Manguard, SweetArberlesque, TFOWR, TGBX, Tandelt, Tanweer Morshed, Taqy33, TheBestVampireDiaries, TheRemnantKid, Theda, Thedeweyfrost, Theenglishway88, Theleftorium, Therealdavo2, Tide rolls, Tinton5, TiraSadiyah, Tommy2010, Uncle Dick, Uncle Milty, Vision14k, Wayne Slam, WereWolf, Werldwayd, White Shadows, WikHead, Wikifan502, Wiwaxia, Wkharrisjr, Woohookitty, XLiveOnDramax, XXMallory13XX, Xenon54, Xoxloverbearxox, XxHeyxXYoxX, Yuoiuysdh, Yusuf Hamzah Anwar, Yvesnimmo, Zac zac03, Zhernovoi, Zidonuke, Zmfltmxlsk, マティ男, 897 anonymous edits

iCarly *Source*: http://en.wikipedia.org/w/index.php?oldid=537561893 *Contributors*: .marc., 0dd1, 190fordhouse, 21655, 22dragon22burn, 22pandrew, 2D, 2tuntony, 3193th, 3jz01bcs, 729JULsparks, 744cody, 7OA, A3RO, ABC1356msep1, ABF, AMK152, ANTMantm, ATC, AVand, Aadilio77, Aaroncortezislame, Aaronkavo, Abcdefghijklmnopqrstuvwxyz10000, Ace of spade114, Acebloo, Acroterion, Acsmappel, Adambadger, Adamthenesgamer, Adcamper92, Addshore, Addyjuly, Ageekgal, AgentPeppermint, Agiorgio, Ahoerstemeier, Aidepikiw07, Airplaneman, Aitias, Akohler, AlRankin, Alan4753, Alansohn, Alec2011, Alex.muller, Alex43223, Alexherrera663, Alexius08, AlixMystical, Allstarecho, Alpha565, Alphius, Altone, Alucard 16, Alxeedo, Amack987, Amanedachi, Amaury, Amcfarlanee, Amdrag568, AmericaIsNumberOne, Amstaton, Amy50632, AnNeLuVr692, Anabus, Anant kamath, Andadundi, Andonic, Andrei.smolnikov, Andrew3054, AndrewAllen15, Andrewrox, AnemoneProjectors, Anesleyp, Angie Y., Angnation, Animum, AnmaFinotera, AnonMoos, AnotherSolipsist, Anthonydyer84, Anyo O, Aoi, Apple1013, Applgeek, Arathun, Ardavu, Arjayay, Armiris, Arogi Ho, Artisol2345, Asenine, AshTFrankFurter2, Ashleyleggat404, Ashleyy osaurus, AsianJanitor, Astros4477, Atd101, AudiR85.2V10, Aunteileen123, Auntof6, AussieLegend, Autoerrant, Avnjay, Awesomeomar, Ayojessie, Azraen, Azumanga1, BR9000, BRG 12, Baa, Backslash Forwardslash, Baileymom2, Bamelephant4, Banana54321, Barneystimpleton, Baseball Fanatic, Baseball Watcher, Basilisk4u, Bat McStar, Batkwak, Battye, Bby11us, Bearcat, Beausalant, Beeblebrox, Beetleborg, Belovedfreak, Bender235, Bep dude1993, Berkunt, Bff101, Bgnkid, Bhall87, Bigbob222, Bigddan11, Bigkhrisdogg, Bility, Billcarey4, Billysuite, Biscuitgirl, Black Yoshi, Blackflyingbats, Blackrose10122, Blake-, Blakecotton, Blanchardb, BluejacketT, Bob987654333, Bobbyzilla, Bobo The Ninja, Bobo192, Bogey97, Boisfilm115, Bongwarrior, Bonusballs, Boo1210, Boogster, Bovineboy2008, Bow-bb, BoxerMan21, Bradysean512, Brambleberry of RiverClan, Brandizzo, BredcaykZ, BriMaster2000, Brian Everlasting, Brianlucas, Bridgetfox, Brittany Ka, Brooklynmw, Bryans-games, Bryantmaquito, BsaPR1996, Bsadowski1, Bubby00000, Bug95, Bulldog73, Butterscotch, ByTheAbyss, C.Fred, CAPRAFILMS, CL, CRRaysHead90, CTF83!, CWii, CaRaNt11, Cacrop, Caknuck, CalSci103, Caldorwards4, Calm123, Calvin 1998, CambridgeBayWeather, CanadianLinuxUser, Candy coated doom, Canuck01, Caponer, Capricorn42, Capt Cajun, Captain Infinity, Captain panda, Captin Shmit, Carlosar45, Carlover08, Carlywg, Carnotaurus044, Carrie2002, Carriefan699, Cartmanatee73, Caster23, Catgut, Cattile, Cbb313, Ccrashh, Ceauntay31, Ceauntay32, Ceauntay46, Celsey05, ChHP211, ChadDylanCooper, Chamal N, Chammack12, Chander Jagtiani, Chantessy, Charitwo, CharlotteWebb, Charvel67, Chatocat55, Checker Fred, Cheesyperson1995, CheezNapkin, Chefmovie, Chibiheart, Chikinpotato11, Chm394, Chris9086, ChrisScorsese88, Chrisisreed, Christianity922, Cinema City Romania, Cinemaniac, Cjesmerio, Ckash, Ckatz, ClapBoy380, Classickrocker, Classicrockfan42, Clerks, Clfan91, Clinity Kane, Closedmouth, Cloverboy19, Cmd11200, CoJaBo, Cole2, Colonies Chris, Cometstyles, Commander Lightning, CommonsDelinker, Computer97, ConCompS, Confession0791, Connorma77, Connorzd, Cookie10114, Cookie81927, CoolZoog, Coolcatevan9, Coolio1996, Coolioride, Cooljason1, Coral Bay, Corpx, Corruptcopper, Corvoe, Corvus cornix, Cory Malik, Cosmo16h12, Cperea1994, Crakkerjakk, Crash Underride, Craziechix01, Crazy4mud, CrazyApple1998, CrazyKid24, CrazyLegsKC, Crazyboy279, Crazyjoe30, Creativity97, Cremepuff222, Crimsonseiko, Csigabi, Cuddly Panda, Cupcakecutie960, Cute34, Cutie546, Cuzuba, Cyrillic, Cyster, Czolgolz, D, DCEdwards1966, DJ WikiBob, DJ1F, DJBullfish, DSFanatic, Dabby, Daisyrose111, Damonluemaxwell97, Dan729, DanTD, DanielAguilar, Danielesteban12, Danieljo2013, Danigro89, Dantheman531, Darth Panda, Darthleroy, Das Ansehnlisch, Davecrosby uk, Davewild, David in DC, Davonte56, DeadEyeArrow, DeannaxTeresa, DeathNomad, Deathlive2, Decibert, Dee6, Deedeedee Steven, Defender Of Justice, Defjam445, DegrassiFreak, Dekisugi, Delcity, Demi818, Dennis55789, Deoxys911, DerHexer, Derekjwhitehead, Devin54321, Df747jet, Dguy3000, Dgw, DiffyFan1, Dimondlover222, DingoateMyBabyyy, Discospinster, Disney avatar, Disneycrules, Disneyfreak96, Disneylove101, Dispenser, Djpez888, Dmdrox!, Doctoroxenbriery, Doglove19, Doman12, Domthedude001, Don-Don, Dontforgetthisone, Doomed Rasher, Dopey9928, Dorftrottel, Dougofborg, Download, Doy-doy people, Dr.drathod, DrFrench, DrWhoJake11, Dragon1027, Dragonex, DrakeBellRocksHard, Dreadstar, DreamStar05, Dreamanderson, DreamsBeginHere, Drmies, DrugFree79, Drumnstas, Dudejerome, Dudesleeper, Duque Santiago, Dusti, Dvpdvp1, Dylan620, Dylan6758, DylanGLC2011, Dylancraigboyes, Dysepsion, E and b, E-man615, ESkog, Eamonster, Easy12345, Easy4me, Eatarock123, Ebe123, Edgars2007, Editfriendly22, Editor2020, Editor510, EditorE, Edokter, Eduardo Sellan III, Eggmanrule, Ejfetters, Ekimberly259, Elephant Talk, Eleventhblock, Elf Taki Taki, Elio97, Elipongo, Elizabeth2345, Elkman, Elvin0420, Emanuebug, Emkat97, Empezardesdecero1718, Enrichyourmind, Enviroboy, Epbr123, Epp, Eric 2 cool77, Eric-Wester, EricCan, Erik the Red 2, Erik9, Erwin, EternalMemory, Eubulides, EvanFinney08, EvanFinney10, Evilmaster23, Explicit, Extremeguy, Eyreland, FaerieInGrey, Faith14la, Faithlessthewonderboy, Falcon8765, Fallen2230, FamFragoso, FamFragoso42, Fastily, Fetchfan88, Fetofs, Ffaadstrbdetete, Ffeifanc, Ffion9, Fieldday-sunday, Fierylemons, Finavon, Finman12, Fishboy 95, Fishmech, Fl, Fladoodle, Flags12345, Fleela, Flewis, Floppyman, Flyby1300, Fn06afranci, For An Angel, Fourthords, Fourviz, Foxhound66, Foxj, Fredgamer5000, Frehley, Freshbakedpie, FreshieSandhu, Frozenevolution, Fuddle, FunPika, Funk1998, Funnybunny44, GLaDOS996, GSK, GVOLTT, GXlighter, Gabester123987, Gaia Octavia Agrippa, Gail, GaryCalcagno, Gazimoff, Geaugagrrl, Geekboy6, Geekrocket, GeisterXfahrer, GeorgeLouis, Geraldo Perez, Gertie1999, Giant89, Gilliam, Gimmetrow, Ginger14, Glane23, Gman1945, Gogo Dodo, Gogo1236665, GoingBatty, GoldFlower, GoodNintendo, Googamp32, Gordan3194, Grashoofd, Greek2, Green Beret 625, GreenBayPackersfan09, Greenleaf547, Greswik, Grooviemania, Groudon199, Gruselfratze, Gunmetal Angel, Gunnar100, Gurch, Guy1423, Gwall49, Gwall77, Gwernol, Gymnasticsmad68, H, H2g2 gabe, HN45, Hadger, Haha169, Haley Lynn, HalfShadow, Hallpriest9, HannahMiley, Hannahfan204, Hannj004, Harmony944, Harold.k.rogers, HayleyMuzik12, Heaven's Army, Heegoop, Heimstern, Heliac, Helland, Helmoony, HexaChord, Hi cool1, Higgins69, Hintss, Hobartimus, Hojmatt, HolmesSPH, Homer saves presidents, Honey Bee Real, Hoppybunny, HorseGirl070605, HouseboatingAsItRocks, Howieandkeyshia, Huchimama, Hueverto, Hughcharlesparker, Hullaballoo Wolfowitz, Hydrogen Iodide, Hyperhippy92, ICarly fan 10, ICarly0246, ICarlytranslator, IFence902, II MusLiM HyBRiD II, IJVin, ILoVeJaCoBbLaCk, IMatthew, IRP, Iamastalker500, Iamcool023, Iamcool234, Ianjones50, Icairns, Icarly and all that rock, Icarlyfan, Icarlyfan01, IceUnshattered, Iceman247, Icep, Ididitmanytimes, Idol 2006, Igoldste, Ihk221, Il223334234, Ilovehi, Ilovepandiebear, Impala99, Imperial Star Destroyer, IndulgentReader, Inferno, Lord of Penguins, Intelati, Iridescent, Irish Souffle, Irishguy, Irishoney13, Iroc24, Irrypride, It Is Me Here, Ivan Eduardo Cuenca, Ivanbeley, J Milburn, J.delanoy, JBK405, JForget, JGossard, JJJ123456789, JNW, JPG-GR, JPINFV, Jabrona, Jacarabeo, JaciFan, JackGuy111, Jackdyson, Jackfork, Jackwillyb, Jacob Koopa, Jafe, Jairo82798, Jakezing, James26, JamesBWatson, Jamesbanesmith, Jammy0002, Janamariepetrosini, Jandbadbay, Japanmovement, Jarkeld, Jason.cinema, JasonXL-V2, Jasonboy678, Jasslyn, Jauerback, Jaxonchikk32, Jay-r101, Jay2009m, Jay2020, Jazzy910, Jclemens, Jcub52, Jdawg97, Jdog9999,

Jedichowder, Jeff G., Jeffq, Jeffrey1992, Jeffreygi, Jeneral28, Jennavecia, Jfarajr, Jim1138, Jimarey, Jina44, Jingle38, Jippiisfriends, Jivecat, Jj137, Jj98, Jjrules08, Jl12w3rrrl8, Jmundo, Jmuppeton, Joedeshon, Joekid23334, Joel macey, Joes a g, Joey Tomson, Joeyandmike, Johnbrechtel17, Johnnywalterboy, Joker Prowess, Jonapello22, Jonathan Harold Koszeghi, Jonathan321, Jonathanjoseph81, Jonc1996, Jonesian900, Jordao095, Josborne2382, Joshua Issac, Joshwim8, Jpharaoh, Jtmt88, Juggler821, Juliancolton, Jungle Thunder, Justinhful, Justme89, K10wnsta, KCSykes, KH1MOVIE, Kaityface, Kalliequeen, Kaponikendo, KariGhso, Karlsolsom, KathrynLybarger, Katydidit, Kball65, Keegan, Keilana, KeltieMartinFan, Kennzoil, Kenyonhero, Kevin2008000, Kevinbrogers, Kevinkid2008, Kgman6, KickAssElite, Kickme1138, Kidlittle, Kidme2, Kildareuser, King of Hearts, King of the Court, KingJFS, KingMorpheus, Kiseki Megami, KittyKo'sCute, Kjinho213, Kking 37, Kletta, KlingonWarrior09, KnowledgeOfSelf, Koavf, Koman90, KoopaCooper, Kurt10, Kuru, Kwil 82, Kww, Kylexy289, L337p4wn, LAUGH90, LAX, LGBLA, LOL, La Pianista, Lady Aleena, Ladyoftrees, Lakeshow13, Lalanie, Landfish7, Lanipearson, Larry Yuma, Larrymcp, Lbrun12415, Leagreen, LeaveSleaves, Leer5454, Legakis, Legoktm, Legoman64, Leila37, Leonard^Bloom, Levodevo, Lewis odane, Likelife, Lilmissrom, Limideen, Limited2fan, LinkSlayer64, LinkToddMcLovinMontana, Liquidluck, Lisa mynx, Little Mountain 5, LittleMan7, Ljb999, Llamadog903, Logan, LokspiritRattle, Lola099, Lonelywheel, Lorraine2721, LostDesmond, LostIntheCityLights, Lotje, Lovebeinchristian120, Lozeldafan, Lt.Kamakaze, Lucas Carranza, Luigifan13, Luisrafael7, Luna Santin, Luvatomi, Lv702, MAN MUSIC, MASQUERAID, MJBurrage, MSHunters, MTVRecorder, MZMcBride, Mack-the-random, Macy, Maddie!, Majin Xezeveir, Majorly, Malcolmxl5, Mandinga, Mandy443, Marcpat1234, Marek69, Marino13, MarixD, Martial75, Martin451, Maryland13, Mastrchf91, Mateo4life, MattieTK, Mattjsrules, Mattokunhayashi, Mattspac, Maxi-media006, Maxis ftw, Maybelle910, McSly, Mcanmoocanu, Mdog13, Me235789065, Meatwod, Meatwood, MegaBasketball03, MegastarLV, Melsaran, Mendaliv, Mentifisto, Merandom, Message From Xenu, Mfrisk, Mg14, Mianghuei, Michaelsbll, Microchip08, Mifter, Mikeifc123, Mikokat, Mileycyrussoulja, Mileyfan222, MimeAdam33, MindstormsKid, Minnesotatwins15, MissyMusic13, Mjbmr, Mk786123, Moanna, Mogism, Mokoniki, Moneymaka21, Monkey32, Monkeys 9711, Monkeyv, Monsterboyroc, Montana's Defender, Moocha, Moocowsrock, Morbeen4444, Morgan York, Mr Unsmiley, Mr. Chicago, Mr. Comedian, Mr. Prez, Mr305worldwide, Mrobamakid, Mrquizzical, Mrschimpf, Mrstonky, Mrules4ever, MsGrizabella, Mspraveen, Muna56, Muppet171, Muppet321, Muppetmasterdc, Musicalmelody, Musicalmelodygirl, MuzikJunky, Myasuda, Mygerardromance, Myra Banks, Mythdon, Myzou, NHRHS2010, NJChristian07, Nana's world, Nari50, Narnia2514, Narsissus, NarutoD444, Nascar1996, Nat682, Natcar112, Natejt08c254, Nato101, Natrat1109, Navy Blue, NawlinWiki, Ncsm4evr, Nealmcb, Neirgb818, Nelliebellie, Nelson2510, Nerdygeek101, Nescio, NetflixSoup, Next-Genn-Gamer, NickPlaya, Nickapo1208, Nickdude45, NickelodeonFan, Nicktoonspl15, Nicktrop, Night Fight, Nmcorp, Nn123645, Noahcs, Nooby101, Noozgroop, NotYouHaha, Notshane, NrDg, NuclearWarfare, Numpty454, Nunquam Dormio, Nxaxtxox, OOODDD, Oanabay04, Obaidz96, ObamaSupporter2, Oceanbeach14, Ohconfucius, Oldspongebob101, OllieFury, Omgdog, Oncesitio889, OneWeirdDude, Ophois, Optimusderf, Orannis, Orphana, Ospinad, Ost316, Ouseraquenao, OverlordQ, Oxfordwang, Oxymoron83, Ozkithar Salas, PMDrive1061, Pablo323, Pakaru, Pantsaklanos, Paper Luigi, Paranomia, Park Crawler, Party, Paul August, PaulPadfield66, Paycheckgurl, Pbroks13, Pdyo, Peaceandjam, Peacerocker12, Peoeagle, Percivl, Peter Deer, PeterSymonds, Phantomevilkingepros, Pharaoh of the Wizards, PhilKnight, Philip Trueman, Piano non troppo, Piazzajordan2, Piblup, Pic Editor960, Pierceybrian23, Pieterhknick, Pikalax, PinkCrustaceanKid, Pip2andahalf, PizzaIceCreamCandyCake1, Planetxdude, Playking616, Pleasant1623, Plong26, Pntjr, PocketRebel, Poison the Well, PokerJoker811, Polarbear97, Polynomial123, Poojapac, Poppa Yami, Possum, Prashanthns, Prcc27, PrestonLong, Princess24163, Printer222, Proofreader77, Pseudomonas, Purple123x, PwilliamQ99, Pwilmot11, Qantasplanes, Qaroberts1995, QuasyBoy, R'n'B, R2D2!, RS485, Radon210, Rafaelsilveira, RaiderTarheel, Raimundo255, RandomXYZb, Randy Jaiyan, Raven23, Razorflame, Rdjere, Realm of Shadows, RedKiteUK, RedRose333, Redskinsdc, Redvers, Redwingsdan, Reedy, Refresh100, Regemet, RegentsPark, Remolaca45, Renojake12, RescueRanger702, Respectthevette, Retro dog, RexNL, Rfsilveira, Rhatsa26X, Rhopkins8, Rich Farmbrough, Richardhuff, Richdiesal, Richmwill, Rigid11494, Ringpop7, RisaPlayer88, RkOrton, Rkofan1993, RobRob94, RobertG, Robertwilkins, Robzthird, Rokcorbust, Ron Ritzman, Rookiez, Rooster13, Ross CJ, Royalsfan121314, Rror, Rtkat3, Rtucker913, Rudolfocortez, Ruffmanfan88, Rumping, Runefrost, RussellAN, Rx4evr, Ry Mac and RJ, Ryan032, RyanCross, Ryguy611, Ryūkotsusei, S3000, SMC, SRASC, Sagittarius95, Sahmeditor, SailorStarFighter, Sakrileg, Salavat, Sami50421, Sandiahead, Sandri, Sangam, Sarapaxtonmusic, Sashpesoj, Saylaveer, Sbrools, Scarian, Sceptre, SchfiftyThree, Scoops, ScottMHoward, ScottyBerg, SearcherAlex, Seattlecinnamongirl, Segafan01, SelenaMusic14, Senator Palpatine, Ser Amantio di Nicolao, Serienfan2010, Seth234, Shadi Potter, ShadowAssassain, ShadowMark-182, Shakeitcecerocky, Shalom Yechiel, Shanefb, Sharkface217, Sharpay Evans, Shawnnicholsonca, ShiningStorm, Shoeofdeath, SidP, Siderz, Signalhead, Silvergoat, Silverknight2113, Silvermoonx, Simon43211, SimonKSK, Simpsons2010, Sionus, Skater, Skulduggery3, Sliem16, Slorange99, Slrkn54, Slyfence, Slysplace, Smartyjeff, Smash, Smashville, Smokizzy, Smurdah, SoWhy, Sohollywood, Soliloquial, Solimoli262, Songwriter693, Sonic100jam, SonicX000000, Soren121, Sparksdontflyup, Spartan, Spears154, Spellcast, Spencer, Split, Sponge8485, SpongeSebastian, Spongesonic277, Sponyge, Sportygirl99, Spottedfeather, Sprite7868, Spyrolivia, Squintin6, Sqwertso, Staffwaterboy, Starsking, StaticGull, StayTunedForDanger134, Steam5, Stephancho96, Stephen85442, Stepshep, Steven Zhang, Stevenghetto257, Stick Figures On Crack, Stolya, Stormbay, Storms15, Strikers5, Subash.chandran007, Sufi34745, Sugarcream, Suiteman, SummerPhD, Sunshineisles2, Super-Magician, Super1092, Superjustinbros., Supermanrulescom, Supermoose101, Superx, Surachit, Susan Capetinga, Swantonbomb444 v1, Sweetest in famliy, Swim33, SympatheticIsolation, THEN WHO WAS PHONE?, THOMASNATOR, TMeyer88, TPIRFanSteve, TRLIJC18, TRLIJC19, TTN, Tabletop, Tae1988, Tajtheman, Taker23456, Talkingbirds, Tamiluvsdanci4, Tardnozzle, Tare44, Tarheel95, Tascha96, Taspozi, Tbhotch, Tckma, Tcncv, Techman224, Teh tennisman, Terrysorange, ThatOneChick87, Thayts, Thdoy2, The R, The Arachnid, The Cool Kat, The Evil Spartan, The Lovable Wolf, The Master of disguises, The Moose, The Obento Musubi, The Rogue Penguin, The Shadow-Fighter, The Wiki Octopus, TheAD1000, TheAnnoying1, TheDiarrheaMan, TheGunn, TheLoverofLove, TheMasterOfAllThingsWiki, TheMightyOrb, TheNewPhobia, TheOtherEgo, TheSuave, TheTVGuy, Theaura, Thedjatclubrock, Thefreakshow, Thefroggiechick, Theleftorium, Theonlynubrox, Theperiodictable, TherealJHONNY, Theryguy512, Theusualroute, Thewhitestripes985985, Thewtfchronicles, Thingg, ThinkBlue, This is Drew, Thomasfan501, Thomasfan5034, Thomasfan5044, Tiddly Tom, Tide rolls, Tikketdev, Timelordlilytennant, Tinton5, Tiptoety, TobyMac35, Toko98, Tokufan, Tombomp, Tomgibbons, Tommy0987, Tommy2010, Tommycrossover, Tonmad, Tony Feld, Tony Fox, Tony1, Tony234567892, Totie, Toughdude, Tpbradbury, TracyLinkEdnaVelmaPenny, Transity, TreoBoy680, Treybien, Triona, Triwbe, Truth247, Truthman14, Truu, Tschow, Tslocum, Tubesurfer, Tucson Arizona Mexico, Tulloch100, Tune juice, Tuxthepenguin933, Tvfreak1, Tvfreak204, Tvstrela, Tvtonightokc, Twaz, Twsx, Uiopklu, Ukexpat, UltimatePyro, Ultraviolet scissor flame, Unreal7, Urkel87, Utcursch, VJ13A, VP44444, ValiantRed600, Vandalizrr4life, Vanilla2, Vanillaman133, Vanished User 8a9b4725f8376, Vanished user 342562, Vanished user sfijw8jh4tjkefs, Vector Potential, Vegaswikian, Veluz330, VeronicaGirl, Versus22, Victorirupp, Vidpro23, Vietxhotgurl, Vincelord, Viper8754, Vishnava, Vivio Testarossa, Vortimaxx, WAVY 10 Fan, WJBscribe, WP Editor 2012, Wack'd, Wackywace, WadeSimMiser, Wafulz, Waggers, Walmwutter, Wamke4, Warregubbi, WeatherBoyWheeler, Webclient101, Weirdy, WereSpielChequers, Weremyjiggins, Westvoja, WhatGuy, Whatever318, Whathevideos, Whiteobama, WiHkibew, WikiMaster500, Wikialexdx, Wikiims, Wikijack847, Wikipedian192, WikipedianMarlith, Wikiweb.09, Wildcat1, Windows.dll, Windows72106, Wingssong, Wjejskenewr, Wkiwikimonster, Woohookitty, Worldstopeditor, Wren Valmont, Write123567, Wyatt915, XDmegaDude, Xaudioxmaniacx, Xbox18000, XenonX3, Xizer, XoXoGossipGirlXoXo, Xokelsokiddox, XxTimberlakexx, Xymmax, YEAHWIN, YUL89YYZ, Yamla, Young V.I.P, ZSoraz, Zabuza0030, ZacTroyLink, Zacgrl1994, Zachary115, Zachb2008, Zaeriuraschi, Zapper 360, Zellfaze, Zidane tribal, Zidonuke, Zii XFS, Zoeyfan101, ZooFari, Zoomanj, Zordon123456789mlw7, Zordon56, Zzguitar14, Zzuuzz, Τις, Ό οἶστρος, 4662 anonymous edits

iParty with Victorious *Source*: http://en.wikipedia.org/w/index.php?oldid=537444256 *Contributors*: 17.ROCO, A520, ABC1356msep1, Akarkera, AlRankin, Aristotle159357, Arjayay, Aspects, Atomician, Awesome444a444, BabyGirl91, Bastian 1929, Bearcat, Beardo, Ben Ben, Bonusballs, Canuckian89, Christopher10006, Chucky30, CityOfSilver, Cleo20, Crash Underride, DJ0215997, DisneyTV2012, DisneyTvNickelodeon, Djtechno95, Dragon1027, Dupewrest, DylanGLC2011, E-man615, Easy4me, Elektrik Band, Epopnidla, Evan615, Fixerupper3000, Fluffernutter, Foxhound66, FromtheWordsofBR, FugaDeAmor, Fylbecatulous, GGFFDDJJKKUU, Gavin.perch, Geraldo Perez, Gkpdjkhg, Grafen, Hallows AG, HannahMiley, Harmony944, HazelEyedKiki, Henryjake121, Hueverto, Hullaballoo Wolfowitz, IFence902, Iknow23, In the shining light, JGossard, JJJ123456789, Jabrona, Jamielynnfan, Jim1138, John of Reading, JosephGoh, Jrvboricua, Juandy004, Katydidit, Kayc9619, Kevinbrogers, KittyKo'sCute, Klilidiplomus, LABS4EVER, LAUGH90, LaloCh, Lalucho Chavarría, Larissa.Chilton, Leer5454, Leles53266, Lewis odane, Logan, Logface5, Maraqua22, Mark Arsten, Materialscientist, Matheus Camcho, Matheus Rodrigues, MeaningOfLife, Mgiganteus1, MikeyMouse10, Millahnna, Muppet321, Musiclover66, Noformation, Notshane, Paine Ellsworth, Pantsaklan, Pantsaklanos, Penguincw, Philg88, Pkfjk, PpeRuiiz, Ptsaklan, QuasyBoy, R'n'B, RHaworth, RadioFan, Ratemonth, Reaper Eternal, Rhatsa26X, Roambassador, Ryanteoh, SM64DSi, Samkletz, Seaphoto, Silvergoat, Simpsons2010, Some jerk on the Internet, Spencer, Spongerupp, Stephanie J Stone, SummerPhD, Sven Manguard, Tae1988, Tbhotch, The Shadow-Fighter, Thine Antique Pen, Tinton5, Ulric1313, Unreal7, Vanished user sfijw8jh4tjkefs, Versegirolanddsdsf, Victorirupp, Vincelord, WKZH4B, WP Editor 2012, WhatGuy, WikiEditor44, WikiMaster500, Wikipelli, Windchaser, 641 anonymous edits

Kool Kojak *Source*: http://en.wikipedia.org/w/index.php?oldid=534913630 *Contributors*: 85Records, AAMediaInc, Al Bombz, Anbu121, Avicennasis, BD2412, Bdwick, Bender235, Blindprwriter, Colbyguarino, Diamondsunderfire, Gorx9395, H2a0t4, ISLANDDJ, Jeff G., John of Reading, KoolKojak, Koumz, Logan, Mattaam, Mcpcp, Mekinas, Minimousedance, N5iln, PancakeMistake, Percxyz, ShelfSkewed, Some jerk on the Internet, WikHead, WillWalker23, Woohookitty, 132 anonymous edits

Last Dance (song) *Source*: http://en.wikipedia.org/w/index.php?oldid=535655022 *Contributors*: Ampdj, Benuliak, Brianhenke, BrothaTimothy, Carlossfsu, Chadwholovedme, Cherrylimerickey, Chillymail, Clarince63, DavyJonesLocker, Delta-2030, Derek R Bullamore, Dreamer.se, Ericorbit, FuriousFreddy, Holiday56, John of Reading, Karldaviesfan, Koavf, MaJic, ManbirS, Megamdrz, Mike Selinker, Oslono, Otto4711, RBBrittain, Richhoncho, Ricky Bobby, Rlendog, SnapSnap, Someguy1221, Starcheerspeaksnewslostwars, Sunshine74012, Tassedethe, Tbhotch, TheKMan, TonyTheTiger, Trivialist, TubularWorld, USS Noob Hunter, Uzerakount, VinnieRattolle, Welsh, WikHead, Wykebjs, Zzyzx11, 64 anonymous edits

Leon Thomas III *Source*: http://en.wikipedia.org/w/index.php?oldid=537506242 *Contributors*: 117Avenue, 12Medbe, 2602:304:AAAD:4879:D086:A638:4D09:BBFD, 2602:304:AAAD:4879:F4B8:BF2E:3B5B:94AF, 2tuntony, 667dave, Active Banana, Afasmit, All Hallow's Wraith, Amy50632, AniMate, Antdhumphrey, Areyouabassishaw, BD2412, BastianSpielbauer, Beanygirl80, Bearcat, Ben Ben, Bender235, Bigkhrisdogg, Bloodbath 87, BrianBMaster7, Briones001, BsaPR1996, Bxstr, C.Fred, Caccrop, Cacrop, Calabe1992, CartoonNetworkFan100, Chaorkid, Colchester121891, Confession0791, Coolbeans443, Coolgirlswren, Cory Malik, Crakkerjakk, Davida1234543678, Dedede672, Denisarona, Dennis55789, Derek R Bullamore, Dimadick, Doncram, Dragon1027, EWikist, EagerToddler39, Enzo Aquarius, Enzo13, Flipflame, Frantzedward.cha, Fyrael, Geraldo Perez, GoingBatty, GoldenChloe4, Good Olfactory, Green Beret 625, Happysailor, Helpful to the spread of information, Impala99, JGossard, Jandbadbay, JavaTenor, Jediknightelectro1997, Joe Decker, KatrinaP1222, KissyQ2, Klilidiplomus, LarryHoward, Legomyeggo252, Lewis odane, Logan, Logic78, Lucas Carranza, MadnessInside, Maraqua22, Materialscientist, Misarxist, Mood122, Mr. Chicago, Mupplan, N5iln, Nasnema, NickelodeonFan, Omnipaedista, Phd8511, Philip Trueman, Pretty bunn, Qaswa, Quaryshon pittman, QuasyBoy, RachJ123, Rawrzzz, Rlg000raz, Ross92, Ruhrfisch, SQGibbon, Serienfan2010, ShelfSkewed, Simpsons2010, Socialservice, Softball babes, Some jerk on the Internet, SonicFan100, Sophus Bie, Spongerupp, Steven Zhang, SummerPhD, Tabletop, Tajay dizzy grant, Tbhotch, Tide rolls, TigersRock5550, Tinton5, Tommy2010, Tontanayw2, Tvtonightokc, Uncle Dick, Uncle Milty, Vanished 1850, Vanished user 194difuh2ruhqwdoinxojakdjncno234r, VictoriousUser, Victorirupp, WOSlinker, Waacstats, Wakawakadis, WhatGuy, Whatever318, WikHead, Wikiims, Woohookitty, Xdelmupp, XenonX3, Xnuala, Zach Benjamin, Σ, 340 anonymous edits

North Broward Preparatory School *Source*: http://en.wikipedia.org/w/index.php?oldid=536824494 *Contributors*: 2602:306:2408:AED9:91BD:CEBF:B5B4:C3CE, Biker Biker, Bnappe, Btestorf, Caneguy64, Copout202, Dexd3, Drunauthorized, Firsfron, Fripri, Hmains, I dream of horses, JohnD.Rockerfeller, Jojafar12, Jprg1966, LilHelpa, Mandarax, Nick Number, PaulJones, Philip Trueman, Postcard Cathy, Prifri, R'n'B, RA0808, Ronmal68, Thattickles, The Illusive Man, TiMike, Variouscatfacts, Weur, WhisperToMe, 117 anonymous edits

Popular Song (Mika song) *Source*: http://en.wikipedia.org/w/index.php?oldid=536438539 *Contributors*: Fraggle81, GoingBatty, IWannaABillionaire, Magioladitis, Rafikirby, 1 anonymous edits

The Christmas Song *Source*: http://en.wikipedia.org/w/index.php?oldid=536562113 *Contributors*: 17Drew, 5tony4ill, A Stop at Willoughby, Adamskiuk2002, Agateller, Alvis, Andycjp, Angel310, Anglicanus, Another Believer, Anotherinkling, Antmusic, Arx Fortis, BRG, Babsdude, Bantosh, Baseball Bugs, Bbruscin, Billy Hathorn, Bleubeatle, Blicarea, Bolafik, Bs308706, CajunGypsy, Captain Cornflake, Carl.bunderson, Cascada0121, Cathryn, Cyde, Dahveed76, DatDoo, Dewelar, Dffb23, Dgsvoboda, Discographer, Donmccullen, Dsp13, Dtwmjb12, Durova, Easy4me, Egorock, Ekabhishek, Elfast, Engineer Bob, Eric444, Esanchez7587, Eschorn, EulerOperator, Extraordinary Machine, FanofCAow, Fortdj33, Froid, FuriousFreddy, Gamaliel, Gareth E Kegg, Gekritzl, Gilliam, Giovannii84, Giusex27sc, GoingBatty, Grafen, Graham87, Granpuff, Grapefruit8, Headbomb, Housewatcher, Husnock, InnocuousPseudonym, It'sOnlyU, J 1982, J Di, J.delanoy, JMyrleFuller, Jafeluv, JamesAlan1986, Jandbadbay, Jayron32, Jazzman2010, Jb413, Jeremyeyork, John, Jozaidins, Kai81, Karldaviesfan, Kikkokalabud, Kitsunegami, Koavf, Kristelzorina, Labalius, Lasersharp, Lfvcl, LongLiveMusic, Lovetoadmire, Martin4647, Martyn Smith, Mathiassandell, Mattbrundage, Mauitunes, Mdumas43073, MegX, Metre01, Mike Selinker, Mr. Frank, Mr. Laser Beam, Mrstickman, Muhandes, Myname808, Nick Number, Nickellmusic, Nunh-huh, OlEnglish, Olafolafsson, Phil Sandifer, Pjoef, PlatinumFire, Preskil, QuasyBoy, Queen2105, Quentin X, R'n'B, RBBrittain, Ral01, Ralphy j, Raul654, Rdsmith4, Rfc1394, Richhoncho, RjCan, RogerSandega, Rsolermo, SchreiberBike, ShelfSkewed, Sk8erock, Sliv812, Smashville, SnapSnap, SquidSK, Status, Stevemko, Supernatural02, Supertrouperdc, TJ Spyke, TMott, Tassedethe, Tertiary7, Tia2, Tjmayerinsf, Trippersham, Trivialist, Trnhgduoc2222, Uzerakount, Vrenator, Wahkeenah, WandaRMinstrel, Wikibryce, Woohookitty, Wysinger, Xeno, Xxmatt2010xx, Yeepsi, Yip1982, Zennon66, Zoe, Zzyzx11, 360 anonymous edits

The Origin of Love *Source*: http://en.wikipedia.org/w/index.php?oldid=534755357 *Contributors*: 2A01:E35:2E09:7400:21FA:CAAB:441D:41EA, 2A01:E35:2E2F:BE00:58DC:7040:1E3F:6F4C, Afavoritaweb, AngelCrying, Bearcat, BionicLotus, CJBR, Canned Soul, DanBLOO, Deejaai, Dl2000, Firsfron, Freshpop, Gonzalo M. Garcia, IWannaABillionaire, Jakor, Jonie148, Koritsi, Liflon, LilTrilly, Madjikly, Magioladitis, Malcolma, Mcmundane, Nick 71, Nick12345213, Ocre, Paul Erik, Phantomsteve, PokerFace3, Rafikirby, RazorEyeEdits, Sdoo493, Silvergoat, SkitChuk, Starcheerspeaksnewslostwars, Stee888, Therealdavo2, Thisiskyle.n, Tigerlemurguy, Widr, Woohookitty, Yaron K., Zak110695, 72 anonymous edits

Victoria Justice *Source*: http://en.wikipedia.org/w/index.php?oldid=537106190 *Contributors*: *drew, 1994student, 1dforlife, 22dragon22burn, 2627f68597, 2tuntony, 5 albert square, ABC1356msep1, ACSE, Acalamari, Achowat, Active Banana, Adambro, Addio, Afavoritaweb, Agallipeau, AgentPeppermint, Agrady8, Ahoskinson 95, AirplanePro, Aitias, Akkthg, Alansohn, Alex27851, Alexa Sprouse, Alexlikesbunnys991, Aliensmoke456, All Hallow's Wraith, Allen4names, Allstarecho, Americanhero, Amy50632, AmyLuvsDeme, Anaiysustetas, Anderstp, Andrewlp1991, Andrewpmk, Andyjsmith, Anen87, Angela6251, Angelinarulz, AniMate, Animefan30, Aoi, Arakunem, Arfn24, Aria1561, AscendedAnathema, Ashlee9, Auntof6, AvatarTeam, Avicennasis, BD2412, Babiiblooma4eva, Barneystimpleton, Bart133, Basakyalcin, Baseballrocks538, Beamike, BeanyFans, Bearcat, Beeblebrox, Ben Ben, Benstiller22222, Betacommand, Bhadani, Biker Biker, BlazeCannon15, Blehfu, BluejacketT, BlurTento, Bobo192, Boing! said Zebedee, Bongwarrior, Bookcats, BoxerMan21, Branson03, Brendan4hsm, Brewcrewer, Briwiki, Bruceyates1, Bsroiaadn, BubblyBerrie, Buttcheekio, C.Fred, C777, CJLUKE93, CaRaNt11, Cajun67, Calabe1992, Caldorwards4, CambridgeBayWeather, CanadianPenguin, Candy coated doom, Canuckian89, CardinalDan, Cesarmaco222, Chanlyn, Charles Sturm, CharlesCasiraghi, Ched, Cheerchick6107, Cheesygold, Chefjordan, Chelo61, Cheriepoon, Chick Bowen, ChrissehJohnson, Chrisstilwell, Christian75, Christina Silverman, Cjc13, Clairedreanne, Clerks, ClosedEyesSeeing, Coasterlover1994, Colchester121891, CollisionCourse, CommonsDelinker, ConCompS, Confession0791, Coolname23, Cooltrainer Hugh, Cosmo16h12, Cotedepabla, Courcelles, Crakkerjakk, Crash Underride, Cresix, Crstsk, CruiseOrGood47, CrunchyCookie, Crystal Clear x3, Cst17, Cureden, Cwluc, Cyberpower678, D6, DARTH SIDIOUS 2, DCEdwards1966, Dadajjj96, DanTD, Danausi, Daniel J. Leivick, Danregal, Danthemankhan, Darrenhusted, Darth Panda, Datattler, Daycd, Dbunkley6, Dcooper, DeadEyeArrow, Debbie rocks, Decltype, Dekan871, DeltaQuad, Demi1993, Dennis55789, Denniss, Deor, DepressedPer, DerHexer, Dethgunz, Dicksoak, Diem nguyen, Dirga Luthfi, Discospinster, Discovermine, Dismas, Disneygalxx123+abc, Divaqueenbabygurl, Djb31800, Dknight192, Dns006, Donovan17, Doomedtx, Dougie korea, Dr.K., Drappel, Drewpac1227, Drillians, Drmies, Drpickem, Dxrocks44, Dylan620, Dylan911123, ERcheck, ESkog, EWikist, Easy4me, Ecallum, Edward779, Eeyore7739, Egpetersen, Eleanorkraven, Elected, Emmawatsonfann, Enauspeaker, Engines On, Enigmaman, Enviroboy, EoGuy, Epbr123, Eposty, Erebus Morgaine, EricSerge, Erik9, Evolution590, Excirial, ExtremeJohnny123, Extremeguy, Ezeu, Ezia, Falcon8765, FamFragoso42, Febbylove12, Fieldday-sunday, FisherQueen, Fnsdbvfvscvwdrsfsdc, Fonduou, For An Angel, Fourviz, Fredrickglaze, Frehley, Fritz Saalfeld, Funnybunny44, Fæ, GCMS1, GD1223, GFOO, Gaius Cornelius, Gazwj, Ged UK, George333jeremy, Geraldo Perez, Gfoley4, Gilliam, Gjbloom, Glane23, Gman1945, Gnowor, Gogo Dodo, GoingBatty, Golde62, GoodGurllyy23, GorillaWarfare, Grafen, Grashoofd, GreenBayPackersfan09, Grizzley1029, HJ Mitchell, HaeB, Haering316, Hahachuckles, Hair, HalfShadow, Hana banana, HannahMiley, Hannahcrazy, Happypan21, Happysailor, HayCray, Hayleydevonne, Heero Kirashami, Heimstern, HelloJelloFell0, Hintswen, Hippie Metalhead, Hmains, Hmrox, Hnismokehash, Hockey champ 2006, Holaamgio, Horkana, Hto9950, Hullaballoo Wolfowitz, Hut 8.5, Hydrogen Iodide, Hypnotizedfilms, Icealien33, Iceboyz, Imaf'inbeast, Impala99, Inferno, Lord of Penguins, Inhabite107, Insanity Incarnate, Instinct, Intelati, Ipatrol, Ischgucke, Ivy odame, Ixfd64, J Milburn, J.delanoy, J36miles, JForget, JGossard, JJW20084, JMS Old Al, JNW, Jack O'Lantern, Jackol, Jacksonori47, Jake.auzzie, Jakehandfg, Jambornik, JamesBWatson, Jandbadbay, January, Jaqcarl, Javiballer411153, Jaxsonista, Jbbmonster7, Jeff G., Jellohello98, Jetman, Jewjamss, Jim Douglas, Jim1138, Jmabel, Jnt329, Joefromrandb, John of Reading, JohnDorianyeah, Johnny0929, Jonathanclarke1, Joshua, Joshua Issac, Jrawgotstacks, Jsayre64, Jtaibl, Juggler821, Junelove, Jusdafax, Justme89, Jwhale9382, Kalliequeen, Kallina17, Katherine, Katydidit, Keishalovespink, Kelly, Kevpark, Kgt4, Killermatt55, Kilopi, King of Hearts, KingMorpheus, Kirsty67y34324, Knowitall911, Koavf, Kollision, Kraka504, Krellis, Ksy92003, Kushboy, Kwiki, Kww, Kylejack1, LAUGH90, LOL, LOL-117, Laceystorm, Lalucho Chavarría, Lamb99, Lando Calrissian, Landon1980, Lauren11467, Lcarscad, LedgendGamer, Legomyeggo252, Lelec92, LeoLady20, Leszek Jańczuk, Lewbertswart45, Lewis odane, Lg16spears, Liamaleman, Life, Liberty, Property, LilHelpa, Liquidluck, Lishowronsakura, Little Professor, Littlecutie212, Living Famously, Lizzy Green, Logan, Logical Fuzz, Lolly949, Lucas Carranza, Luckas Blade, Lugia2453, Lugnad, Lugnuts, Lunchscale, Lupin, Lyssa2314, M.Sunshine, MJ136, Magicmat, Magioladitis, Maimai009, Manway, Maraqua22, Marek69, MariGaleano, Marine 69-71, Mariokart110, MarkGallagher, Marknutley, MarnetteD, Martarius, Martin451, Maserati21, Materialscientist, Matredsoxfan, Matt Kake, Matthewzients, MattieTK, Mbinebri, Meckstroth.jm, MedinaG, Megaocher, Melii kendall12, MelissaSnider, Mentifisto, Merlinme, MesabaFan146, Mets501, Michaelsbll, Michaelsimmons, MickWithoutGlasses, Mifter, Mihalaych3345, Mike 7, Mike Rosoft, Miken32, Mikkibear444, Mileyfan19920012, MissIndependent537, Mizzesawesome, Mjbmr, Mmiller20910, Moonriddengirl, Morning277, Mr. Prez, Mr. Unknown, Mrschimpf, Msutton92, Mylatka, Mythdon, Mz perfection42, Nancy, Naraht, Nashapapa, NawlinWiki, Nelle8, NickelodeonFan, Nickfan24565, Nickroop, Nights Not End, Nightscream, Ninetyone, NitRav, NoodleLuvsMuffins, Notshane, NrDg, Nsaa, NuclearWarfare, Nymf, ONE-FOUR, OOODDD, Ohconfucius, Only, Orphan Wiki, Oxymoron83, PCHS-NJROTC, PL290, POPOEs, PaintedLadder, Paranomia, Part of me 2, Pavel92, Pax85, Peeekaboo, Penguinsmarlene, Perumalism, PeterGriffin11298, Pharaoh of the Wizards, Phd8511, Philip Trueman, Philip.t.day, Piandcompany, Piano non troppo, Piast93, Pinethicket, Pinkbluegreencolourz, Pinoy Pride, Pioneersbrog, Pirateogta, Pknkly, Playtime3701, Poshspiceneverythingnice, Postdlf, Potterharrymorion, Prince Ludwig, Princesa yolita, Pristinegoal, Purple123x, Putmalk, Q8love, QuasyBoy, Quentin X, Qwyrxian, RadioKirk, Rafatisd, RainbowOfLight, Raving Monster 2, RayeRaye121, Rbb1181, Rbccgodwin, Reach Out to the Truth, Reconsider the static, Riveramagic13, Rlg000raz, Rman1234567890, Rmm81, RobertGustafson, Rocketry, Ronhjones, Rosepuff12, Ross92, Rrburke, Runndover, Ruy Pugliesi, Rvir0522, RyanCross, S1D3winder016, S1l3ntx5, SQGibbon, Salvio giuliano, Sam Korn, SamanthaRamrajVevo, Santryl, Save-Me-Oprah, SchnitzelMannGreek, ScottSteiner, Seaphoto, Seblini, Seddie Shipper, Serene78, Serpenthia, Sethjohnson95, Sg2sb2000, Shadowjams, Shaericell, ShakataGaNai, Shanes, Shaq91, Shawncvl, Shelbyeah, ShelfSkewed, ShuffleStop, Shyla Weikum, SickGamingTom, SilverOwl001, Silvergoat, Simpsons2010, Skb8721, Skomorokh, SkyWalker, SkyeSweetnam4ever, Slfxox13, Smalljim, Smart food, Snigbrook, Snowolf, Soccer22dman, Soliloquial, Solunitica, Sparkie963, Spears154, Spiderboi, SpikeToronto, Spitfire19, Sr200179, StAnselm, Staka, Starsking, Steam5, StefanX112, SteinbDJ, Stephanie J Stone, Stephcheung512, Stephe1987, Steven Walling, Streamerlovesmusic, Stunt, Stwalkerster, Sugar51995, SummerPhD, Sunnylover11, SupremoJunior, Susan Capetinga, Swimmerwinner72, Syrthiss, THEN WHO WAS PHONE?, TMC1982, TWMM91, Tariqabjotu, Tastewrongroom, Taylor Hailey James, Taylorselenataylor, Tbhotch, Tdinoahfan, TeaDrinker, Tedder, Teenboy5000, Tenebrae, Thadius856, Thatguyflint, The Illusive Man, The Shadow-Fighter, The Thing That Should Not Be, TheFeds, Theaura, Theaveng, Thebozz, Theflash4647, Thefreakshow, Thesmatestguy, This lousy T-shirt, Tide rolls, TigersRock5550, Tihi lol, TimYanX, Timrollpickering, Tinton5, Tommy2010, Tommycrossover, Tony1, TradyM888111, TradyM888221, Transity, Travelbird, Travistraytray, Tubby23, Twispace3000, Ufi03, UltraCody, Uncle Dick, Usb10, VJ13A, VJisamazing, VP44444, Vacation9, Varlaam, Versus22, Victoria0507, VictoriaJusticeFan, VictoriaJusticeFan1, Victoriajustice, VictoriousUser, Vj2009, Vjusticeorg, VladDoskov, Volleyballgirls, Volpe5, Vreddy92, Vrenator, Vwolf3, WCW1969-2002, WadeSimMiser, Wakawakadis, Waltermelon, Watermellonanna, Wayne Slam, Webclient101, Wellneededpat, Welsh-girl-Lowri, Werdan7, WhatGuy, Whitesox30pk, Widr, Wikien2009, Wildhartlivie, Wilhelmina Will, Wolfentoad66, WonderBuono!, Woohookitty, Wooodddd222222, XMirandaxCosgrove, Xcvista, Xkyliex21, Xoxomabel, Xxbrokenwishesxx, Yaksar, Yamla, Yeahflorida, Yellowweasel, Yintan, Yksin, Yodus, Yopug, Zach Benjamin, Zozomileyfan123, ~Ryan Mckenzie~, Σ, Вика Смайлик, 2292 anonymous edits

Victorious *Source*: http://en.wikipedia.org/w/index.php?oldid=537487951 *Contributors*: -bentleyboo-, 1007D, 100Edgar, 1989 Rosie, 1exec1, 2001:5B0:24FF:EF0:0:0:0:3B, 2002:1806:3BC:1234:217:F2FF:FE96:5F76, 2602:304:5E42:8ED9:58C2:8260:DF88:BD1F, 2tuntony, 3jz01bcs, 5 albert square, 729gabby, 744cody, ABC1356msep1, Abortman, Active Banana, Agent192, Ainsworth anderson, Airplaneman, Alamon23, Alansohn, Albertus Aditya, Ale 03, Alec2011, Alex Daire, AlexJFox, Alexonion, Alicelove303, Aliensinyourcloset, Aliensmoke456, Allens, Alpha 4615, Alphius, Altaïr, Altorrocks, Alvaro.rodriguez91, Americanhero, Andadundi, AndrewAllen15, Andrewhottie, Andrewwiki123, Angel28065, AniMate, Anisaowens, AnishaLovesMakeup, AnonMoos, Anthony Appleyard, Apostnikov1, Arjayay, Arthena, Aschulman17, Asdlfkj;lk, Astros4477, AussieLegend, AutoGeek, AvatarTeam, Awesomedude321, AxelBoldt, Azeruth42, BDE1982, BLACK N RICH, Babyphatlove0707, Bananastalktome, Barek, Barneystimpleton, Baseball Fanatic, Bdwick12, Bender235, Bento00, Bes7est, BettyMoo101, Bgnkid, Bgwhite, Biker Biker, Billy Liakopoulos, Bjrnet, Black Yoshi, BlazeCannon15, BlowingTopHat, Boing! said Zebedee, Bollyjeff, Bongwarrior, Bonusballs, Booby101, Boobye, Bovineboy2008, Britannic124, Broof5js, Brunette16, Buffywillowtara, Bulldog73, Bungiedog9898, Burningview, C.Fred, CNGLITCHINFO, Calabe1992, Candace401, CarlosPenaftw, Carlosalvrezforever, Carlysam49, CartoonNetworkFan100, Cassie17364, CennoxX, Chander Jagtiani, Channelboy, CharCharOverOver11, Chebforeva, Checker Fred, Chloegmoretzfan, ChrisCarss Former24.108.99.31, Chzz, Cit helper, Clfan91, Cmd11200, Cntras, Coasterlover1994, Colchester121891, CollisionCourse, Comm1098, Confession0791, Cookie10114, Coolio1996, Coral Bay, Corvoe, Corvus cornix, CorwinDruzil, Craft Sword, Crash Underride, CrazyApple1998, CrazyFunny, Crazyjoe30, Crushgirl98, Cst17, DC Fan 5, DVdm, Daddypigstummy, Dakuro, Damonluemaxwell97, Dan6hell66, DanTD, Davida1234543678, Dbunkley6, DegrassiFreak, Dennis55789, Derek R Bullamore, DerekB2010, Diannaa, Dicepter, Discospinster, DisneyTV2012,

Disneyfreak3496, Disneynicklatino, Divad20, Djtechno95, DoRD, Dobie80, Dogster070, Dplcrnj, Dragon1027, Dubulge, Ducknish, Dudefacepotter, Dudejerome, DylanGLC2011, DylansTVChannel, Dylanwen, E-man615, E. Ripley, Eagles247, Easy4me, Ebp112002, Eddisonn, Edenkorcari, ElBarco2011, Elektrik Band, Elizabeth2345, Emaan100, EoGuy, Eomon, Epopnidla, Erielhonan, Essops, EvanFinney10, EverAllMupp, Everythingproud, Falcon8765, FansVictoriaJustice, FantageJapanRox, Favonian, Fetchfan88, Ffion9, FinalRapture, Flipflame, Fluffernutter, Footballfreak97, Forever awesome, Francis Jay Acosta, Francisco97, Frantzedward.cha, FreshBeatKiki, Frostheartx, Funandtrvl, Funnybunny44, Fæ, GGFFDDJJKKUU, GOTHICMUSICGIRL, GSF4LIFE, Gabbymz, Gareth Griffith-Jones, Ged UK, George2001hi, Geraldo Perez, Gkpdjkhg, Gogo Dodo, GoingBatty, Gordan3194, Gounc1994, Grachifan, Grafen, Grashoofd, Gwen-chan, HJ Mitchell, HOVariel, HannahMiley, Harmony944, Harryaslim45, Heelylover117, Hfdhfdhhfh, Hfdhfdhhfh again, Hi im zim, Hi4231, Highlighter Fresh, Hoafan123, Holaamgio, Holysaget, Hoo man, Hoppybunny, Hueverto, I am rockin skittles!, I dream of horses, IGeMiNix, IMikee, Ihalm, Iknow23, Il223334234, Iluvmarchingband, Impala99, In the shining light, Inka 888, Isabelissa, J4lambert, JGossard, JHUbal27, JHunterJ, JJJ123456789, JJWest56, Jab7842, Jabrona, Jack Greenmaven, Jackodon, Jadewest.catvalentine, Jadipro, Jakew, JamesBWatson, Jamesbanesmith, Jamiemae123, Jandbadbay, Jared martinez gwapo, Jeff G., Jennette*Cyrus, Jfarajr, Jj137, Jj98, Jnorton7558, Jobin RV, Joefromrandb, Joes a g, Joey836, Johanne23, John, Johnello, Johnlongbond, Jojhutton, Jon23812, Jonah22, Jonas kam, Jose Monreal, Joseph BB Ferri, JpGrB, Jprg1966, Jschnur, Juandy004, Julian6789, Juragraf, Jusses2, JustinReed1234, KH1MOVIE, KTo288, Ka Faraq Gatri, Kak1328, Kalliequeen, Kallina17, Kamaki, Kamiv922, Katloveswiki89, Katydidit, Kayla21314, Keinerfrei, Keith D, Kelvin245, Kendo el demonio de la tinta, Kentiall, Kevinbrogers, Kiki360, King Shadeed, Kingawesome100, KittyKo'sCute, Kk26995, Kkllmmnn98, Klilidiplomus, Kolbykooz, Kristen287, Kubigula, Kww, Kyyabearr, L Kensington, LAUGH90, LGBLA, Laceystorm, Lasy, Lazaris117, Legomyeggo252, Lelec92, Lewis odane, LilHelpa, Limited2fan, Lindsayoris15, Linguisticgeek, Liquidluck, Lisica in pes 5000, Living Famously, Locco Mocco, Logan, Lolaidiotick, Lonelywheel, Loohcsnuf, LuK3, Lucas Carranza, LuvCandyzz, M.Mario, M.V.E.i., MJ94, MZMcBride, Magioladitis, MagnusA, Maraqua22, Marco Guzman, Jr, Marcula, Marek69, Maricar56739273, Marigbooth, Mario14Party, MarnetteD, Materialscientist, Matheus Camcho, Matredsoxfan, Maxrideboytoy, Mclucas603, Me235789065, MegastarLV, Meowsi34, Methecooldude, Metricopolus, Mglangl, Michaelsbll, MickWithoutGlasses, Mike Rosoft, MikeyMouse10, Misawadaichi, MisterMod, Mockingjaybonnott, Moe Epsilon, Mogism, Monk19, Moorglade, Mr. Prez, Mr.nickdaking, Mrschimpf, Mrt3366, Mryoung2002, Mth1997, Muppet171, Muppet321, Mupplan, Mypasswordisgood, Mysterytrey, N-HH, Nagaieh786, Nancy, Nasnema, Nathan92295, NawlinWiki, Ndukey, Neeesaaan, NeilN, Nelle8, NellieBly, Nick Number, NickConfaloneNealDusedau, Nicktoons, Nicktropolis, Night Fight, NinjaTazzyDevil, Ninjawarriordex, Nitefirre, Nnffll, NrDg, Ohconfucius, Oliveolivia, Opeaina123, Orphan Wiki, PMDrive1061, Pantsaklanos, Patrickmgaddis, Peter Karlsen, Petrb, PeytonMaslow, Phd8511, Philg88, Phillnyx Web Production, Pinkadelica, Pleasant1623, Pleasethen200, Pntjr, Poop poop786, Poopsandwich123, Popcorn44, Popper54321, PpeRuiiz, Prcc27, PrestonLong, Princessimmadolla, Pswiney, Qazkjlg5, QuasyBoy, QueenArianaG, QuiteUnusual, Qwyrxian, R'n'B, Rafy, Rahuloof, Rainbow015, Randomhairflipping, Rangermups, Ratemonth, Raven2578, Rayjman1, Reader 21, Rhatsa26X, RickyYayo3, Rickyhillhouse, Riku&sora1212, Rmorash, Rob827, RobBon1232, RobinHood70, Rocio44, Roguemaster83, Ron2, Ronnywiki, Roshele tenney, Rouge2, Roy1944, Ruffmanfan88, Russellethan13, Ryulong, SQGibbon, Sallylockhart1, Sanjana1505, Sanybel9, SaucyQueenNumber5, Saylaveer, Sbze14, Scarlett2Emma, Scjessey, ScottMHoward, Seaphoto, Selenagomezgonzalez, Sequinedchick, Sergay, Serienfan2010, Serpent-A, Seth234, Sethjohnson95, Sgs101, Shara25, Shortie43504, Shsilver, Silvergoat, Simon.hess, Simpsons2010, Sinjin135, Sion8, Sjones23, Skizzik, SkyMachine, Slakr, Sleddog116, Solarra, Sole Soul, Someonewithme, Sonicyouth86, Sonny1412, Souleater12343, Ssjtk, Starbuckslover123, Starranger00, Streamerlovesmusic, Stroppolo, SummerPhD, SuperHamster, Swimmerwinner72, TPIRFanSteve, TRLIJC19, TV Shows Fan, Tabercil, Tabletop, Tacoboobsack, Tardnozzle, Taylorselenataylor, Tbhotch, Tcnorden, TeeheeChick, Temmy34, TenPoundHammer, Tgeairn, The Shadow-Fighter, The Stick Man, The Thing That Should Not Be, The Trent Gaines Show Characters, TheUncivilizedHermit, Thecheesykid, Thecoolkids13, Thedude346, Thegreatgeek, Theguywhohatestwitter, This lousy T-shirt, Thomas888b, Tide rolls, Tidefave59, Timothytheasian, Tinton5, Tommy2010, Tommystar, Trezjr, Trivialist, Trusilver, Ttonybl, Tvstrela, Tvtonightokc, Twispace3000, Ultimatelains09, Ultimatetroll909, Uncle Dick, Unreal7, Usb10, VP44444, ValiantRed600, Velella, Versegirolanddsdf, VictoriaJusticeFan1, Victoriatuler, Victorious fan 2011, VictoriousUser, VictoriousVNick, Victoriousgirl98, VideoGameMaster6, Vincent byrd, Vjusticeorg, Volkovp56, WP Editor 2012, Warregubbi, Wayne Slam, Waywardhorizons, Wazzup101, WeatherBoyWheeler, Webclient101, WereWolf, What 2 do Next, WhatGuy, Whatever318, Whisky drinker, WikHead, Wiki13, WikiMaster500, Wikialexdx, Wikiims, Wikijack847, Wikilover223, Wikipedian Penguin, Windows72106, Wtmitchell, WweLoser96, XDREIVAJ17, XDmegaDude, XMirandaxCosgrove, Xdelmupp, Xjenniferdinh, Xoxomabel, Xxposhikaxx, Yaddasy, Yaksar, Ycbaby619, Zachlipton, Zeitlupe, Zumiezboy, Σ, 2943 anonymous edits

Victorious (soundtrack) *Source*: http://en.wikipedia.org/w/index.php?oldid=536204884 *Contributors*: 3jz01bcs, ABC1356msep1, AussieLegend, Awesome444a444, Bastian 1929, Bdwick, Biker Biker, Braincricket, Bubbleoui, Christopher10006, Crash Underride, CrazyFunny, DanTD, Dbunkley6, Djtechno95, E-man615, Easy4me, Elektrik Band, Eric444, FallenWings47, Flipflame, Gareth E Kegg, Geraldo Perez, Gersende, Go-btr, GoingBatty, Iknow23, Iluvselenagomez1234, Impala99, In actu, In the shining light, IzzyRail, Jared martinez gwapo, Kiki360, Kilopi, King of the Court, Koavf, Kubek15, Legoman64, Logan, LuckyBluJay05, Maraqua22, Marc-André Aßbrock, Mike-Man12, Mild Bill Hiccup, Mileyfan19920012, MrF1shIsFish, Ninjawarriordex, Ozkithar Salas, PixieLottFan, QuasyBoy, Ron Ritzman, Silvergoat, Ssilvers, Stephanie J Stone, SummerPhD, SupremoJunior, Theo10011, TutterMouse, VictoriaJusticeFan1, VictoriaJusticeFan311, Warregubbi, WhatGuy, Woohookitty, XMirandaxCosgrove, Youknowmyname657, Zach464, 296 anonymous edits

Winx Club *Source*: http://en.wikipedia.org/w/index.php?oldid=537482065 *Contributors*: 117Avenue, 1oddbins1, 2, 2001:558:6012:3:141B:A676:B572:57B4, 2009rubygirl, 2600:E00F:4008:10:0:0:0:3B, 2602:306:CE20:4C90:CCE2:9C29:3D88:E04E, 28bytes, 29fleury, 2D, 31Gabe, 5 albert square, AAA!, AKGhetto, ALoopingIcon, AOL Alex, APT, Aalstar, Aavalenzuela, Adamfinmo, Addict 2006, Addshore, Adyniz, Aftkm, Alai, Alansohn, Aldebaran66, Aleksa Lukic, Alessia2002, AlexB531, AlexLevyOne, Alexius08, Aliya bloom, Allens, Alpha92613, Alyssa hoffel, Amibite, AmyRose's, Anamona, AndreniW, Androzaniamy, Andy4789, Angelblue142, Angelo Michael, Angie Y., Anir1uph, Anjalit2624, Ankaton55, AnmaFinotera, Antandrus, Antiuser, Antiwinx, Arcee jazz365, Ari3lsss, Asenine, Ashyflora, Aspects, Asuka56, Atomician, Auric, AussieLegend, Azumanga1, BBTV90, Backslash Forwardslash, Bazzargh, Bearcat, BelieveInWinx, Believeflora, Bellng, Ben Ben, Benpiwari01, Bento00, Benzy19, Bhumi0618, Bigbrifsx, BigrTex, Bisbis, Blackeykittie, Blackgaia02, Blah yap dribble, Bleubeatle, Bloom of Sparx, Bloomenchantixpics11, Bloomergil, Bloomwinxgirl, Blossomingspring, Blue eyes gold dragon, Blue-Shark, Boardor, Bobking1384, Bobo192, Bono24, Bovineboy2008, Braceout, Braincricket, Brandotaylor, Bratztvgirl, Bri1995, Brianhe, Bsadowski1, Bulldog73, Bunnyhop11, Burning Amber, C-M, Cabbacaleb, Cailunet, Calabe1992, Calum MacÙisdean, Camw, Can't sleep, clown will eat me, Captainwarsaw, Carly Greene, Cartoonborg, Causa sui, Cclarke, Cding318128, CharlYnn nic0le, CharlotteWebb, Charms21, Che829, Cheautyan, Ched, Chiharu2shi, Chip123456, Cholmes75, ChrisGualtieri, Chubzhac, Ckatz, Cmdrjameson, Coallen, Cod777, Codelyokofan, Commander Keane, CommonsDelinker, CooKeeN, Cookie3xx, Cookiecrumbs1530, Cookietiara, Coolak, Copycatloki, Coralwinx, Crashsnake, CrazyChinaGal, Cryptic C62, Crystallina, Cupcake12winx, CureStarscape, Cute koala, D-Master94, DARTH SIDIOUS 2, DVdm, DabMachine, Darcy4life13, Darkness2005, Darknyss, Darth Panda, DeadEyeArrow, Deadlyaaron, DedleaDragoria, Deltabeignet, Demonraiser, Denelson83, Deor, DerHexer, Deryck Chan, Deyyaz, DikiMonah, Disavian, Discospinster, Disinclination, Dlae, Dogaroon, Donbonzi96, Doniago, Dorem11, DorothyAnn64116, Doyne, Dreadstar, Drmies, Droplette73, Drpickem, Drpryr, Drstuey, Duncan, Durin, DylanGLC2011, DylansTVChannel, DynamoDegsy, EEMIV, EPO, EVula, EagerToddler39, Echolot, Ecopetition, Edderso, Edenc1, Egon Eagle, Eilonwe, Electrode Light, Elen of the Roads, Emarsee, EmmaBloomWinx, Energybender, Epolk, Este99, Eugenekoh12, EurekaLott, Evanh2008, Everyking, Excirial, ExclusiveInformation, Exeunt, Extreme Unction, Falcon8765, Faster2010, Fastilysock, Fatmagulunsucune, Feezo, Feinoha, Felicia parker, FeliciaAkira, Ferreal, FetchcommsAWB, Feudonym, Fiery bobcat, FinnWiki, Flami72, Flewis, FloraXOXO, Flower Priest, Flowerparty, Fluffernutter, Frood, Frozen Flower, FudgeFury, FunnygirlM, Furber15, GLaDOS, GMc, GVnayR, Gadget850, Gail, Gaius Cornelius, Gali00, Gareth Griffith-Jones, Geoffman13, Geopgeop, George The Dragon, Gfoley4, GhostPirate, Gidonb, Gilliam, Gimlei, Giovanazzi kid, Glacialfox, Gladrius, Glane23, Gogo Dodo, GoingBatty, Goldom, Good Olfactory, Goody3333, GothicAngeloftheDead, Grafen, Gromlakh, Guil2001, Gundersen53, Gune, Haein45, Hailey C. Shannon, Halo 2 Ops ANBU Itachi, Harasegawa, Haseo9999, Heaven19733, HelenaAnneValentine, HexaChord, Hexadecimalmonkey, Heyfaa, Hiding, Hinatax01, Hmr, Hohenloh, Homered1, HopeSeekr of xMule, Hotfireball1, Hyju, IW.HG, Ian Lopez, Ian Pitchford, Icantbeliveijoindwiki, IceUnshattered, Icep, Ilovecheese2012, Iluvzelda123, Imacoolchick, Imperial Gift, InShaneee, IndulgentReader, Iohannes Animosus, Iridescent, Islamisgr88, Island Monkey, J.delanoy, J4lambert, JForget, JSH-alive, Jacob9594, Januarian Winter, JasonLong2468, Jasper Deng, Jenny206, Jenrzzz, Jessepinky, Jessicapierce, Jhsounds, Jj98, Jmlk17, Joe Decker, John of Reading, John254, JohnCD, Josep Maria 15., Joseph mitchell9, JoshWiki6, Jpikachu, JuJube, Judgeking, Jusses2, Juze, KATkanga, Kafziel, Kagome2720, KaleidoMagic, Kariteh, Katanzag, Katep1997, Katie.cute, KaySL, Kbh3rd, Kehrbykid, Kencaesi, Kenriolover789, Kingpin13, Konrad149, Krenair, Kubek15, KuduIO, Kurtking, Kusma, Kwiki, Landon1980, Lauraac2110, Laurek68, LedgendGamer, Legrammarnazi, Lenakrons, Leszek Jańczuk, Levalley, Lgfuhrmann, LiD0T0ny, Lights, LilHelpa, LinnFan432, Lionking23411, Litsy4218, Livy, Lizburtjess, Lockley, Logan, Logical Cowboy, Lonelywheel, Lovecandy555, Loveprincess66, Lovewitchie, LowerStateGood, Lugia2453, Lullabying, Lunamaria, Luv4TakuyaK, MMG1196, MZaplotnik, MacintoshApple, Madchester, Magioladitis, Malkinann, Maniesansdelire, Maplerdarkness, Mark Arsten, Mark Grant, Matchesthedragon, Materialscientist, Matt Deres, MattParker 119, Matty-chan, Mattyhiphop500, Maxamegalon2000, Mayur, Mboverload, McSly, Mechamind90, MegaHL90, Melaen, MelbourneStar, Melody.Song, Mentifisto, MewMewStrawberry, Mike Rosoft, MikeyMouse10, Mild Bill Hiccup, Minimac, Miquonranger03, Mkill, Mmxx, Moe Epsilon, Mogism, Morning277, Movingimage, Mr. Carter4, Mr.Z-man.sock, Mrt3366, Mspraveen, Mygosh123, Myohmyooh, Myscrnnm, N. Harmonik, NCurse, Nana's world, Nascar1996, NathanoNL, Neelix, Neo Geo, NeoChaosX, Neoguest, Neojeran, Ngyikphang, Nicie98, Nick Number, NickDibuv, Nikkoneeko35, Nisa Tunesque, Noman953, NoseNuggets, NrDg, Nsaa, Nutiketaiel, Nwwaew, Ocean Shores, Old Jacques, Olipop25, Onedirectionrockz, Onomatopoeia500, OpinionPerson, Orenburg1, Oreos, Oxymoron83, Ozerovocka, Paishu, Paralympic, Parker1297, Peace551, Perfectblue97, PeruAlonso, Pevernagie, Pgk, Piano non troppo, Pieguy96, Pinethicket, Pinkyblu, Pix3, Pjvpjv, Plong26, Pointillist, Pokemonv3, Polly102, Prateekshya Ayushi, PrestonLong, PrestonLong501, Pride the Arrogant, Princesa-Calistro, Princessofsparks, Private Sweety, Puffin, Pumpkin3110, Quatonik, Quiz63allday, R'n'B, R.G., Rabukurafuto, Racerx11, Rachael7982, Radiant!, Ramaallbboo, RandomXYZb, Randy121, Raphael1123, Razor X, Rcsprinter123, Rdsmith4, Red Angel, RedWordSmith, Redbird 41, Redkidrocks1, ReesRose, Renatokeshet, Retired username, Rettetast, RexNL, Rhapsodyinpink, Rholton, Rich Farmbrough, Richybenno54, Riverstepstonegirl, Rjwilmsi, Rlove, Rocketrod1960, Rockman.exe, Roepers, Rouenpucelle, Roxy4everpuppy211, Roxyandflorawinx123, RoyBoy, Rtkat3, Rudi argento, Rwalker, Ryulong, Sadaf winxclub 12, Sailor Angel, Sailoranjo, Salamurai, Sam Hocevar, Samqwe4, Sarai134, Sashstables, Sceptre, Sergecross73, Shadowjams, Shaiel004, Shellymayo81984, Shii, Shirik, Shiroi Hane, Simeondahl, Simoncursitor, SingCal, Sjones23, Skinny McGee, Skraz, Slgrandson, Slon02, Smash, SolAcid, SolarianSunshine, Some jerk on the Internet, Soniccis, Soupfan101, SpaceFlight89, Sparkley gurl, Sparthorse, Sparx101, SpikeJones, Srushe, Staffwaterboy, Starionwolf, Starry maiden Gazer, Stella345, StellaBloomMusaFloraLaylaTecna, Stifle, Stolya, Strike Eagle, Supremecouncil, Svick, Swiftink, Swimstr98, SwisterTwister, Syakirah939, TBrandley, TJRC, TPIRFanSteve, Tabercil, Tabletop, TacticalMaster, Tech1995, Technopat, TexasAndroid, Tgeairn, Thaf, The 80s chick, The Chinchou, The Illusive Man, The JPS, The Thing That Should Not Be, The wub, TheFarix, TheLoverofLove, TheRanger, TheRealFennShysa, Thecheesykid, Thedjatclubrock, Themusicdiva67, Theopolisme, ThermoNuclearWar, Thingg, Thinkpinkgirl, Thomasfan5044, Thorncrag, Tide rolls, Tiffamswart, Tiggerjay, Tikiwont, Tim Q. Wells, Times1, Tinkerbell52589, Tinton5, Titodutta, Torreslfchero, Trevor MacInnis, Tricksy.fire.princess, Trivialist, Troyanni, Trusilver, TutterMouse, Tuvalkin, Twilight obssed, Twilightforever123, Tyman 101, TyrannoRanger, UDScott, UltimatePyro, Ungvichian, Unotwotiga, Useight, Usotsuki, Utcursch, UtherSRG, V! The Vile, VAcharon, Valtor'scuppycake, Vannamoo, Varshkumar, Vary, VernoWhitney, ViperSnake151, Wack'd, Waggers, Walord0, Warregubbi, Wer900, WhisperToMe, White Shadows, WiNxClUbFaN!0!, Widr, WikHead, Wiki libs, Wiki4Blog, WikiKatie4, WikiLeon, WikiNerd231, Wikialexdx, Wikihelper134, Wikihobby, Wikismartfairy, Wildthing61476, William Avery, WilsCast88, Winx Bloom Club, Winx Club Girl, Winx4ever, WinxClubFlora, WinxClubGirl1990, WinxFlora672, Winxclub17, Winxclubforever2011, Winxclubrulez, Winxhorse, Winxrocker, Winxrockswitchsux, Winxsirenix775180, Winxwikigirl, Winxy, Wjejskenewr, Woohookitty, Wwane, Wwoods, Xelgen, Xiong Chiamiov, Xoalyssagirlxo, Xuanwu, XxCookie3xX, Xyzzyplugh,

Yamatochem, Yogosan, Ytic nam, Yumiifofinha, Yz2907, Zalgo, Zanimum, ZenTronOne, Zerachielle, Zsero, Pappap, 4902 anonymous edits

Image Sources, Licenses and Contributors

License

CPSIA information can be obtained at www.ICGtesting.com
Printed in the USA
LVOW09s1943291113

363228LV00014B/919/P